The P
of Social
Problems

The Economics of Social Problems

The Market *versus* the State

SECOND EDITION

Julian Le Grand
Department of Economics
London School of Economics
and Political Science

and

Ray Robinson
School of Social Sciences
University of Sussex

MACMILLAN

First edition 1976
Reprinted 1977, 1979, 1981, 1982
Second edition 1984
Reprinted 1985, 1986, 1987, 1989

Published by
MACMILLAN EDUCATION LTD
Houndmills, Basingstoke, Hampshire RG21 2XS
and London
Companies and representatives
throughout the world

Printed in Hong Kong

ISBN 0-333-35305-6

Contents

Introduction

This book is an extensively rewritten and expanded version of our *Economics of Social Problems* which first appeared in 1976. We have taken the opportunity to incorporate numerous changes and extensions suggested by colleagues, students and reviewers who have used and commented upon the original edition. Our ideas have also been sharpened through writing a US version of the book in which problems similar to those faced in Britain are often resolved within a very different institutional framework. However, our basic approach to the analysis of social problems remains the same. Indeed, we believe that this approach – which is designed to encourage systematic analysis of alternative methods of economic organisation within the social policy area – is of even more relevance now than when we first wrote the book. Since then, privatisation proposals in health care, housing, education, etc. – which we discussed originally as possibilities suggested by academic inquiry – have, with the election of a radical right-wing government, assumed a central position on the policy agenda. As such, the topics covered here are of considerable contemporary concern.

The basic aim of the book is to introduce students to certain key economic concepts and methods of analysis through the study of a range of contemporary social problems. It is our deliberate intention to move away from the more abstract theorectical approach that is a feature of many introductory economics textbooks and instead try to provide a book that emphasises 'learning-by-doing'. This is done through the simultaneous development of the relevant theory and its application to particular social issues. The success of the first edition of the book has shown this approach to be both popular and effective.

All the relevant concepts and theories are explained in the text, and so no prior training in economics is required. Accordingly, the book may be used as a basic text for an introductory economics course. If it is used in this way, the student will acquire many of the basic skills of economic analysis that are usually obtained in a rather less appealing manner from a more conventional introductory textbook. Alternatively, it may be used as a supplementary text to provide students with an appreciation of the relevance of economic analysis to a range of instrinsically interesting social problems not normally dealt with in introductory textbooks. We believe that the book will prove of interest and value not only to students who will go on to specialise in economics but also to students in other disciplines, such as sociology, politics and social administration who would like to consider the contribution that economics can make towards understanding some of the pressing social problems that confront us today.

Although the book has been designed primarily for use at the introductory level, we hope that it may also be of interest to those with a more extensive background in economics and/or the problem areas studied. We believe that the approach we have adopted for the study of each topic is a useful way of clarifying the issues involved and has some claim to originality. This approach is discussed more fully below.

The Topics Chosen

We have called the issues discussed in this book 'social' problems, so as to distinguish them from the more conventional 'economic' problems (such as inflation, unemployment and economic growth) that are usually dealt with in introductory principles books. This is not a distinction we would seriously defend – all problems faced by a society, including economic ones, are presumably social problems by definition – but we feel that it has some support from popular usage. A more important common feature of the areas studied is that they are all amenable to a similar analytic approach, as explained in the following section.

Structure and Approach

In the process of teaching the material on which this book is based, we have learned a great deal about the difficulties that the study of our topics involves when used at the introductory level. In particular, we have found that students usually lack any framework that would enable them to introduce some order into their inquiries about particular problems. Teachers whose earlier education has provided them with such a framework sometimes forget the sense of confusion that the student feels when confronted with highly complex issues. For this reason we believe it to be imperative that a consistent approach for examining problems should be used throughout. This is a key feature of this book and its main claim to originality. We have not produced a set of separate essays on individual topics or a discursive examination of 'Some economic aspects' of each of the problem areas. Instead we have adopted an integrated and systematic framework for studying each problem in a consistent way.

Thus the reader will find that each chapter contains three basic sections. *First,* we ask what are society's objectives in the area concerned. In most cases we decide that these objectives can be conveniently summarised under two main headings: the achievement of *efficiency* and of *equity*. Efficiency considerations refer to the provision of the quantities of housing, hospitals, schools, roads, and so on that yield the greatest level of aggregate (net) benefit to the community. Equity issues are concerned with the justice or fairness of the way that these goods and services are divided between different members of society – for example: Who receives a university education? How should health care be divided between different patients? Which areas of the city should receive different amounts of policing? Who should receive council housing? However, while we concentrate upon efficiency and equity, there will be other objectives that society will also wish to pursue. The preservation of freedom or liberty and the promotion of altruism, for instance, are two others that figure in some of the areas in this book. Consequently, attention is drawn to them when it is considered relevant to do so. Having so specified society's objectives we can say that a social problem exists whenever the existing system fails to meet the objectives set for it.

Once we have defined a society's objectives, the next question to ask is: 'What kind of system could meet these objectives?' Since the private market system is the dominant means of providing the goods and services that we use in our everyday lives, it is the obvious place to begin an examination of alternative systems. In some of the areas we examine, the market is the main means actually used (housing and energy, for example); in others, the market has been either replaced or stringently regulated (education and health care, for example). Hence, the *second* main section of each chapter considers the arguments for and against the use of the market system as a means of allocating and distributing the good or service in question. Then in the light of certain shortcomings of the market, in the *third* section we examine the desirability of government intervention. Although we consider numerous forms of public policy, ranging from minor adjustments in the market's operation to its complete replacement, we show that they all fall into one or more of three general categories: that is, tax or subsidy policies, market regulation or direct public provision. But each of them is shown to be subject to the same tests of efficiency and equity that were relevant to the private market.

The first and last chapters do not have this structure since they are not concerned with specific problem areas; but they are none the less an integral part of the whole approach. Before students begin to study a particular problem, we feel it is important that they have at their disposal some general discussion of society's objectives and their relationship to the operations of the market system. Chapter 1 is an attempt to provide this. Students will find it useful to look at this chapter before they consult the one dealing with the area in which they are interested. The last chapter, Chapter 12, is an attempt to pull together the links between all the previous chapters. In the context of a general discussion about the merits and demerits of market and non-market allocation systems, it draws attention to the common elements in the discussions of each problem area and to their wider implications.

We believe that this format has two advantages. First it has the unity of approach that, as we emphasised above, is essential for the student to obtain a good understanding of the generality of economic analysis and indeed of the specific problems themselves. Second, it does in fact enable us to cover most of what economic analysis has contributed to these subjects. Much of the debate between economists has been about market versus non-market systems of allocation. Hitherto, however, the contributions to this debate have been dispersed among countless books and journals. As far as we are aware no one has previously brought together the disparate strands of this debate in a single integrated study. By doing so, at the introductory level, in the context of social issues of wide concern, we hope to make accessible to the maximum number of readers a systematic critique of market and non-market economic systems.

Note to the Teacher

Each of the chapters is largely self-contained and hence can be read quite separately from one another. This feature – which is deliberate – has involved some repetition in the later chapters of theoretical material that appears in the early ones; however, our experience suggests that when students are 'learning-by-doing', repetition is no bad thing. Within each chapter, sections and sub-sections have been carefully indicated so that, if necessary, they too could be read independently. Moreover, each chapter contains suggestions for further reading and a set of questions for discussion. Some of the questions relate directly to material presented in the relevant chapter, whereas others are designed to extend discussion beyond the limits of the chapter. Those familiar with the first edition of this book will note that many of the chapters have been extensively re-written in order to incorporate more up-to-date material and current issues – and, in some cases, to tighten the analytical structure – and that two extra chapters on crime and energy have been added.

If a full course is to be taught from the book, the following advice as to the order of topics might be helpful. We have found that it is useful to begin the course with a brief examination of society's objectives and the operations of the market, as in Chapter 1, then to continue with health and education – the discussions of which have strong analytic similarities and which also arouse passionate debate (and hence student interest). Poverty, as one of the fundamental issues underlying the discussions of most of the other topics, is a good subject with which to culminate the course; if there is time, it can be followed by a summary session, along the lines of Chapter 12, reviewing the first week's discussion of the market system in the light of subsequent course work.

Notes and References

When reference is made to an article or a book, we have simply specified the author's surname and the date of publication. A full bibliography is provided at the end of the book. Thus William Baumol and Alan Blinder's book, *Economics: Principles and Policy,* published in 1982, is referred to in the text as Baumol and Blinder (1982).

Acknowledgements

Again we are massively in debt to the many colleagues and students who have commented on earlier editions and on the manuscript of this one. In particular, Julian Le Grand would like to mention Kurt Klappholz and Alan Marin for most helpful comments on specific chapters. Ray Robinson would like to thank the members of the Urban Research Unit, Australian National University – especally Pat Troy and Peter Williams – who provided a stimulating environment during his stay as a visiting research fellow during the summer of 1982 when some of this book was written. Barbara Hammond, Christine Moll, Pauline Hinton, Pat Bennett and Jill Burford typed the manuscript with efficiency and equanimity. To them all, many thanks.

Julian Le Grand
Ray Robinson

Society's Objectives and the Allocation of Resources

1

Introduction

This chapter describes the analytical framework which is used in each of the subsequent chapters for the study of particular social problems. Those readers who have studied economics previously will recognise certain parts of the analysis (such as the theory of demand and supply), but are unlikely to have seen it incorporated within the general framework presented here. This is because we have endeavoured to explain at an introductory level the relationship between social objectives and methods of resource allocation, notably the market system. Explaining this relationship involves dealing with a number of theoretically complex issues and it is for this reason that most economics textbooks delay dealing with it until the inter-mediate or advanced level. However, the study of social problems is greatly assisted if some appreciation of the subject is acquired at the outset. Moreover we feel that it is possible to retain an acceptable degree of theoretical precision and at the same time convey certain key elements of the subject to a more general readership.

Accordingly, this chapter proceeds as follows. After a brief consideration of the concepts of scarcity and choice, we begin by specifying society's objectives in relation to economic activity. We suggest that it will want to select the quantity of output for each good and service that results in the highest attainable level of economic welfare. We term this the *efficient* level of output. We also suggest that it will want to distribute the goods and services it produces between the members of society in a way that is considered to be fair or just. This we term the *equity* objective. Finally, we suggest that other objectives within the social policy area are likely to include the desire to preserve *freedom* or *civil liberty* and the encouragement of *altruism*. Having considered these objectives we go on to explain the way in which a private market system of economic organisation – the *market system* – will organise economic activity, and to consider the extent to which it can be expected to realise these objectives. We conclude the chapter by anticipating some of the arguments that appear later in the book, which suggest that a market system cannot be expected to fulfil these objectives to a satisfactory extent, and consider the forms that government policy may take in its effort to realise these objectives more fully.

Scarcity and Choice

Economics is concerned with the way in which we use society's scarce resources to produce the goods and services which satisfy our material wants. Because it is through the consumption of various goods and services (commodities) that people satisfy their wants, we can say that these commodities yield economic benefits. Moreover the amount of benefit enjoyed by society may be expected to increase as the quantity of goods and services made available for consumption increases. Thus additional housing, improvements in the quality of education or health care, and increases in energy supplies will all yield positive benefits. Unfortunately, however, the resources of land, labour and capital which are used to produce these commodities are not available in unlimited supply, and so we cannot hope to produce a sufficient quantity to satisfy all our wants. The scarcity of resources in relation to the demands made on them leads inevitably to the need to make a series of choices about the quantities of different commodities that are to be produced. Production of a particular commodity will therefore have costs in the form of the other goods that could have been produced with the resources it uses up. For example, labour time or machinery that is devoted to car production is obviously not available for providing hospital facilities or schools. Because it is possible to look at the costs of production in terms of the alternative goods and services that could have been produced, economists have devised the term *opportunity cost*: the cost of producing cars is the forgone opportunity of providing other commodities such as hospital facilities.

In many situations the market price that is paid for the use of a resource reflects its opportunity cost. Thus we may expect the price a hospital has to pay for the services of a plumber or carpenter to be the same as he would receive when employed in the construction of new housing. Therefore the price paid by the hospital measures the value of the plumber or carpenter's service, not only to the hospital, but also in its alternative use in the housebuilding industry. But market prices do not always measure opportunity costs. In situations where society's resources are not being utilised fully, the decision to employ an additional resource in, say, the provision of hospital services will not necessarily imply a reduction in the availability of resources for alternative uses. So if there is unemployment of labour, or machines are standing idle, the decision to put them to work may incur a zero opportunity cost (for otherwise they would be producing nothing) even though the market price for their services will almost certainly be positive. In any discussion of the costs of resources used in production, the concept of opportunity cost should always be borne in mind.

Efficiency

When deciding on the quantity of a particular commodity that should be produced we will need to consider the way that both benefits and costs vary at different levels of output. In general, benefits are desirable and costs are to be avoided, so it would seem logical to try to select that output at which the excess of benefits over costs, called the *net benefit*, is largest. When society has selected this level of output and has allocated its resources accordingly, we say that there is an *efficient* allocation of resources or, alternatively, an efficient level of output. In the next two sections we shall investigate a little more closely the level of output that will satisfy this condition by considering the way that benefits and costs arise through the consumption and production of an everyday foodstuff – butter. Butter has been chosen because it is fairly simple commodity familiar to most people, although this is only for purposes of illustration – those cholesterol-conscious people who have forsaken butter will find that the arguments presented here are equally applicable to margarine! Indeed, as we shall show in the remainder of this book, the arguments can be extended to practically all commodities.

Benefits to Consumers

If we look at a typical person we will probably find that the total benefit (*tb*) he or she derives from eating butter will vary according to how much is eaten. In general we would expect *tb* to increase as more is consumed. However let us look a little more closely at the way in which benefits increase; specifically, let us consider the benefits which are derived from each separate gramme that is consumed. Most probably, this will depend on the quantity of butter that has been consumed already. If the person has had no butter at all, considerable satisfaction is likely to be obtained from spreading it on bread or toast. As the amount that is available already increases, the options facing the consumer will tend to satisfy less mouth-watering needs: spreading it a little more thickly or using it for purposes (such as cooking) for which inferior substitutes were used previously. By and large, we would expect to find that the benefit derived from each gramme becomes less as more immediate needs are satisfied. Hence each additional gramme will yield less benefit than the previous one. If we define the last unit of butter consumed at any level of consumption as the *marginal* unit, we can say that the benefit derived from the marginal unit – that is, the *marginal benefit* (*mb*) – declines as the quantity of butter consumed increases. Note, to say that *mb* declines does not mean that the consumer does not derive positive benefit from the marginal unit; it simply means that the benefit is less than was derived from the previous unit.

Now we can extend this analysis beyond the individual consumer to society as a whole. If we define society's benefits as the sum of the benefits received by each consumer of butter, we can add up each person's *tb* to obtain the *total social benefit* (*tsb*). Similarly we can add up the *mb*s derived by each person to obtain *marginal social benefit* (*msb*) – that is, the increase in *tsb* recorded as we increase society's consumption by a marginal unit. (Note that this process of adding up does require us to be able actually to add the amounts of benefit received by different consumers. Usually this is facilitated by expressing benefits, which are obviously subjective, in terms of a single objective unit of measurement, i.e. £s. However, this procedure can present problems if not everyone derives the same amount of benefit from a £.)

When we are considering society's consumption of butter, we are more likely to ask what is the *msb* of increasing consumption of a thousand tonnes than by a single gramme; but although the scale of analysis is different from that of the single consumer discussed above, the general principles of the example are unaffected. In particular, just as we would expect *mb* to decline as butter consumption increases, so we expect *msb* to decline. Society will also derive successively less benefit from each marginal unit as the total level of butter consumption increases. This information is depicted in Figure 1.1.

In Figure 1.1(a), *tsb* is measured in £s on the vertical axis and the quantity of butter consumed per week – in thousands of tonnes – is recorded on the horizontal axis. The *tsb* curve shows that as butter consumption increases *tsb* also increases, but that the increases in benefit become less at successively higher levels of consumption. For example, compare the increase in benefit between 40 000 and 60 000 tonnes with that between 120 000 and 140 000 tonnes. These increases in *tsb* are of course the *msb* at each level of consumption; the pattern of *msb*s implied by the *tsb* curve has been extracted and presented separately in Figure 1.1(b). This time the vertical axis measures *msb* while the horizontal axis continues to measure the quantity of butter consumed. The *msb* curve slopes downwards from left to right, showing that the *msb* declines as the level of butter consumption increases.

FIGURE 1.1
Benefits and Costs of Butter Consumption

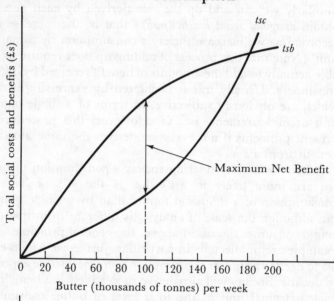

(a)

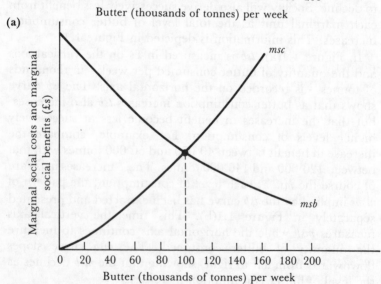

(b)

Costs of Production

Let us now look at the costs incurred in the production of butter – that is, the resources of land, labour, and capital that are used up. The actual chain of production of even a reasonably commonplace foodstuff will be quite complex – extending from the dairy farmer, and the equipment and labour that is used, through the manufacturing process, to the packaging and marketing in retail shops. It is not our intention to get involved in a detailed examination of all these costs, but instead to draw some broad conclusions about the way we can expect costs to vary as output increases.

If we take the typical firm engaged in the process of butter production, we would expect to find that its costs of production increase as its level of output expands, for it will need to employ a greater quantity of resources. Hence *total costs (tc)* will increase with output. But how will the costs of producing each additional unit of output – the *marginal cost (mc)* – vary as output increases? Numerous studies by economists have shown that when we take a reasonably short period of time (in our example it is one week), although the *mc* of production may at first decline as output increases, there is a level of production beyond which it becomes increasingly difficult to expand output without incurring heavier costs per unit produced. This phenomenon is commonly known as *diminishing returns* and it is caused by such factors as the need to bring older, less efficient equipment into service and to pay higher wages to induce people to work overtime or to attract new labour to the firm quickly. Therefore, over an important range of possible outputs, we can expect to find the firm experiencing rising *mc*.

Now in the same way that we added up individual consumer's benefits to obtain social benefits, so we can add up the individual firms' *tc*s to obtain the industry's *tc*. Moreover if we assume that all the costs of butter production are borne by the industry, its costs will represent *total social cost (tsc)*. Similarly the individual *mc*s can be added up to obtain the *marginal social cost (msc)* at each level of output. The *tsc* curve of Figure 1.1(a) shows the way that *tsc* is expected to increase with butter output and the *msc* curve of Figure 1.1(b) shows the corresponding behaviour of *msc*.

The Efficient Level of Output

Given the above description of the way in which social benefits and social costs vary as butter consumption and production increase, we are now in a position to identify the level of output at which the excess of *tsb* over *tsc* is greatest – that is, where net social benefit is at a maximum. This will be the *efficient* level of output. This position is most easily identified by again considering Figure 1.1(a). The level of output at which the *tsb* curve is at the greatest distance above the *tsc* curve is 100 000 tonnes per week. At any other level of output the excess of *tsb* over *tsc* will be less. A glance at the corresponding *msb* and *msc* curves in Figure 1.1(b) will show that this point of maximum net benefit will occur where *msb* = *msc*. A moment's thought should confirm why this must be so: as long as the *msb* of a unit of output is greater than its *msc*, society will gain by more being produced, for each unit will add more to benefits than to costs. Conversely, if *msc* is greater than *msb*, society will gain if butter consumption is curtailed, for in this situation the last unit produced is adding more to costs than to benefits. Only where *msb* is equal to *msc* will it be impossible to increase net social benefits by changing the level of output. Hence an equivalent way of defining the efficient level of output is to say that it occurs when marginal social benefit equals marginal social cost.

This analysis of the efficient level of butter output is, as we said earlier, not only relevant to the production of butter but to all goods and services. Hence we can define the socially efficient output of cars, health care, education, housing or any other commodity in exactly the same way. Overall efficiency is achieved when the market for every commodity is producing its efficient amount. In such a situation it will be impossible to increase net social benefit by reallocating resources from one area of production to another, for the reallocation of a resource will lead to a reduction in output in the market from which it is taken (and hence a departure from its efficient level) and an increase in the market to which it goes (and, once again, a departure from the efficient level).

Thus to say that we have an efficient allocation of resources is a powerful statement, for it means that net social benefit cannot be increased by a reallocation of resources and/or a rearrangement of production. This would indeed seem to be an important aim that any economic system should set itself. However this will not be society's only objective. It must be stressed that an efficient system does not necessarily imply a fair or *equitable* one. At first sight this may seem to be a strange statement, for we have said that an efficient system is one that produces the maximum net benefit for society. This might be taken to imply that it will be equitable, because a society in which there are gross inequalities of income – where Rolls Royces exist alongside widespread poverty – is hardly likely to produce the maximum benefit for all its members. But such a conclusion would misunderstand the meaning of maximum net benefit. It only refers to the overall level of net benefit for a given distribution of income; it does not concern itself with the way it is distributed between the individual members of society. The notion of equity is not dealt with by the efficiency criterion in the way the latter is generally used by economists. Let us examine more closely why this is so.

Equity

The distinction between efficiency and equity can probably be explained best by means of an example. Suppose there are just two members of society – Adam and Eve – who produce and consume all their own butter (with, of course, a little help from their four-legged friends). Now assume there are a variety of ways in which Adam and Eve can organise their time and work, but that the amount of butter produced per week for which their total benefit is greatest is ten kilograms (kg). Therefore, following our earlier discussions, we can say that the system of work that produced ten kg per week is an efficient system. Now there are a number of ways in which they could divide these ten kg between themselves for consumption. For example, they could have five kg each, or Eve could have six kg and Adam four kg, or Adam ten kg and Eve none. They are all possible, and all could occur at an efficient level of output, but we would probably not consider them all to be fair. Questions concerning the distribution of butter between Adam and Eve are matters of *equity* and must be considered as distinct from the question of efficiency.

The distinction is stressed in Figure 1.2. On the vertical axis we measure the quantity of butter consumed by Adam and on the horizontal axis the amount consumed by Eve. The straight line *UU* is called the *consumption possibility frontier*, for it traces out the maximum combinations of consumption (and hence benefit) open to Adam and Eve. For instance, at point *A* they both receive five kg, while at point *B* Eve receives eight kg and Adam receives only two kg. Now clearly any combination, such as *C* (where both receive four kg and there are two kg left over), is an inefficient combination because it would be possible to move to a point on the frontier, such as *A*, at which both Adam and Eve are better off. The same will be true for any other combination inside the frontier: it will always be possible to make at least one person better off without affecting the other, or to make them both better off. Only when a combination on the frontier is selected will we have an efficient solution. But of course this does not mean that it will be equitable. There will be many combinations lying on the frontier, but a number of them will involve quite uneven distributions. One's view about the equity of these various combinations will depend on one's ethical views about the way that butter, or benefits, should be distributed between Adam and Eve. It is because questions of equity involve personal value judgements about the way in which benefits should be distributed among members of society that many economists claim them to be outside the realm of their professional competence. Economists, it is argued, are no better equipped to supply answers to these questions than are any other citizens. Accordingly they have confined their attention to the allegedly value-free efficiency condition claiming that questions involving the distribution of benefits are matters for the political process. However, one should always be wary about claims of value-free (and hence superior?) social science. Some people who recommend the pursuit of efficiency imply that this is a value-free, technical matter without apparently realising, or revealing, that their prior acceptance of a given income distribution (often

FIGURE 1.2
Efficiency and Equity

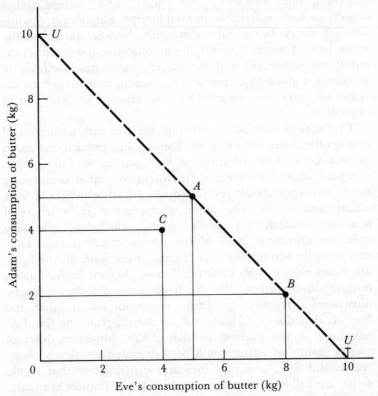

the existing one) itself involves a value judgement. In fact the only difference between the objectives of efficiency and equity – in terms of their dependence upon value judgements – is that there is greater consensus among economists about what constitutes efficiency (as described in the previous section) than there is about what constitutes equity: but this is a difference of degree not kind.

Consequently the view taken in this book is that the economist's methods of analysis may be used to evaluate alternative methods of economic organisation in terms of their success in achieving both efficiency and equity; and, indeed, other objectives such as freedom or civil liberty. Furthermore, while we shall always be careful to distinguish between the inevitably value-laden process of specifying an objective (be it efficiency, equity or whatever) and the largely value-free methods of achieving a given objective, it is relevant to note that economic reasoning may also actually serve to clarify the definition of objectives.

To illustrate this point, consider the two interpretations of equity often associated with the social policy areas investigated in this book. One of these is the concept of full *equality*: everyone should have equal treatment for equal health care needs, everyone should receive equal education subject to their ability and so on. The other interpretation is in terms of *minimum standards*: no person should fall below a socially specified minimum level of income or consumption. Thus every family should live in a decent house with all the basic amenities even though some families would have better quality housing than others. Now both of these objectives can be illustrated in terms of our earlier discussion about Adam and Eve. This is done in Figure 1.3. In the diagram the line OE, running from the origin at an angle of 45°, shows how different total amounts of butter could be distributed equally between Adam and Eve, and thus indicates distributions that would satisfy the full equality criterion. With 10kg of butter available, it would obviously indicate that 5kg each was the most preferred combination on both equity and efficiency grounds. On the other hand, assume that in this two-person society agreement has been reached specifying a minimum level of consumption of 2kg of butter below which no-one should fall. This minimum standard objective is depicted by the two lines $M_A M'_A$ and $M_E M'_E$. They indicate that only combinations of consumption enclosed by the two lines to the north-east of their point of intersection will satisfy the minimum consumption constraint. And with a consumption possibilities frontier UU defined for 10kg of butter, they indicate a range of distributions on the frontier that will be considered equitable and efficient.

FIGURE 1.3
Full Equality and Minimum Standard Definitions of Equity

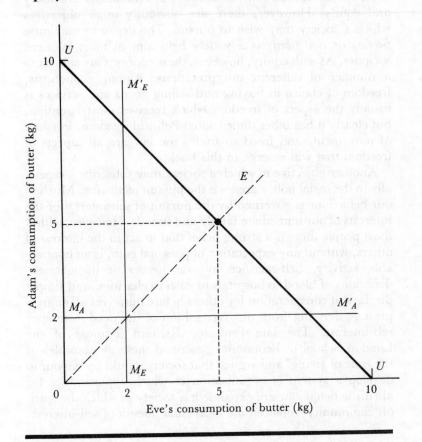

Other Social Objectives

Because this book is concerned with the economic analysis of social problems most of our attention is devoted to the two objectives most commonly considered by economists: efficiency and equity. However, there are obviously other objectives which a society may wish to pursue. The desire to maximise *freedom* or *civil liberty* is a widely held aim in most Western societies. As with equity, however, these concepts are subject to a number of different interpretations. Among economists, freedom of choice in buying and selling goods and services is usually the aspect of freedom which receives most attention, but clearly it has other dimensions. Political freedom, freedom of movement, and freedom under the law are all aspects of freedom that will emerge in this book.

Another objective to which a society may subscribe – especially in the social policy area – is the pursuit of *altruism*. Much of our behaviour is governed by the pursuit of self-interest or the interests of our immediate family and friends. However, within most people there is a strong belief that to act in the interest of others, without any expectation of personal gain, is an honourable activity. Self-sacrifice by war heroes or lifeboatmen, donations of blood to hospitals or cash to charities, and simple displays of consideration for others before ourselves all enjoy a prestige deriving from our recognition of the need to temper self-interest. The late Professor Richard Titmuss of the London School of Economics described these as examples of the 'role of giving' and argued that society should endeavour to develop a system of organisation in which opportunities for altruistic behaviour are expanded: a society in which the spirit of 'community' replaced the individual pursuit of self-interest.

The Market System

As we stressed earlier, wherever scarcity exists society is confronted with problems of choice. A variety of ways have been devised, at different times and in different places, to provide particular societies with a set of rules or laws by which these choices can be made. For instance, in certain primitive societies chiefs or councils of elders typically made decisions about what foods should be grown, gathered, and hunted. They also decided how their members were to go about these tasks and who was to receive the food and other goods produced by the community. At a slightly more complex level, feudal societies also operated on a similar system of central direction.

Among the large-scale societies of today two dominant methods of performing these tasks of allocation can be identified. On the one hand there are the *planned* economies of Eastern Europe, the Soviet Union and China in which primary emphasis is placed upon the administrative planning of production by government appointed decision-makers. Within these societies the main means of production are in public ownership and decisions about what and how goods are produced, and to whom they should be allocated, are made via a government bureaucracy. Obviously the particular systems of individual countries vary quite considerably, especially in relation to the amount of decentralisation of power they display, but they all – to a greater or lesser extent – share a common reliance upon government decision-making as a means of co-ordinating everyone's activities. In contrast, the economies of North America, Western Europe, Australia and Japan, and Third World countries such as India, employ a system of economic organisation in which the majority of allocation decisions are made through the ostensibly unco-ordinated actions of large numbers of individuals and private firms. The co-ordination of activities within these countries comes about because each factor of production (land, labour and capital) and each commodity has a *price* to which diverse groups respond in a way that reconciles their separate actions. Once again, of course, the systems of particular countries display considerable variation: in Britain, for example, there is a much larger element of public ownership and decision-making than in the United States. But all these countries have a central feature in common; that is a dependence upon the price or *market* system as the dominant form of economic organisation. Because of its dominance within our society our primary focus of attention in this book will be on the way in which the market system operates (or could be expected to operate), especially in areas where social problems arise. In the meantime, however, the remainder of this chapter is devoted to an explanation of some of the essential elements of the market system.

Let us continue to use the butter example for illustrative purposes. As in the case of all commodities we shall distinguish between those people who buy and eat the butter, the *consumers*, and those who provide the butter for sale, the *producers*. In general, consumers comprise private households while the producers are usually organised groups known as firms. Of course, a particular individual will be both a consumer and producer at different times; the categories refer to the actions taking place while performing a particular role rather than to distinct categories of individuals. By looking at each group in turn we can see how their respective, apparently unco-ordinated actions are reconciled by the market system.

Consumer Demand

Each individual has a set of tastes or preferences that will determine, among other things, how much butter he would like to consume. However, a general preference for acquiring a commodity only becomes a *demand* for the commodity when the consumer is willing and able to pay for it. Hence the price of butter and the amount of income the individual possesses, as well as his tastes, will also determine how much he demands. Also the prices of other commodities, such as margarine, may affect the quantity of butter he demands.

Let us for the moment confine our attention to the way the demand for butter varies as its price varies, with all the other factors remaining unchanged. There is a certain amount of intuitive appeal in the proposition that a consumer's demand will increase as the price falls: thus as butter becomes cheaper a person is induced to buy more of it. If we then add up all the individual demands that would be forthcoming at each price we should be able to see how much butter would be demanded within the economy at each price. This information will be embodied in a *market demand curve* of the type presented in Figure 1.4(a). In this diagram the vertical axis measures the price of butter per 250g packet and the horizontal axis

FIGURE 1.4
The Demand and Supply of Butter

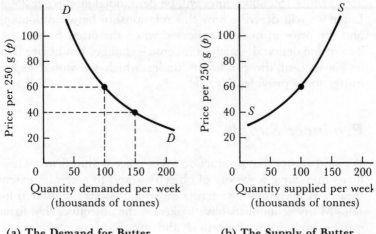

(a) The Demand for Butter

(b) The Supply of Butter

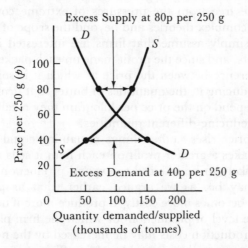

(c) Market Equilibrium Output and Price

measures the quantity demanded in thousands of tonnes. The demand curve slopes downwards from left to right, showing that the quantity demanded will increase as the price falls. Thus 100 000 tonnes will be demanded at a price of 60p per 250g, while 150 000 tonnes will be demanded at 40p per 250g. Later we will describe how this relationship between demand and the price of butter is affected when the other factors that determine demand – such as income – change, but before then let us look at the conditions under which we would expect butter to be provided for sale.

Producer Supply

We said earlier that production takes place within firms. These firms may have a variety of objectives and to a certain extent these will determine the terms on which goods are offered for sale. Many economists have looked at the objectives that firms pursue both from theoretical and empirical points of view. Some claim that firms aim to maximise profits; others maintain that they try to maximise sales; still others believe that firms do not pursue maximising targets at all but are more interested in a quiet life free from the pressures of extreme competition. These are complex theories and beyond the scope of this book. We shall simply assume that firms are interested in making some profits, and since the profit made on each packet of butter is the difference between the price at which it is sold and the cost of producing it, the quantities of butter that firms offer for sale will depend on the price per kilogram they receive and the costs of producing different quantities.

As the price rises – other things remaining equal – the firm initially makes a greater profit on each item it sells and therefore it is likely to be induced to expand production. Furthermore it may be, as we argued earlier, that as production expands it becomes more costly to produce more if output goes beyond the level of production for which the firm planned. In this case production costs may be increased by the need to pay overtime wages and to use older, less efficient equipment to supplement that used in normal times. For these reasons we may expect the firm to offer more for sale as the price it obtains increases or, put alternatively, to ask a higher price as its output increases. By adding up the quantities that each firm is willing to supply at different prices, we can see the quantity that the industry will supply at various prices. This information, commonly presented in the form of an *industry supply curve*, is depicted in Figure 1.4(b). The curve slopes upwards from left to right, showing that a greater quantity of butter will be offered for sale as its price rises.

Market Price and Output

We have now established a relationship between the quantity of butter that would be demanded and supplied at different price levels. By combining these two figures we can see how much is *actually* bought and sold and at what price. This is done in Figure 1.4(c), where both the demand and supply curves are shown on the same diagram. The point where the two curves intersect represents the price and quantity at which both consumers' and producers' requirements are met. In this case, consumers are willing to buy 100 000 tonnes of butter at 60p per 250g packet and firms are willing to supply that quantity at that price. This price–output combination, known as the point of *equilibrium*, is the one that will be established in the market and it will persist until some outside influence disturbs the situation. We can see why the equilibrium point is the one towards which market price and quantity will move by considering what would happen if the market price were *above* the equilibrium, say at 80p per 250g. At this price firms are willing to supply 125 000 tonnes of butter but consumers are willing to buy only 75 000 tonnes. If this price persists firms will overproduce and stocks will begin to pile up. The only way to rectify the situation is to lower the price. This has two effects: it increases the demand for butter and at the same time reduces the supply coming on to the market. In this way the discrepancy between demand and supply is reduced until it is eliminated at the equilibrium price.

The same process will also ensure that price cannot remain *below* the equilibrium level. If, for example, the price were 40p per 250g consumers would demand 150 000 tonnes per week while firms were only willing to supply 50 000 tonnes. In this situation butter would be snapped up as soon as it was offered for sale and shelves and stockrooms would soon be bare. The more astute firms would soon notice that a lot of demand was remaining unsatisfied at this price and that they could, in the next week, sell all they had to offer at a higher price and thereby make larger profits. Prices would therefore begin to rise. Once again this would have two effects: it would reduce the demand for butter and induce producers to supply more. The tendency for prices to continue to rise would only end when the equilibrium price was reached, for then demand and supply would be equated.

Such are the rudiments of the way the market system operates: the ostensibly unco-ordinated actions, and possibly conflicting interests, of consumers and producers are reconciled by the way they both respond to common price 'signals', and in this way market output is determined. For simplicity we have confined our discussion of the way the market system operates to the case of butter, but obviously the application is far more general. In each commodity market, whether it is butter or bread, health care or housing, decisions regarding the level of output can be decided by the interaction of demand and supply. Furthermore this operation is not only confined to markets for commodities. It also applies to the markets for factors of production. If one looks at the number (that is, the quantity) of construction workers or lawyers who are employed, and the wage or salary (that is, the price) they receive, one can see that demand and supply factors often play a key role. (The way in which the amount of income received by owners of factors of production is determined is discussed in Chapter 10.)

The discussion thus far of the way in which consumers and producers react to price levels different from the equilibrium price has shown how their respective actions tend to move market price and output to the equilibrium level. These same reactions can also be expected to establish a new equilibrium price–output combination if a change in market circumstances renders the existing one inappropriate. Indeed, one of the most important attributes claimed for the market system as an allocator of both commodities and resources is its ability to respond quickly and smoothly to change. In the next section we look at the way in which it does this.

The Market System and Change

For the sake of continuity we shall ask for the reader's tolerance and continue with our butter example. When the demand and supply curves of Figure 1.4 were constructed it was stated that they showed the way in which the demand and supply of butter were likely to vary as its price varied, when all the other factors that might be expected to affect demand (and supply) remain unchanged. We shall now relax this assumption and see what happens when one or more of these factors changes. We will consider one example of a change in the determinants of demand and one of a change on the supply side of the market. First, let us look at demand.

Suppose that for some reason the incomes of a large section of the population increase. We would expect that some of this additional income would be used to buy more butter: that is, some consumers who were not able to afford to buy much before will be able to use butter instead of cheaper substitutes and others will be able to become more lavish in their use of it. In terms of our diagrams society's increased affluence can be conveyed by constructing a new demand curve to the right of the original one. (This is sometimes referred to as a *shift* in the demand curve although, strictly speaking, it is a new curve.) Thus in Figure 1.5(a) the curve $D'D'$ shows that a greater quantity of butter will be demanded at each price – at the new higher level of income – than at the previous level. Now at the original equilibrium price of 60p per 250g packet there is a new, higher level of demand – 150 000 tonnes. However, since there has been no change in the conditions under which producers supply butter, the quantity they are offering for sale is shown by the original supply curve (SS). So at a price of 60p per 250g, they still offer 100 000 tonnes. Thus we have a situation in which demand exceeds supply at the prevailing market price. And, as we know from our earlier discussion, we can expect some upward movement in the price until a new

FIGURE 1.5
Change and Market Equilibrium

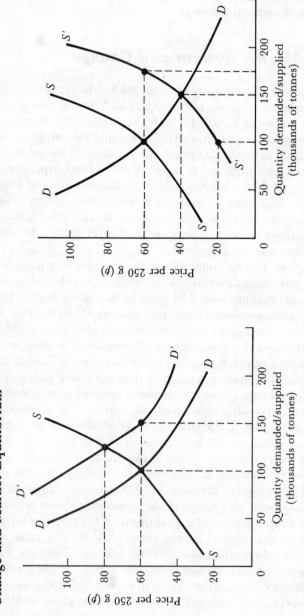

(a) Market Equilibrium following a Change in Demand

(b) Market Equilibrium following a Change in Supply

equilibrium is established. This is shown in Figure 1.5(a) by the point of intersection between $D'D'$ and SS – that is, an output of 125 000 tonnes at a price of 80p per 250g. The 20p rise in price has induced producers to supply more and 'choked off' some of the excess demand that existed at the old equilibrium price.

Second, let us look at the effects of a change in supply. Consider a new discovery in butter-making technology that enables firms to produce butter at less cost. This may be expected to lead firms to lower their prices and still make the same, or even greater, levels of profit. Thus, at each level of output, firms will charge a lower price. This information is conveyed by the new supply curve ($S'S'$) in Figure 1.5. (Verify your understanding by checking to see that each quantity is being offered at a lower price than before. Where would the curve lie if a change in supply conditions led to higher prices being charged?) Now producers are willing to sell the old equilibrium output of 100 000 tonnes at 20p per 250g or to offer 175 000 tonnes for sale at the old market price of 60p per 250g. However, neither of these alternatives is compatible with consumers' willingness to buy, as indicated by the unchanged demand curve (DD). At the new lower price of 20p there would be too much demand, and at the old price of 60p not enough demand for the larger amount being offered for sale. Clearly an intermediate price needs to be found. Such a price is given at the point of intersection between the unchanged demand curve DD and the new supply curve $S'S'$ – that is, 150 000 tonnes at 40p per 250 g. The new equilibrium price is lower than the previous one, but the lower production costs permit firms to produce a larger equilibrium output.

The two examples given above show the way in which changes in the determinants of demand and supply – other than price – can be incorporated into an analysis of the way the market system functions. We have only considered two such changes but, obviously, many are possible. (Again, test your understanding of the way that changes in external factors may be accommodated by considering the effect on the initial price–output equilibrium of the following events: (a) an increase in the price of margarine, (b) an increase in the price of cattle foodstuffs, and (c) a publicity campaign linking the incidence of heart disease with the consumption of foodstuffs containing animal fats. After considering the effect of each of these events separately, suppose they happen simultaneously!)

As mentioned earlier, the way in which the market system reacts to change is often claimed to be one of its main attributes. There is no need for a complex administrative system to make decisions about changes in the composition of output. This is achieved by the supposedly unco-ordinated, individual actions of a vast number of consumers and producers, each acting in response to price 'signals'. If butter production becomes more costly, price will reflect this and demand and output will probably fall while the production of some other good increases. The system is automatic or, in the words of Adam Smith – the father of modern economics – there is 'an invisible hand' at work.

The Market System and Social Objectives

We have now discussed both the concept of an efficient level of output and the level of output that will be established in a market system in terms of our butter example. However, the link between the two approaches is far more fundamental than this choice of an arbitrary example might suggest. It will no doubt have been noticed that the marginal social benefit and the marginal social cost curves have the same general appearance as the demand and supply curves. The benefit and demand curves slope downwards and the cost and supply curves slope upwards. This is no coincidence. In fact an essential part of the theory underlying the market system is that in certain circumstances the demand curve is an alternative presentation of the marginal social benefit curve and the supply curve is an alternative form of the marginal social cost curve. In that case *the equilibrium output obtained through the market system will be the efficient level of output.* Let us look at the system a little more closely to see why this is so.

For any rational individual who wants to maximise the net benefit obtained from consumption, it must be the case that the maximum price he or she is willing to pay for a commodity is determined by the *mb* derived from it. An individual will not be willing to pay a price greater than the *mb* received because this would lead to higher costs being incurred than benefits obtained. Similarly a rational consumer will always be willing to pay the market price if it is less than the *mb* obtained, for net benefit will be increased through each extra unit of the commodity consumed. In such a situation a person will continue consuming additional quantities of the commodity until the *mb* derived falls to the level of the price. At this point there is no further possibility for increasing net benefit. Thus the price a consumer is willing to pay for different quantities of a commodity, or the demand curve, is defined by the *mb* curve. Now when we discussed the marginal social benefit (*msb*) curve we said that this was obtained by adding the individual *mb* curves of each consumer. Similarly the market demand curve is obtained by adding all the individual demand curves. So if each individual *mb* curve is identical to the individual's demand curve, the *msb* curve must be identical to the market demand curve. From society's point of view the price that consumers collectively are willing to pay, or their demand, is determined by the sum of their individual marginal benefits, or the marginal social benefit.

Moreover, as long as there are many firms in competition with one another, the link between the marginal cost and supply curves can be established in a similar fashion. For each firm, the price at which it will sell a particular quantity of a commodity will equal the costs of production it incurs on the last unit of output as production increases, or the marginal cost (*mc*). For if it were to sell a commodity at a price less than the cost of producing the last unit it sells, the firm would lose money on that last unit. If it were to sell the commodity at a price more than the cost of producing the last unit, other firms could undercut it by reducing their prices to the level of marginal cost. Therefore under competitive conditions the marginal cost and supply curves must be the same thing. Further, if the marginal social cost (*msc*) is the sum of the individual firms' *mc*s at each level of output the result is that the *msc* curve and the market supply curve also are identical.

Thus the interaction of demand and supply can be expected to lead to an efficient level of output. Now this is obviously a very important prediction. We are saying that an unfettered competitive market system in which both consumers and producers are intent on maximising their *individual* net benefits will lead to the maximisation of *society's* net benefit. Or as Adam Smith put it:

> **It is not from the benevolence of the butcher, the brewer, or the baker that we expect our dinner but from their regard to their own interest. We address ourselves not to their humanity but to their self-love, and never talk to them of our own necessities but of their advantages.**

It is the claim that a market system will produce an efficient allocation of resources which provides the major theoretical basis for preferring it to other methods of economic organisation. But because this claim is often obscured in emotion-laden debates between ideologues of the political left and right, it is important to establish exactly what it asserts.

First, it is important to recognise that the prediction that a market system will achieve efficiency rests upon certain assumptions about the way in which the market operates. These have not been spelt out in this chapter because an examination of them, and the possibility that they will not be met in specific problem areas, constitutes a major element of the remainder of this book. However, to anticipate our conclusions, the reader will find that we identify a series of important *market imperfections* which can be expected to prevent it achieving efficiency. Second, we must emphasise again that despite its dominance in the economics literature, efficiency is likely to be only one of society's objectives. From among the others we have selected the aim of equity for special attention. And as we have seen, an efficient system is compatible with a number of different distributions of benefits between the members of society, many of which may be highly inequitable.

We have also indicated other objectives such as freedom, civil liberty and the promotion of altruism. Professors F.A. Hayek and Milton Friedman have argued forcefully that it is only through a market system that economic and political freedom can be preserved. But this view has its opponents. In particular they criticise the concepts of freedom employed by Friedman and others, and claim that under rather different interpretations of freedom the market system performs less well. Take, for example, the claim that a citizen of the United States has a freedom of movement that is not enjoyed by a citizen of the Soviet Union. Thus an ordinary US citizen may visit the Soviet Union as a tourist but his Russian counterpart would probably be denied the exit visa necessary to travel abroad and visit the United States. However while the *formal* freedom of movement may differ considerably, the *effective* freedom may vary less so. A member of a poverty-line family living in a US urban ghetto has the formal freedom to tour the Soviet Union but income limitations are likely to effectively prevent him from so doing. In fact, a Soviet party member, sportsman or woman, or concert musician is likely to enjoy greater freedom of movement than many low-income US citizens. In short, freedom depends upon the nature and extent of the *constraints* facing an individual: in a market system income limitations constitute a major constraint whereas in a socialist economy political constraints are likely to be more important.

Finally, there is the objective of altruism. For many of the social reformers who were influential in the establishment of the 'welfare state' the market system, with its dependence upon the pursuit of self-interest, was inconsistent with the objectives of caring and altruism which they wished to promote. This belief is still held strongly by present day supporters of the welfare state who maintain that government finance and provision of services such as health care, housing and education is far more likely to produce a sense of community than is private provision. And so once again, the ability of the market system to realise one of society's objectives is called into question.

Government and the Market System

The failure of the market system to realise satisfactorily the objectives which our society has set itself has led to various types of government intervention. The precise form of government policy in the areas of health care, education, housing, etc., will be the subject of discussion in the individual chapters of this book. However, because it is easy to become immersed in the detail of individual policies at the cost of losing sight of the general principles they are meant to embody, it may help the reader if we specify at the outset the general categories within which all government policies fall. First there is *regulation* of the market system. This involves specifying, via law, what activities may, or may not, or have to be undertaken. Examples of regulation include pollution control standards (for example, smokeless zones), rent control restrictions, compulsory schooling until 16 years of age and public health legislation. Second, a government may use *tax* or *subsidy* policies to deter those activities it wishes to restrict and to encourage those activities it wishes to expand. Examples of the use of tax/subsidy policies are student grants, tax concessions to house owners, home insulation grants, congestion and pollution taxes, and taxes on scarce energy resources. Third, the government may seek to achieve the desired allocation of resources through *direct provision* which actually replaces the market system. The National Health Service, the provision of council houses and public transport provide examples of this policy.

Now through the use of regulation, tax/subsidy policies or direct provision the government tries to achieve, more fully than the market system by itself can achieve, the social objectives it has set. But it should be stressed that it does not always realise this aim. So far we have discussed only the potential failings of the market system but, as we shall see, sometimes government policies designed to rectify these failings actually exacerbate the situation. We can only hope to identify the best system – whether it is private, public or mixed – by careful analysis of the theoretical and empirical evidence. This is the task of the remainder of this book.

Summary

In this chapter we have argued that most societies pursue a number of objectives in the allocation and distribution of resources. From these we have selected *efficiency* and *equity* for particular attention, although we have also discussed *freedom* and *altruism*. We have defined the efficient level of output as the one which yields maximum net social benefit; that is, where the marginal social cost of production equals its marginal social benefit. We have shown that, *under certain conditions*, the inter-action of demand and supply within the market system will achieve an efficient level of output. It may also promote freedom, according to some definitions of that term. However, there is less reason to be confident that it will achieve an equit-able distribution of resources or promote altruism and a sense of community. Given the likelihood that a market system will be able only partially to meet the objectives set for it, we have anticipated methods of government intervention that may be used to meet these aims more fully viz, *regulation, taxes* and *subsidies*, and *direct provision*. These will be examined more thoroughly, within the context of specific social problems, in the remainder of the book.

Further Reading

There are a large number of introductory textbooks that develop the ideas contained in this chapter at greater length and depth. Individual students and teachers will no doubt have their favourites and so we have just provided some suggestions for the reader who is totally unfamiliar with these texts. Probably the most widely used introductory textbook in Britain is Lipsey (1979). A recent American textbook, Baumol and Blinder (1982) covers similar ground and includes a number of interesting applied examples, albeit frequently with a North American emphasis. Hunt and Sherman (1981) is a less com-plete formal text but it does include some discussion of matters of *political* economy that social problems inevitably involve. Sandford (1977) and Gordon (1982) are both concerned with the economics of social policy and include chapters on the macro-economic constraints which affect its formulation. Professor Friedman's ideas may be found in Friedman and Friedman (1980) and those of Professor Titmuss in Titmuss (1970).

Questions for Discussion

1. The concepts of *social* benefit and *social* cost involve the summation of individual benefits and costs. What problems does this procedure pose?

2. 'The specification of an efficient allocation of resources, unlike the definition of an equitable distribution, does not involve personal value judgements.' Discuss this claim.

3. How would you go about specifying an equitable distribution of income for Britain today?

4. The price system is based upon consumer *demand*; how does this differ from consumer *need*?

5. Will the achievement of an equitable distribution of resources inevitably involve inefficiency and a restriction of personal freedom?

6. Explain how you would expect maximum price controls to affect the operation of the price system.

7. Do you think that reliance upon the price system precludes the promotion of altruism?

8. Contrast the view of society presented in Chapter 1 with a Marxian view.

9. In what ways would you expect the development of large firms to affect the model of the price system presented in Chapter 1.

10. Consider the concept of freedom and the extent to which it is promoted by alternative economic systems.

Health 2

Good health is one of the most important factors contributing to individual welfare. It is an essential prerequisite for enjoyment of almost every other aspect of life. A high income or a good education yield little satisfaction to the chronically sick. And, at the extreme, ill health that leads to death will make all other sources of satisfaction irrelevant.

It is not surprising, therefore, that throughout the world considerable resources have been devoted to the maintenance and preservation of health. In Britain and in most other European countries health care expenditures take up about six per cent of the Gross National Product; in the United States they take up nearly 10 per cent. Despite the amount of resources involved, however, the area has only become of interest to economists relatively recently. It is not clear why this is so. Perhaps because it involves dealing with highly emotional and sensitive issues, economists have not traditionally viewed it as suitable for the application of economic analysis. Even now there is a strong feeling among many non-economists that health is a matter of 'social' and not 'economic' concern, and therefore that the tools economists use for studying problems of resource allocation in other areas are simply not appropriate for the field of health.

It is one of the aims of this chapter to show that this feeling is mistaken. The fundamental problems of resource allocation apply to health just as they do in any other area of life. What proportion of the nation's resources should be devoted to the

31

maintenance of its citizens' health? What is the best method of achieving a given level of health care from limited resources? Should health care be privately or publicly provided? All these are 'economic' problems in the sense that they are problems of resource allocation, and they are all therefore problems for which the economist's tools can contribute to finding the answers.

Many factors contribute to individuals' states of health. These include diet, work situation, public health measures (such as sewage disposal and rubbish collection) and the availability and quality of health (or medical) care. Resource allocation problems arise in each of these areas, and to treat them all adequately would be beyond the scope of this chapter. Accordingly we shall concentrate on the last of them: health care. First we look at the objectives society might have with respect to the provision of health care. Then we examine the possibility of using the market system to allocate such care: its advantages and disadvantages as a means of achieving the objectives. Finally, in the light of certain market shortcomings, we discuss the various ways in which the state can intervene.

Objectives

We saw in Chapter 1 that two important aims that have to be considered in any question of resource allocation are the attainment of efficiency and the promotion of social justice or equity. Let us see how these can be interpreted in the context of health care.

Efficiency

A common definition of an efficient health care system is one that provides the highest possible standard of care, regardless of cost. As an American doctor has put it:

> It is incumbent on the physician ... to practice not 'cost effective' medicine but that which is as safe as possible for that patient under the particular circumstances. Optimiza-

tion of survival and not optimization of cost effectiveness is the only ethical imperative ... A physician who changes his or her way of practising medicine because of cost rather than purely medical considerations has indeed embarked on the 'slippery slope' of compromised ethics and waffled priorities. (Loewy, 1980, p. 697)

This point of view has a strong influence on the way that medical practitioners actually behave; understandably so, since it is of obvious ethical appeal. Unfortunately as a policy guide it is a non-starter, for costs cannot be ignored in making policy choices. The building of hospitals, the training of doctors and nurses, the manufacture of drugs and technical equipment – all off these consume scarce resources. That is, they use up land, labour and capital: resources that could have been put to other uses, such as building schools, training teachers or making cars. The 'best possible' standard of health care could only be achieved by devoting all of the economy's resources to it; hardly a wise course of action, since no other commodities (including those vital to health, such as food) could be produced.

Even within health care itself the idea that physicians should always provide the best possible treatment regardless of cost makes little sense. Doctors who give their patients 'Rolls-Royce' treatment are likely to be depriving other patients of treatment they need. The cost of one heart transplant, for example, could keep twenty or more sufferers of kidney disease on home-dialysis for a year. 'Optimisation of survival' cannot be a target for the allocation of resources, even within the health sector, for the survival prospects of one patient can only be increased at the expense of the survival prospects of others.

What is needed is a definition of efficiency that takes account of the costs of, as well as the benefits from, health care. An obvious starting point is the definition suggested in Chapter 1. There an efficient level of production of a commodity was defined as one where the difference between benefits and costs is greatest: that is, where the marginal social benefit (msb) from a production of the commodity equals its marginal social cost (msc). A simple example will show how this might be applied in the field of health care.

Suppose we are trying to decide what is the efficient number of hospital beds to provide in a paricular town. Imagine that we can measure the benefits and costs of providing hospital beds in terms of money (how this might be done is discussed below). Looking at these benefits and costs, we find that to provide 1000 hospital beds would yield a social benefit of £20 million and would cost only £10 million. To provide a second 1000 beds would benefit the town rather less than the first: say, by £12 million. It would cost slightly more: say, also £12 million. To provide a third 1000 beds would cost yet more – £16 million – and create benefits of only £8 million. Thus the benefit from providing each extra 1000 beds, the *msb*, declines while the cost, the *msc*, increases. This is as would be expected. Once the major needs of an area have been satisfied the benefits from providing more and more hospital beds are likely to diminish, while with each new hospital built the resources available for building yet another one become increasingly scarce and, therefore, more expensive.

These figures, together with their equivalents for a fourth and fifth thousand beds, are summarised in Table 2.1. From this table we can deduce what would be the efficient number of hospital beds to provide. The gain (the *msb*) from providing the first thousand beds is £10 million greater than the cost (the *msc*). So those beds are worth providing. The *msb* from the second thousand equals the *msc*; hence they are also (just) worth providing. However, the costs of the third, fourth, and

TABLE 2.1
Social Costs and Benefits of Hospital Beds

Number of hospital beds (000)	Marginal social benefit (£ million)	Marginal social cost (£ million)
1	20	10
2	12	12
3	8	16
4	6	22
5	5	30

fifth thousand beds are greater than the benefits, and so it would not be efficient to build them. Therefore the efficient number of beds is two thousand, the point at which the marginal social cost of providing more beds begins to exceed the marginal social benefits.

We can make the same point by use of a diagram. In Figure 2.1 the curve running downward from left to right shows how the *msb* declines as the number of beds provided increases, while the curve running upward shows how the *msc* increases.

FIGURE 2.1
Social Costs and Benefits of Hospital Beds

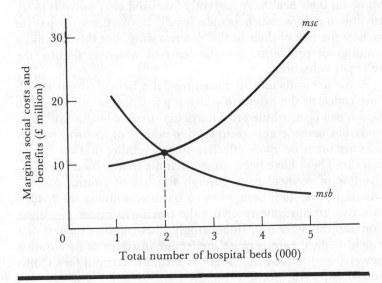

The point at which the two curves intersect is the efficient number of hospital beds. This is an example of how the conception of efficiency outlined in Chapter 1 could be applied in the field of health care. It is in fact perfectly general; in principle at least, it could be applied to any problem of allocating resources in the area (such as that of determining the efficient number of doctors to train, or of kidney machines to provide). But to use the concept in practice is not so easy. Difficulties arise in measuring the quantities involved – particularly the benefits – and these we must now consider.

The benefits from a course of medical treatment are the value of the improvements in health that result from the treatment. Any attempt to measure these benefits therefore requires information concerning the value people place on improvements in their health. But this is not easy to obtain. Ill health usually involves a loss of earnings or earnings-potential, and a common method of measuring the benefits from a particular health improvement is to calculate the associated reduction in lost earnings. However this takes no account of the value of any reduction in pain and suffering; moreover it assumes that individuals with no earnings or earnings-potential place no value on their health. A currently favoured alternative is to try to find out how much people would be prepared to pay to reduce the risk of their health deteriorating; but this also has a number of problems, not the least of which is finding the relevant valuations.

A further difficulty in measuring the benefits from health care concerns the extent to which a particular improvement in health can be attributed to a particular item of health care. The body has considerable recuperative powers of its own, powers that are often far more effective than anything that the doctor can do. There have been some attempts to ascertain the effectiveness of medical care through the use of control groups, whereby patients suffering from a particular illness are divided into two groups, one receiving the treatment under investigation and the other not. Interestingly, these studies suggest that much medical care is quite ineffective in terms of its curative powers, and indeed that some is actually harmful (see Cullis and West, 1979, pp. 6–14).

But the fact that measuring the benefits from health care is difficult should not obscure the essential truth that it is impossible to make any reasonable decision concerning resource allocation in the health field without taking some view (however crude) of the benefits involved. The hospital administrator who decides to allocate money to heart transplants rather than to kidney machines is making an implicit judgement about the relative benefits to be derived from each. The decision to use labour and capital to build a clinic rather than, say, a school or a mile of motorway implies that the benefits from an extra clinic are greater than those from an extra school or more motorway. The difficulties in measuring benefits do not invalidate the definition of an efficient level of health care as one that maximises the difference between benefits and costs, for that definition is simply a formal way of stating a social objective already implicit in most decisions concerning resource allocation. That being the case, it is worth attempting to measure benefits, however crudely, for the alternative is simply to rely on what are often ill-informed and arbitrary assessments.

Equity

Most people would agree that the health care system should be fair or equitable. However there would be much less agreement concerning the appropriate definition of fairness or equity. In Chapter 1 we discussed two ways of defining the equitable allocation of a commodity: one in terms of a minimum standard – everyone should have at least a minimum quantity of the commodity concerned – the other in terms of full equality – everyone should consume the commodity equally. Both of these have figured in discussions concerning the equitable allocation of health care. Some believe that there should be a *minimum standard* of treatment for those in need. Others prefer the broader objective of full equality, usually phrased in the health care context as *equal treatment for equal need*.

A third interpretation of equity found in discussions concerning the organisation of health care is that it should promote *equality of access*. What is meant by this is rarely specified, but it seems simplest to define it in terms of the costs or sacrifices that people have had to make to get medical care. These include any fees or charges that may be levied, any money lost through having to take time off work, and the costs of travelling to the medical facility concerned. If these differ between people – for instance, if some individuals have had further to travel than others – then there would seem to be inequality of access. Hence equality of access implies equality of cost.

The Market System and Health Care

In the United Kingdom the market system is used to allocate a wide range of basic necessities including clothing and food: it is not employed (by and large) in the allocation of health care. In the United States, on the other hand, much health care is provided by the private market in a similar way to food and clothing. In contrast to the United States, therefore, it is apparently believed in Britain that food and clothing will be distributed roughly in accordance with social objectives under the market system, but that health care will not be. The purpose of this section is to examine the basis for that belief. Is health care in some way fundamentally different from food, clothing or any other commodity which is distributed through the market? Are there special characteristics distinguishing medical care from these other goods? Why should society's objectives be better achieved by non-market provision? To many people the answers to these questions might seem obvious, but they are by no means as simple as they appear.

First let us see how a private market might operate in health care. Hospitals would become profit-making organisations and charge a price to their patients, the price varying according to the type and the length of the treatment. Doctors would operate similarly, charging for consultations and treatment. People in need of medical care could go to the doctor or to the hospital of their choice, provided only that they pay the appropriate charge. Drugs and other medicines would be produced, as now, by pharmaceutical companies who would sell them either to hospitals and doctors or to the patients direct.

The principal argument of the proponents of such a system is that it would be efficient. Since people would be free to pick and choose, doctors and hospitals who provided inferior treatment at high prices would lose customers to those who provided better and/or cheaper services. For instance, a doctor who acquired a reputation for making wrong diagnoses, holding half-hearted consultations, and overcrowding the waiting room would lose patients to one known for his or her medical successes and ease of access. A hospital that did not use cost-saving technology would have to charge higher prices than would its more efficient competitors and would eventually be driven out of business. Thus medical practitioners of all kinds would have a strong incentive to improve their standards of service and/or reduce their costs.

Furthermore there would be freedom of choice; people could choose the doctor, hospital, and treatment that suited them best. Doctors and hospital staff, knowing that their livings depended on it, would be more attentive to their patients' desires and preferences. In short the result would be a system of health care that catered for individuals' wants at the least possible cost – an efficient system.

These arguments are essentially the same as those used in Chapter 1 to demonstrate that the market would allocate butter efficiently. They imply, for instance, that the *msb* curve in Figure 2.1 coincides with the market demand curve for hospital beds, and the *msc* curve with the market supply curve. Hence the point of intersection of the supply and demand curves – the quantity of hospital beds that would actually be supplied under a market system – will be the same as the efficient quantity. Therefore, its proponents argue, if the allocation of health care is determined by the market, the outcome would be efficient.

But can health care really be allocated in a fashion similar to butter? Many argue that it cannot. They claim that health care possesses certain characteristics that render market allocation inefficient: in particular, *uncertainty of demand, imperfect consumer information* leading to *monopoly*, and *externalities*. Moreover, they continue, efficiency is not society's only objective: there are others, such as *equity*, whose requirements are generally violated in the market. Let us look at those arguments in more detail.

Uncertainty of Demand

One feature of health care that makes it different from other commodities is that the demand for it is likely to occur unexpectedly. Generally people cannot predict when they are likely to want health treatment, and it is difficult for them to plan their expenditure and savings so as always to ensure that they could meet any unexpected medical expenses. This perhaps would matter little if the sums involved were small, but many forms of health care – such as those requiring long stays in a hospital – involve the payment of sums that can be very large indeed.

Now within the market system there is an institution for coping with the problem of uncertainty: insurance. In theory – and indeed in practice in some countries such as the United States – the majority of families could have some kind of insurance plan to help them cope with expenditures for medical care. However, there are two difficulties with private insurance that may reduce its efficiency: what is rather quaintly termed *moral hazard*, and *adverse selection*. Moral hazard is the phenomenon that to insure against an eventuality makes it more likely to occur. It arises in the health-care field because if a person is fully covered by insurance the incentives to both patient and doctor to economise on treatment are virtually eliminated. The insured may visit a doctor for frivolous ailments; the doctor, secure in the knowledge that the patient does not have to pay, may recommend highly expensive treatment. Both factors may raise utilisation and costs well beyond the efficient level. The problem of adverse selection arises from the facts that (a) insurance companies often find it difficult to distinguish between high- and low-risk individuals and (b) that the former are more likely to demand insurance than the latter. This leads to a majority of high-risk people in an insurance pool, which increases the premiums of all those insured and may induce some people not to buy the insurance they require.

Imperfect Consumer Information

Health care is also considered to be different from other commodities in that there is an imbalance between the knowledge of the supplier of the treatment (the doctor) and that of the consumer (the patient). With many commodities, consumers have a fair idea of what constitutes quality. Even if they do not, provided that the commodity in question is one that is bought repeatedly, they can acquire knowledge of its quality from their use of it and then employ this information in deciding whether to purchase the commodity again. For instance, if the shoes bought from a particular store quickly wore out, consumers would acquire this information through several purchases of shoes – and presumably would shift their custom elsewhere.

But with health care the situation is very different. Before the treatment starts consumers usually have little idea of the suitability of the treatment for their illness or of its likely effectiveness. Rather, they have to rely upon their doctor for this information – that is, upon the supplier of the treatment. Furthermore much medical care is not repeated, so that even if a consumer finds out that a treatment was not suitable, it will in many cases be too late to change to another. In other words, neither before nor after the treatment can consumers easily acquire information that will enable them to make an informed choice. That being so, the claim that a market in health care provides an incentive to doctors and hospitals to provide good service becomes of doubtful validity. If consumers do not know (and cannot find out about) the difference between good treatment and bad treatment, then they are unlikely to shop around for better service.

Monopoly

The existence of the information imbalance confers considerable *monopoly* power on the suppliers of medical services. The fact that patients find it difficult to shop around intelligently makes it less likely that doctors and hospitals will compete with one another. Instead, each can operate as a monopoly, raising prices and perhaps offering a lower quality of service without fearing a substantial loss of customers. This is not to imply that all doctors act as rapacious exploiters out to extract as much profit as possible from their patients. Rather it is simply acknowledging that many of the incentives for efficiency normally present in a competitive market are conspicuously absent in that for health care.

Externalities

Another feature of health care that creates problems for market allocation is that it has 'external' benefits or *externalities* associated with its use. The consumption (or production) of a commodity is said to create an externality when a third party who is in no way involved in the decision to consume (or produce) it is none the less affected by it, without compensation or payment. If the effect is adverse, it is described as an *external cost*; if it is beneficial, as an *external benefit*.

Certain types of health care, and particularly those concerned with communicable diseases, can create external benefits. For instance, if you decide to be vaccinated against whooping cough, then not only do you reduce the probability of your getting the disease, but you also reduce the probability of others getting it. The vaccination has thus benefited you (an 'internal' or private benefit); and it has benefited others (an 'external' benefit). Similarly, a hospital treatment that cures someone of a particular communicable disease confers external benefits, since it reduces the probability that others will contract the disease.

Since society includes both those who undertake any externality-generating activity and those affected by the externality, the total *social benefits* (or costs) of an activity is the sum of the *private (or internal) benefits* (or costs) and the *external benefits* (or costs). Thus:

private benefits (or costs) + external benefits (or costs) = social benefits (or costs)

The greater the size of the externality, the greater the divergence between social and private costs or benefits.

What are the implications of this for market provision? Simply that, if these externalities exist to any significant extent, the market can no longer be relied on to operate efficiently. Suppose, for instance, that charges were levied for vaccination against whooping cough. Now in trying to decide whether to be vaccinated, individuals would take into account the private benefits (the reduction in the probability of my getting the disease) and the private costs involved. The latter would depend on the charge, the inconvenience of going to the vaccination clinic, and any risk that might be associated with the vaccination. Suppose a particular individual decides that it is too expensive and hence that he or she will not be vaccinated. As a result, not only is the probability of his or her getting whooping cough increased but so is that of everyone with whom he or she comes into contact. Now if there had been some way of including the benefits to these others in the calculations, the sum of the private and 'external' benefits might have outweighed the private costs. In that case it would have been more efficient for the individual concerned to have been vaccinated, yet, under the market system, this did not occur. Hence, in the presence of externalities, the market cannot be relied on always to produce the most efficient solution.

This can be illustrated by our example of hospital beds. Suppose that treatment in hospitals confers external benefits: that is, it benefits not only people who become patients, but also the rest of the population (through, say, the reduction in the spread of communicable diseases). Let us assume that the size of the external benefit created by each extra thousand hospital beds – the *marginal external benefit* – decreases as more beds are provided, ranging from £22 million for the first thousand to £14 million for the fifth. Suppose, also, that each hospital still confers the same benefits on patients as before; but we now have to call these the *marginal private benefits*. Then we must draw up a revised cost and benefit statement, as shown in Table 2.2. From this table we can see that the socially efficient quantity of hospital beds has changed. It is now four thousand, where the *msb* – the sum of the marginal private benefits and the marginal external benefits – equals the *msc*. For each

TABLE 2.2
Social and Private Costs and Benefits of Hospital Beds

Number of hospital beds (000) (1)	Marginal private benefit (£ million) (2)	Marginal external benefit (£ million) (3)	Marginal social benefit (£ million) (4) = (2) + (3)	Marginal social cost (£ million) (5)
1	20	22	42	10
2	12	20	32	12
3	8	18	26	16
4	6	16	22	22
5	5	14	19	30

thousand of the first four, the *msb* is at least as great as the *msc*; whereas for the fifth thousand, the extra cost is greater than the extra benefit.

But under the market system only two thousand beds would be provided. While it would be socially profitable to provide the third and fourth thousand beds, it would not be privately profitable. Why not? We saw in Chapter 1 that the market demand for butter equalled the sum of the marginal benefits that individuals derived from butter. However in this case, when external benefits are present, the market demand only equals the sum of the marginal private benefits, because under a market system a hospital only receives payment from its patients. It has no way of making non-patients (those who receive the external benefits) pay. Hence the maximum revenue that could be extracted for the third and fourth thousand beds would be only the amount that the patients using them are prepared to pay (that is £8 million and £6 million, respectively). Since in both cases this would be considerably less than the costs of providing the beds no profits could be made by any firm providing them; hence they would not be provided.

Again this can be illustrated by a diagram. In Figure 2.2 the marginal social benefit (*msb*) and the marginal private benefit (*mpb*) curves are plotted along with the marginal social cost (*msc*) curve. The point of intersection of the *msb* and *msc* curves shows the socially efficient quantity of hospitals; the point of intersection of the *mpb* curve (which, for the reasons explained above, is the same as the market demand curve) with the *msc* curve shows the quantity that will be provided under a market system. Thus, when there are external benefits, the market demand curve and the marginal social benefit curve are no longer identical. The result is that the quantity provided under a market system will not necessarily be at a socially efficient level. So the existence of externalities can prevent the market from operating efficiently. The degree of inefficiency will depend on the size of the externality (that is, on the divergence between the *msb* curve and the *mpb*, or market demand, curve in Figure 2.2).

Now some have argued that in fact the external benefits from health care are relatively small and hence the degree of

FIGURE 2.2
Social and Private Costs and Benefits of Hospital Beds

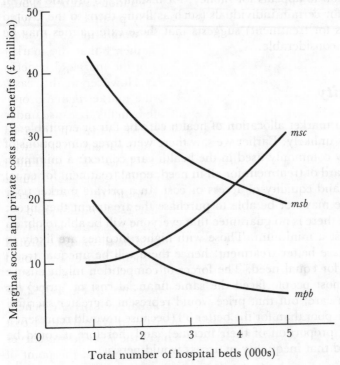

inefficiency from this source will also be small. The basis for this argument is that (a) communicable diseases are now fairly rare and (b) their treatment is the only form of health care that confers external benefits. But both claims have been challenged. Some communicable diseases are still widely prevalent (such as venereal diseases) and others might become more so if a market in health care were operating. Furthermore, communicable diseases may not be the only form of health care to create external benefits. Many people feel concern when others fall ill, even if they themselves are not directly threatened. They feel that the sick should always receive the medical care they need; that the poor, for instance, should not be deprived of care simply because they are poor. These 'caring' externalities are likely to be associated with most forms of medical treatment; moreover, the scale of the reaction to appeals for money, for instance, to provide special care for certain individuals (such as flying them to the United States for treatment) suggests that these externalities may be quite considerable.

Equity

Will a market allocation of health care be fair or equitable? It seems unlikely. Earlier we saw there were three conceptions of equity commonly used in the health care context: a minimum standard of treatment for all in need, equal treatment for equal need and equality of access or cost. In a private market poor people may not be able to purchase the treatment they need: hence there is no guarantee that everyone will be able to obtain at least a minimum. Those with higher incomes are likely to purchase better treatment; hence there will be unequal treatment for equal need. The forces of competition might ensure that most people faced the same financial cost or 'price' for health care; but that price would represent a greater sacrifice for the poor than for the better off (because it would represent a larger proportion of their income), and therefore it could be argued that inequality of access would persist.

The Role of Giving

A further argument that has been put forward against the use of a market system in health care is that the introduction of commercial considerations would destroy the relationship between patient and doctor – or more generally the relationship between the supplier of the service and its recipient. The late Professor Titmuss of the London School of Economics – the principal exponent of this view – claimed that to give (and to receive) a service where no financial renumeration is directly involved is a more satisfying form of human relationship than one involving direct payment for services rendered, and because of this is ethically superior.

The basis for the argument is this. To introduce a system linking payment to the quantity and quality of treatment provided is to relate treatment to the supplier's self-interest. The main argument in favour of this is that it would make the system more efficient; and, as we have seen, there are counter-arguments denying the likelihood of any increase in efficiency. But what this view is saying is that even if there is an increase in efficiency, the social welfare might none the less be reduced by the use of the price mechanism. This is because its use diminishes the role of altruism and increases the role of self-interest. In a society such as our own where, ostensibly at least, altruism is valued more highly than self-interest, to decrease the opportunities for the exercise of the former while increasing those for the latter might be a retrograde step.

To develop this view further would require finding a satisfactory definition of altruism and the undertaking of a closer study of its existing and potential role in the supply of medical services – a task beyond the scope of this book. Here we can simply acknowledge the existence of the view and point out that it has to be added to the anti-market side of the scales when weighing up the balance between market versus non-market provision.

Government Policies

We have now established that there may be reasons why the allocation of health care by the market may not achieve society's objectives. This suggests that we must examine other methods of allocating health care, and particularly various forms of state intervention. In so doing we must consider the advantages and disadvantages of each type of intervention in the same way as we did for the market system. In doing so it is important to remember that the mere fact of the market system's failure to achieve social objectives does not automatically imply that state intervention is desirable; the policy alternatives open to the state might be equally (or more) unsatisfactory.

As we saw in Chapter 1, the government may intervene in

the allocation of a commodity in any of three ways: provision, regulation or taxation/subsidisation. In the case of health care most governments use all three. Under the National Health Service, for example, the government owns and operates most of the country's hospitals; it also employs most medical personnel. It regulates the quality of medical practitioners by requiring them to undergo specified training leading to recognised qualifications. And it provides health care free or (as, for instance, in the case of prescription drugs or dental services) at heavily subsidised prices. Even in the United States, where the system of allocating health care is more market-oriented, there is extensive state regulation, some public hospital provision, and programmes subsidising the medical expenses of the poor (Medicaid) and the elderly (Medicare).

Now each of these forms of intervention can be viewed as a response to the problems of market allocation that were discussed in the previous section. Thus regulation is an attempt to deal with the problem of imperfect consumer information; provision, with that of monopoly; and subsidy with those of uncertainty of demand, externalities and inequity. Let us examine the arguments more closely.

The problem of imperfect information identified earlier was that consumers of health care do not have the information adequately to assess the quality of the treatment they receive. In this situation, the government could act as a guardian of consumers' interests by itself assessing the quality of treatment; but this would be impractical for each and every case. Instead, governments prefer to assess the quality of those who supply the treatment, through licensing procedures. Thus people generally have to obtain officially recognised qualifications before they can call themselves doctors; nurses have to be trained in a specified fashion; and so on.

The difficulty with this kind of intervention is that it is almost impossible to avoid using as regulators those already involved in the activity to be regulated. Thus doctors determine the curricula and set the exams in medical schools; they sit on regulatory committees and panels that monitor other doctors' performance. This is in part inevitable for they are likely to be better qualified to do the job than anybody else; but it means that the regulatory agencies may operate more in the interests of those they are supposed to be regulating than in the interests of the consumers. For instance, there is evidence to suggest that the medical profession's power over the length of training required to qualify as a doctor has been used more to restrict the supply of doctors (and hence raise their incomes) than to protect the public against poor quality treatment (see Cullis and West, 1979, p. 259).

The imbalance of information contributes to the monopoly power of the suppliers of medical care. One way of counteracting this monopoly is for the state to provide health care and therefore become the sole buyer of the services concerned – what economists term a *monopsonist*. It can then use its power to counteract the monopoly power of the suppliers, and to reduce the price they are able to charge for their services. There is some evidence that in fact the National Health Service has been a relatively effective monopsonist. For instance, it purchases drugs at about half the prices paid in other countries and, relative to the earnings of manual workers, doctors in the UK earn only about half as much as their counterparts in Western Europe and the United States.

State provision, though, is not without its problems. Because there is no competition there is less incentive for efficiency. Because their incomes do not depend on meeting consumers' wishes the state's employees are often insensitive to those wishes. And the size of the administrative machinery often renders the system bureaucratic, cumbersome and inefficient.

The difficulties that can arise under state provision are illustrated by the system of payment to general practitioners under the National Health Service. Under this system doctors are paid according to the number of people registered with them, and not with the amount of treatment they give. Hence they have an incentive to maximise the numbers of people on their register, but to minimise the amount of time spent with each person. In other words, they have an incentive to 'under-doctor' – in contrast to the market system where, due to the fact that their income depends entirely on the amount of treatment they give, they have a strong incentive to 'over-doctor'. Both systems are thus likely to be inefficient, though in different directions.

A major justification for state subsidy of health care is the existence of externalities. It will be remembered that the fact that there are external benefits from health care implied that in a private market the amount of health care consumed will be less than the socially efficient level. Reducing the price for a service by a subsidy will increase the demand for the service. For instance, suppose a charge is made for treatment for a contagious disease: if you have the disease and weigh up the costs and benefits to me of having the treatment, then, because of the expense, you may decide to have less treatment than you should. As a result other people are put at an increased risk of getting the disease, and hence they are worse off by your decision. However, if the charge is removed, you may find that the benefits to you now outweigh the (reduced) costs; you will have the full treatment and other people will be better off. The provision of free treatment may therefore move society closer to the efficient level of health-care provision.

Against this it could be argued that to achieve efficiency it is not necessary to reduce the price to zero, as in the vaccination example and throughout much of the National Health Services. It may be possible to persuade people to consume the efficient amount of treatment by only lowering the price a little. Indeed, lowering the price to zero for all medical treatment may increase the demand for health care well *beyond* the level that it is efficient to supply. If the response to this increase in demand is to increase supply correspondingly, then medical care will be provided that costs society more than it benefits and there will be inefficiency. If the extra demand is not met by any increase in supply, then queues and waiting lists will develop (as they have done, notoriously, under the National Health Service) creating frustration and arbitrary allocations.

Another important reason why governments subsidise health care is a concern for equity or social justice. Whether such subsidies are an effective way of promoting equity will depend on the type of subsidy and on the definition of equity. Some subsidy schemes, such as Medicaid in the United States, involve a means test; that is, they are confined to people with income ('means') below a certain level. Others, such as the British National Health Service, are universal; that is, all those who need treatment receive it free or at a heavily subsidised price. Both universal and means-tested subsidies can be justified on the grounds that they promote equity defined in terms of minimum standards, for they both reduce the price of medical care to the poor and therefore encourage their consumption. However, it is likely that universal subsidies will be the more successful of the two in this respect. For means tests are often regarded by those eligible as stigmatising and socially humiliating; moreover the procedures involved in decisions over eligibility are often complex and time-consuming. Hence the take-up of the service by the poor will not be as large as it would be if there were no means test.

On the other hand, means tests are possibly superior to universal subsidies in meeting the other interpretations of equity – equal treatment for equal need and equality of access or cost. For means tests imply a lower financial cost of health care to the poor; they therefore make the actual sacrifice involved more in line with that incurred by the rich (thus creating greater equality of access) and perhaps also thereby increase the poor's use of the service relative to that of the rich (thus promoting greater equality of treatment). However, this will only apply if the reduction in financial cost to the poor is not offset by the increase in the non-financial costs of stigma and complexity mentioned above.

There is some evidence to suggest that the National Health Service has not achieved either the objective of equal treatment for equal need or that of equality of cost. One study (discussed in Le Grand, 1982, Ch. 3) shows that the top socio-economic groups (professionals, employers and managers) receive about 40 per cent more National Health Service expenditure per person ill than do the bottom groups (semi- and unskilled manual workers). This arises largely because, even though the service is free, or largely so, there are still major differences in the costs people face when using it. Manual workers, for instance, are more likely to lose money when they take time off work to go to the doctor than are professionals, employers and managers. Working class areas are less well endowed with medical facilities than middle class ones; hence manual workers and their families have to travel further to obtain comparable treatment. Moreover, working class families are less likely to have telephones or cars than middle class ones; hence they find it more difficult to make appointments or to even get to the doctor in the first place.

Hence inequalities of cost (and thus of access) persist even under the National Health Service, and these contribute to inequalities in treatment. Of course these inequalities might – very likely, would – be worse if there were no Health Service; however, it is important to be aware that even a universal system of state provision and subsidy cannot guarantee equity.

Summary

There are two principal objectives with respect to health care: *efficiency* and *equity*. An efficient level of health care is one where the *marginal social cost* of further care begins to exceed the *marginal social benefit*. Equity can be defined in a number of ways in the context of health care: the most common are a *minimum standard* of treatment, *equal treatment for equal need* and *equality of access* or *cost*.

Health care has certain characteristics which in general mean that it will not be allocated efficiently by a market system. These include *uncertainty of demand, imperfect consumer information* leading to *monopoly*, and *externalities*. Nor is the market likely to achieve equity under any of its interpretations.

The state may intervene through *provision, regulation* and *taxation/subsidisation*. Under the National Health Service all three are used. Each can be seen as a response to the various failures of the market. Thus state provision is a means of dealing with the problem of monopoly; regulation, with the problem of imperfect consumer information; subsidy, with uncertainty of demand and externalities. However, each has problems of its own. Thus provision can create inefficiency due to the absence of competition; regulation often serves the interests of the regulated; and unrestricted subsidies can lead to over-use and an inequitable distribution of public expenditure.

Further Reading

Two useful books that deal with the issues involved in health care from an economic point of view in a non-technical fashion are Abel-Smith (1976) and Culyer (1976). Wilson and Wilson (1982) contains a chapter on health services. On the specific question of efficiency, Williams and Anderson (1975) contains much useful material; Le Grand (1982) discusses equity. The Institute of Economic Affairs has published numerous critiques of the National Health Service: an early but still important example is Lees (1961), and a later one is Seldon (1981). Useful institutional material on the National Health Service (and a defence of its record) can be found in the Report of the Royal Commission on the Service (1979). For those with some economics, and even for those without, an important text that surveys the whole field of health economics is Cullis and West (1979).

Questions for Discussion

1. How would you define health?
2. Should a doctor's aim be 'optimisation of survival' or 'cost-effective medicine'?
3. What is an equitable distribution of health care?
4. 'To place a money value on human life is both immoral and impossible.' Discuss.
5. Discuss the various ways in which the benefits from health care can be measured.
6. 'In the market medical care will tend to be undersupplied relative to the efficient level.' 'Profit-maximising doctors have an incentive to over-supply treatment.' Reconcile.
7. Are there any reasons on the grounds of efficiency for replacing the National Health Service by a system of private health insurance?
8. 'Food is as essential to health as visits to the doctor, yet under the N.H.S. the latter is provided free while the former is not.' Is this an argument against the National Health Service, for a National Food Service or neither?
9. Should blood donors be paid? Should users of donated blood be charged?
10. Why do the poor apparently use the National Health Service less, relative to need, than the rich?

Education 3

In 1890 the leading English economist, Alfred Marshall, wrote:

> There are few practical problems in which the economist
> has a more direct interest than those relating to the prin-
> ciples on which the expense of education of children should
> be divided between the State and the parents. (Marshall,
> 1890, p. 180)

Since Marshall's time the education system in Britain has
expanded beyond recognition and come to depend over-
whelmingly upon state provision and finance. In 1980 there
were nearly 13 million children or students in a public
education system which includes nursery, primary and
secondary schools, colleges of further education, polytechnics
and universities. As one would expect the costs of this system
are substantial: in 1980–81 public expenditure on education
was over £12 000 million, this represented approximately 13
per cent of total public expenditure or 7 per cent of national
income. Not surprisingly, costs of this magnitude –
particularly in a period of general economic recession – have
attracted the attention of those people concerned with the
methods of provision and finance of education. In consequence, Marshall's comment has once again assumed topical
relevance.

Our examination of this subject will begin with an attempt to
define the objectives of the education system. Is it designed to

train the future workforce? Or should it be more concerned with the provision of more general social skills? To what extent should it be used as a means of equalising opportunities in subsequent adult life? Having considered issues such as these, we shall go on to consider how far a market system of provision can be expected to realise the particular aims set for the system. As few societies have left the provision of education exclusively to the market, it should come as no surprise to the reader to learn that we conclude that there are strong reasons for some form of government intervention. But what form should this intervention take? Is the present system of state dominance satisfactory? We deal with this issue in the final part of the chapter where we look at two controversial current proposals designed to introduce a greater element of the market system into the education sector. These are proposals for the introduction of education 'vouchers' with which parents or students could buy education at fee-charging schools – instead of it being provided free to the user and financed from taxation as at present – and the proposal that grants to students in higher education should be replaced by some form of loan scheme.

Objectives

Just as in the case of health care, we can discuss the objectives of the education system in terms of two main categories – those concerned with *efficiency* and those concerned with *equity*.

Efficiency: Production and Social Benefits

Stated in general terms, the efficiency objective will be to try to specify the amount of education (that is, the size of the education system) that will maximise net social benefit. To translate this into a working definition we need to be able to identify both the costs and the benefits of providing education. Now while the costs are relatively easy to specify – being the costs of teachers' salaries, books and materials, school and college buildings etc. – the benefits are less tangible. Basically, however, it is possible to distinguish two categories of education benefit that any system will be expected to produce. We may term these *production* benefits and *social* benefits. (Note, incidentally, that many discussions of educational objectives concentrate simply upon the benefits produced whereas our discussion in Chapter 1 shows that, in a complete analysis, benefits should always be considered alongside their costs.)

Production benefits accrue because one of the main functions of any education system is the training of the future workforce. Through education individuals acquire knowledge and develop skills that will increase their productivity when they enter employment. Thus expenditure on education is an *investment* that yields benefits in the form of additional production in the future. Of course, the link between education and production benefits is more pronounced in some forms of education than in others; clearly it is stronger in engineering or medicine than in English literature or history. But most education will contain some job training element. For example, research carried out in developing countries shows that substantial benefits are obtained from progammes teaching basic literacy and numeracy as well as more clearly vocational training. For when communication through reading and writing becomes possible, there is scope for the use of more efficient techniques in a whole range of economic activities. Similarly, basic numeracy makes access to an increasing range of computer-based production techniques possible. Furthermore, an increase in the number of people with the elementary qualifications which are a necessary prerequisite for more advanced training will lead eventually to a larger number of highly trained personnel. Economists refer to this as the 'option value' of elementary education; that is, it provides the option of further education or training.

In most cases it is not possible to identify the social benefits of an education system with the same degree of precision as the production benefits. They tend to assume far more diffuse and less tangible forms. But this should not be allowed to diminish the importance attached to them. For example, most forms of education perform an important socialisation function; that is, they seek to provide pupils or students with a set of values and range of skills that will enable them to function effectively in the wider society outside the school or college. These may be

expected to extend from consideration of major ethical and
moral questions to more mundane advice on out-of-school
leisure activities, job application procedures etc. Of course the
precise form of socialisation can be expected to vary between
different parts of the education system. Thus while certain
values are likely to be shared by all institutions within a given
society (e.g. a belief in the superiority of reasoned argument
over emotional prejudice), others will vary between institutions, depending upon the social context in which they expect
their students to find themselves. For some, the attributes of
punctuality, reliability and discipline will be important
whereas others may be encouraged to question and criticise
rather than conform. In addition to this socialisation function,
many people would argue that the transmission of knowledge
through education is a good thing in itself, irrespective of
whether or not it serves any ulterior objective. Thus an
appreciation of literature, the arts, the discoveries of science
and technology and so on are seen as desirable ends in themselves. In fact these two views of education's social benefits
were neatly summarised by the Robbins Committee on Higher
Education who in their Report wrote:

A proper function [of education] ... is to provide in
partnership with the family that background of culture and
social habit upon which a healthy society depends.
(Robbins, 1963, p. 7)

Equity

In Britain certain basic human rights guaranteeing equality of
treatment have long been recognised. The right to vote and to
receive justice before a common law are two examples. More
recently it has been argued by many people that *equality of
opportunity* in education should become a basic right. This view
recognises that education is not just another consumer service
but a process that has a fundamental effect on the recipients' –
and their children's – lives. For many people it is not only a
major determinant of their lifetime incomes (and hence their
access to market goods and services), but also the quality of

their lives. Tastes cultivated through education enable individuals to enrich their lives in numerous ways.

Given the importance attached to education for these reasons, it is hardly surprising that society should require that it is allocated equitably. This would seem to be both an aim in itself and a means of promoting an objective of civil liberty. But what is the equitable allocation implied by the frequently cited aim of equality of opportunity. Just as in the case of health care, this is not usually taken to mean that everyone should receive exactly the same amount, because their needs and capabilities may vary. Not everyone wants or is able to benefit from a three year university course. Rather it is usually taken to mean that there should be universal *equality of access*. That is, no student who is willing and able to benefit from a particular course should face higher costs of access because of irrelevant or discriminatory criteria, such as income, race, sex, or religion. Sometimes, however, it is felt that although this objective is desirable it is not possible to achieve with the limited resources that are available for education. Accordingly, the less stringent definition of equity presented in Chapter 1 is often adopted; this states that everyone should have access to a certain *minimum quantity* of education. Some students may obtain more education than others but no one should be denied access to the minimum amount considered socially necessary.

The Market System and Education

The general advantages claimed for a market system were discussed in the introductory chapter. In the context of education it is claimed that the quantity provided, its form, and (with some reservations) the people who receive it will be determined best by a free market. Two main reasons are usually cited in support of this claim. First, the need for consumer freedom of choice is emphasised. In a market system consumers are able to express their preferences when they make decisions about the type and quantity of education they purchase, and through the expression of these individuals' choices the socially efficient quantity of each type of education will be indicated. The second and related point ensures that the required education is, in fact, made available. Educational institutions will be in competition for students (as this will be the source of their income) and will need to respond by offering those types of education that are in demand. Moreover, as students will be deterred by unnecessarily high fees, schools, colleges and universities will need to ensure that they are not wasteful or extravagant in the way they provide the students' education. Thus it is maintained that, in this way, an efficient system responsive to consumer needs will be established.

But can we be confident that the market will operate in this way? Critics of this view argue that there are specific failings that will prevent the market in education from operating efficiently: these are *capital market imperfections*, widespread *imperfect information, externalities* and *monopoly* in the supply of education. Moreover they also question the ability of a market-based system to achieve an equitable distribution of education. Let us look at each of these points and try to assess their validity.

Capital Market Imperfections

We have seen already that education can be expected to increase students' future productivity. Thus they (or their families) know that through education they can acquire knowledge and learn skills that will widen their future employment choices and, in most Western societies, increase their future earnings. Therefore when considering whether to undertake further or higher education beyond the age of 16, individuals are effectively faced with an *investment* decision; should they incur costs in the present in the expectation of receiving additional income in the future?

We may depict the situation confronting a typical individual in the following fashion. Consider a student who has obtained the necessary entrance qualifications for a three-year degree course in economics and wants to decide whether to accept the offer of a university place or to enter a firm directly on a school-leavers' trainee management scheme. Confronted with this choice, the student will want to know the relative costs and benefits of each option. First, he or she will want to consider the additional costs that would be incurred through following the university course. These are likely to include certain books and study materials, possible additional costs incurred through living away from home (if the students would remain at home otherwise), and tuition fees if these are not paid for by a grant-awarding body. But the major cost item will be the salary forgone through undertaking education instead of going directly to work. (Note this is an opportunity cost of the type discussed on p. 3. For most students, however, this cost will be reduced by the amount of any maintenance grant they receive while at university. After considering the costs, the student will want to know about the likely benefits of a three-year degree course. These will generally accrue in the form of higher expected earnings over his or her working lifetime. A plausible time profile of the flow of costs and benefits is shown in Figure 3.1. In the figure the potential graduate's annual costs and benefits are compared with those he would expect as a non-graduate. The shaded areas A + B represent the costs to the student of a

FIGURE 3.1
Investment in Education

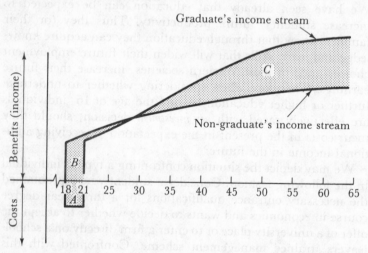

three-year degree course; A is the additional cost of attending university compared with working as a management trainee (books, additional living expenses, fees etc.) whereas B is the opportunity cost of forgone income, (the non-graduate's net income *minus* the student's grant between the ages of 18 and 21 years, and thereafter the lower income received initially by the graduate compared with the non-graduate who is already established in the workforce). Area C represents the benefit of a degree course. It indicates that from his late 20s until retirement the graduate can expect a higher annual income than his non-graduate counterpart. By comparing C with $A + B$ the student can estimate the likely rate of return on an investment of $A + B$ in education – that is, the extra income received per pound 'invested'.

Now this discussion is not meant to imply that every student consciously makes these calculations before choosing an education course. Rather it is intended to demonstrate the economic implications of education choices, some of which are almost certainly taken into account, albeit implicitly, by prospective students. It also allows us to investigate the rates of return obtainable on different types of education. One study (Ziderman, 1973) estimates that the post-tax private rate of return on a university degree in Britain is between 18 and 24 per cent – clearly a much higher return than could be obtained on almost any other form of investment. (The existence of student grants which reduce private costs obviously increase the rate of return. However, this may not make much difference because in the United States – where grants are not generally available – private rates of return of around 17 per cent have been estimated for comparable degree courses.)

But what are the implications of these results for a private market in education? Simply that if returns of this magnitude can be obtained from investment in education we would expect students to be willing and able to borrow money to finance their studies and to repay these loans from their subsequent increased earnings. In general there would be no need for government financial assistance to students in further or higher education. However this presupposes that the capital market (banks or other lending institutions) would be willing to offer loans on these terms. In practice financial institutions tend to be very cautious about lending to low-income borrowers with little collateral. (Try persuading your bank manager to lend you £10 000 on the sole basis of your future earnings potential!) At the same time many students – especially those from low-income households – will be unused to entering this type of credit arrangement and are likely to be reluctant to commit themselves to long-term debt. For these reasons we cannot be confident that the private market would finance the efficient amount of investment in education.

Imperfect Information

It is a basic assumption in economics that consumers know their own interests better than anyone else. However, in most cases consumers of education are not mature adults; consequently most people would be a little wary about ascribing to them all the usual attributes of sound judgement and rationality that consumers are usually assumed to possess. Generally, however, this problem is overcome because decisions regarding education are made by, or in close consultation with, parents. But in some cases the need for an adult to act on behalf of a child does present problems of its own, for adults may not always act in their children's best interests. This may be particularly important in the case of education, which has been described by one writer as a process that protects children from their families. The failure to act in their children's best interests may result from neglect or malevolence on the parents' part, but it is more likely to arise because parents cannot be expected to possess all the information necessary to make wise decisions.

Education is a complex process with many facets that are not readily apparent to those viewing it from the outside. To collect all the information on courses, teachers, facilities, out-of-school activities and so forth – which would be necessary to make wise choices – can be very time-consuming, even if we assume that all parents are able to assimilate and evaluate the information. Against this it is sometimes argued that the complexity of choice is just a matter of degree and that choosing a new video recorder or stereo set is an equally complex task which is, nevertheless, left to the consumer's discretion. Moreover, if educational institutions were competing for students there would be an incentive for them to disseminate information more effectively via advertising than they do at present. Furthermore, it might also be argued that only by giving parents the responsibility for making choices can they be expected to have sufficient interest to develop the expertise necessary to make wise decisions.

How convincing is each of these counterarguments? Certainly video recorders are complex pieces of machinery of great variety about which the average buyer has only superficial knowledge. But are the consequences of the decision as to which set to buy quite as important as those concerning education? If we accept that education goes a long way towards determining subsequent job opportunities and the quality of an individual's life, we may well feel that the scope for individual mistakes of judgement should be minimised beyond those considered permissible in the case of purchasing a video-recorder. Clearly this involves an element of paternalism; a constraint is being placed on the expression of consumer choice on the grounds that consumers may not always act in their own best interests.

Because they dislike such restrictions upon freedom of choice, most economists prefer strategies that simply provide consumers with the information necessary to make wise choices. But these obviously require effective methods for the dissemination of information. Would such methods be produced within a market system? Certainly we would expect the amount of advertising to increase but would this lead to a greater amount of relevant information being made available? Discussions of advertising practices usually distinguish between informative and persuasive advertising. And so while most people might favour the production of prospectuses in which information was provided on teaching staff, courses offered, out-of-school activities etc., the existence of certain college advertisements which emphasise the quality of skiing facilities or the merits of the local beer give some cause for concern. Moreover, current debates in Britain about the desirability of publishing school examination results – which critics claim will result in an undesirable polarisation between 'good and 'bad' schools (see the discussion on segregation in the final section of this chapter) – suggest that additional information may jeopardise some of the equity aims of education. Finally, we can accept the claim that individuals can be expected to collect information and act responsibly only if they are given the opportunity to do so, without necessarily accepting that the best way of encouraging responsibility is by making people paying consumers. There are other ways of encouraging parents to participate more fully and responsibly in their children's education; for example, parent-teacher associations and other non-market systems of mutual involvement in the education process.

On balance, therefore, it seems that problems of lack of parental judgement and/or information are likely to inhibit seriously the role that consumer sovereignty can play in deciding the amount and type of education each individual receives.

Externalities

As we saw in the case of health care, wherever external costs or benefits exist, a private market cannot be expected inevitably to produce an efficient allocation of resources. This is because the incidence of externalities will cause private and social costs and benefits to diverge. Neither producers nor consumer will normally take these externalities into account. However, from society's point of view, they will have a substantial effect on the level of welfare enjoyed by each member and so they need to be considered. In the case of education there is a range of external benefits that do not accrue directly to the student but that instead are passed on to others in the community. We may divide them into two main categories: *employment* benefits and benefits to *society in general*.

Employment benefits arise because modern production techniques require a high level of co-operation between workers. People who have been educated, as well as increasing their own productivity, will be able to increase the productivity of their fellow workers through their contact with them. The educated worker may achieve this by the use of more efficient methods of supervision and management that permit his relatively uneducated colleagues to use their time more productively. Alternatively, it is sometimes argued that education increases a person's flexibility and adaptability, and hence the educated person is likely to be more able to accommodate the changes that arise through rapid technological progress. This will prevent breakdowns or 'bottlenecks' in the production process. Against this view some economists argue that although these benefits are a result of education they are not externalities because they will be reflected in the earnings of the people who have received the education. Thus the benefit will accrue to them as a *private* benefit and not to others. It is difficult to resolve this disagreement because measuring the different components of earnings presents substantial problems. Clearly, separating the components that are attributable to the education of others from those attributable to the worker's own efforts, his own education, and other factors affecting his productivity is no easy matter. None the less, given the interdependence of modern production techniques it is difficult to believe that everyone is paid strictly in accordance with his or her own contribution to productivity and is not affected by others working for the same firm or organisation.

There will also be external benefits that accrue to society in general. Certain aspects of education can only be realised fully if other people share them. Our scope for communication will be severely restricted if we can write but you cannot read! So if communication is in our mutual interests, we benefit from the literacy you acquire through education. On a more general level, we have already spoken of the socialisation function of education, and this obviously provides a benefit to society at large. What the Robbins Report called 'a common standard of citizenship' will tend to produce a degree of social stability that is in most people's interests. Of course, education does not always produce stability. It also leads to the questioning of accepted practices, sometimes resulting in social unrest and even the unseating of governments. Those politicians who clamp down on universities in times of trouble clearly believe they impose external costs rather than benefits.

Even more than in the case of employment externalities, the measurement of these social externalities poses enormous problems. In consequence, economists' attempts at quantification have tended to concentrate on the more tangible items, which are not always the most important ones. For instance, the benefits of socialisation have been approximated in terms of 'crime-avoidance costs' – that is, the police and other law-enforcement costs that do not need to be incurred because people are more law-abiding. Again, literacy benefits have been measured in terms of the cost savings that arise through people being able to fill in their own income tax returns. These obviously represent highly imperfect measures of external benefits. However, for our purposes we do not need to dwell on the problems surrounding the precise measurement of these externalities; we simply require to establish that they exist – and this seems undeniable.

Monopoly

In a market system competition between firms can be expected to lead to each firm adopting the most efficient method of production. To do otherwise would lead to higher than necessary costs and a need to charge higher prices, with a consequent reduction in demand for its products. However, if a firm enjoys a monopoly position it is protected from the competition of rival firms and is able to charge higher prices without a substantial loss of trade. Now monopolies can arise for a variety of reasons but they all introduce the danger of prices being set higher than would obtain in a competitive market.

Within the education system there is reason to expect monopolies to develop because certain areas are not sufficiently densely populated to support more than one school. Thus without certain pupils making very long journeys to more distant schools, or becoming boarders, one school may have an effective monopoly of education in its area. Such a monopoly is known as a spatial monopoly because it is space – or distance – that is protecting the monopolist from its potential competitors. Wherever a spatial monopoly exists there is reason to fear that a market system will not produce an efficient allocation of resources.

Equity Considerations

It will be recalled that the principal objective concerning equity is that there should be equality of access to educational facilities. Now if education is sold on the market, access will be dependent on household income. In a world where there are unequal incomes, access to education will also tend to be unequal. Alternatively, the less stringent definition of equity could be adopted; that is, there should be universal access to a minimum quantity of education. But even with this restricted definition it is virtually certain that a large number of families could not afford the minimum of ten years of schooling that our society feels is necessary if they are required to pay for it from their own resources. In short, wherever access to education is determined largely by incomes that are distributed unequally, or where large numbers of families are on low incomes, we are likely to get a socially inequitable allocation.

Thus we may conclude that there is a case for government intervention in education on both equity and efficiency grounds. But this does not establish the form that this intervention should take. Debates on this subject have covered much ground. In the remainder of this chapter we shall consider the way in which the government has chosen to deal with the problem in Britain, and look at some proposals for reforming the system which have attracted the support of a number of economists.

Government Policies

The discussion in the previous section has established that a market system in education is unlikely to achieve the objectives society has set itself. This provides a case for government intervention. But what form should this take? In Britain the government dominates both the provision and finance of education. Nearly 95 per cent of children attend state schools in which education is provided free to the user and financed from central government taxes and local government rates. In further and higher education, the vast majority of home students receive education free of charge in government-financed colleges and universities; in addition, many students also receive maintenance grants from the government to cover their living expenses while studying.

As we have shown there are a number of efficiency reasons (imperfect capital markets, external benefits etc.) why the government will want to ensure that individuals do not underinvest in education. But probably the main reason for the adoption of the present system is on equity grounds – that is, to provide equality of access to education. By controlling the provision of education and making it available free of charge the government seeks to ensure that no one is denied access because of income limitations.

Recently, however, a number of people have questioned whether existing methods of direct provision and subsidisation represent the most effective way to achieve this aim. In particular, criticism has been directed at the alleged lack of responsiveness of the state monopoly education system to the demands of students, parents and employers. This dissatisfaction has resulted in a number of proposals for the reform of education finance designed to increase education's accountability to the consumer. In this section we shall consider two such proposals: the first of these – the voucher scheme – aims to reduce dependence on tax-financed, direct state provision. It has usually been discussed with reference to the school system, although, as we shall see, the main arguments surrounding it extend to further and higher education. The second proposal – the introduction of student loans in place of grants – aims to reduce subsidisation and is of major relevance to students in colleges and universities although, once again, it will have implications for the school system.

The Education Voucher Scheme

A voucher scheme is designed to retain the advantages of a market system while at the same time making sure that everyone is able to obtain at least the minimum quantity of education considered socially necessary. It does this by allocating education vouchers to families with which they can 'buy' education services for their children at the schools of their choosing. Thus the consumer chooses a school instead of being allocated one on the basis of administrative criteria. The voucher would entitle each student to a given quantity of education services and would be presented to a school as payment for the services it provides. The schools – which could be state run or owned privately – would then redeem the vouchers from the government for cash. Assistance rendered through an education voucher is usually preferred to a straight cash payment to the family because, in this way, it is possible to ensure that the expenditure is in fact made on education instead of being used on (from the government's point of view) less desirable purchases. Thus the scheme does involve some restriction of consumer choice. This may be justified on the grounds that government has better information about the benefits of education than the individual parent. Alternatively, it may wish to encourage people to obtain more education than they would choose freely because of external benefits. Finally, it may be that government takes a paternalistic view and encourages individuals to obtain at least the minimum quantity of education because it feels that it is good for them whether they agree or not!

There are a number of variants of the basic voucher scheme. In a flat-rate scheme every family would receive a standard voucher for each child of school age equal in value to the average cost of a year's schooling. Alternatively, an income-related scheme would link the value of the voucher to the family's income, with higher valued vouchers being provided for lower income households. Some proposals seek to combine administrative simplicity with assistance to low income families by offering standard vouchers to the majority of households and supplements of specified amounts (25 per cent, 30 per cent, etc.) to certain qualifying low income households (for example, those in receipt of supplementary benefit payments). Finally, many schemes are designed to enable a family to supplement its voucher allocation with cash and thereby purchase more education services than the government-specified minimum if it so chooses. In this way a voucher scheme could combine the guarantee of access to at least a minimum amount of education for everyone with the freedom for some to obtain more.

Many of the general arguments for and against a market system can also be cited in favour of or against a voucher scheme. On the credit side, it is claimed that low-income households' interests are protected while all parents are offered greater freedom in their choice of schools, that the schools would become more responsive to consumers' demands, and through their competition for pupils would be encouraged to offer a high quality of education with cost-effective techniques. Against these claims it is alleged that even if such a scheme removed some of the difficulties faced by low-income families within a market system, it would still fail to produce an efficient education system because of imperfect information among parents and the existence of spatial monopolies. However, apart from these general arguments, much of the dispute between proponents of a voucher scheme and those in favour of the existing system of direct provision and tax finance has centred on the rival claims about the type of school system that is (or would be) produced by each method of organisation. Specifically, it is possible to identify two main areas of contention. One refers to the *diversity* of the schooling that would be provided, and the other to the *relative quality* of education received by different groups.

It is often claimed that a voucher system will produce a diverse education system with a variety of curricula and methods of teaching catering for differing needs, whereas the present system offers a more or less standard education to everyone irrespective of their particular preferences. The Weiller Report on the first education voucher demonstration scheme in Alum Rock, California, expressed this view as follows:

> **Vouchers will overcome rigidities in the education system brought about by the public (i.e. state) schools' virtual monopoly of elementary and secondary education ... The quality of schooling will improve because vouchers will promote educational innovation and diversity, parental interest in education, and school responsiveness to parent and student needs. (Weiller *et al.*, 1974)**

However, there is no absolutely convincing theoretical reason why shifting the balance of control from teachers and educationalists to parents should necessarily produce a more diverse and varied school system. A feasibility study of a voucher scheme carried out for Kent County Council in the Ashford district expressed a counter view:

> It is possible ... that parents would generally opt for the 'safety', as they perceived it, of a traditional curriculum and this would result in many schools following similar paths, all competing for the 'middle ground' of educational style. The idea of innovation tends to produce concern among a large number of parents. (Kent County Council Education Department, 1978, p. 4)

Moreover, empirical evidence on the subject is inconclusive. There is no doubt that within the existing state school system there is great diversity of schools and courses, whereas numerous small private schools offer a uniformly dull, examination-dominated type of education. On the other hand, however, there have been examples of exciting innovatory forms of education pioneered in the private sector while similar schemes have been strangled by Local Authority temerity and bureaucracy in the public sector. At present both sides of the argument can find sufficient evidence favourable to their cases to continue to believe in their own veracity.

Finally, however, on the subject of diversity and the ability of the school system to respond to differing needs, it is important to point out that the claims about schools' ability to respond to consumer demands under a voucher scheme may well have been exaggerated. Schools with substantial investments in buildings and fixed plant would find it costly to expand or contract in response to short-run changes in parents' tastes. To illustrate the scale of the problem, the Kent study estimated that following the introduction of a voucher scheme between 20 and 46 per cent of the population of some secondary schools would move. They concluded that 'if most of the moves were to the schools already most popular, this could produce an unmanageable situation'.

Those in favour of vouchers point to the scope for using

mobile class-rooms which could be moved from the less to the
more popular schools, but these would have clear educational
disadvantages. In an attempt to cope with short-run excess
demand, some advocates of the voucher scheme suggest using
the price mechanism – that is, schools for which there is excess
demand could raise their fees. This, however, introduces the
spectre of qualitative differences in the education received by
different social groups. This is the second area of contention we
mentioned above.

One of the main fears of those opposed to a voucher system is
that it would lead to a hierarchy of schools, based on fees,
which would leave those who could not afford to supplement
their vouchers receiving an inferior education at schools with
poor facilities and less able teachers. According to this view,
guaranteeing a *minimum* standard of education would not yield
the social benefits or establish the genuine equality of access
that society has set as its goals. Once again the Weiller Report
gives voice to these fears:

> **Vouchers could foster segregation by race and class ... and
> destroy the shared democratic values fostered by the tradi-
> tional system of [state] schools.**

In reply to this charge supporters of a voucher scheme often
point out that the present system of state provision in Britain is
already hierarchical and far from equitably distributed. There are
gross inequalities in the amount and quality of education
received by children from different socio-economic groups.
Despite the widespread introduction of comprehensive
schooling in recent years, children at schools located in middle-
and higher-income catchment areas tend to be educated in
better schools and stay at school longer (and hence receive
more education) than the children from lower-income homes.
For example, in 1978–79 over 50 per cent of children in the
16–18 age group with fathers in the 'professional, employers
and managerial' socio-economic group were in full-time education compared with under 30 per cent of children in the same
age group whose fathers were in the 'semi-skilled, manual,
personal services and unskilled' group (*Social Trends*, Central
Statistical Office, 1981, p. 62). Thus it seems that both systems

can work to the disadvantages of lower-income groups. None the less, if we wish to reduce inequality of access we need to adopt the arrangement that is likely to minimise it. Given this aim, it seems that a system of state provision at zero prices – which at least eliminates inequalities on the direct basis of ability to pay – is more likely to do this. But the foregoing account suggests that it is likely to require complementary policies on income redistribution if it is to succeed. Moreover it also requires that those in positions of political and administrative power have a genuine commitment to this aim.

Subsidies to Students: Grants or Loans?

Most students in full-time further or higher education in Britain receive subsidies in the form of non-repayable grants which pay their tuition fees and make a substantial contribution towards their living expenses while they are studying. Although they are not usually described in such terms, these grants are a form of education voucher; they are allocated to students to enable them to buy education services at approved institutions, and these institutions – which are increasingly dependent on fee income – are in competition for students. Unlike the voucher schemes described in the previous section, however, they are not available to every potential student, only those who obtain the educational qualifications necessary to gain admission to a college or university.

Now as we have seen, government subsidisation of education is necessary to ensure that the socially efficient amount is undertaken and to make sure that it is distributed equitably. These are the criteria in terms of which any assessment of the grants system must be conducted. However, because there is excess demand for higher education and its supply is rationed by the government which, through finance, controls its provision, we may assume that the government is able to ensure the efficient level of provision. It may be, of course, that the government fails to do this; those who argue for a larger private sector in higher education operating on market principles as in, for example, the United States maintain that this is the case. But we shall not be addressing this argument here. Rather it is the second objective – the equity of the subsidisation of students through grants – that we wish to consider.

The grant system is frequently defended in terms of the need to equalise access to further and higher education by ensuring that students from poorer families are not discriminated against because of their limited ability to pay tuition fees and finance a period of study. But to what extent can the grant system – which has been in operation in its present form since 1960 – be said to have equalised access? One source of information is provided by international comparisons. In the United Kingdom approximately 20 per cent of the relevant age group enter some form of higher education. While this is higher than the German percentage and is broadly comparable with the French, it is considerably below Canada (34 per cent), Sweden (38 per cent) and the USA's 47 per cent (Verry, 1977, p. 68). Of course there are many factors which determine the participation rate in higher education and international comparisons are always hazardous, but it is relevant to note that the three latter countries all rely on loan schemes rather than grants. Alternatively, it may be more germane to examine the percentage of students from lower socio-economic backgrounds who enter higher education in Britain, for these are surely the group who require assistance to ensure equality of access. Once again the figures do not support the case for grants; approximately 25 per cent of university entrants are from families where the head of the household is in a manual job, whereas such families represent around 60 per cent of the general population, and this percentage has remained fairly constant since the grant system was introduced (Verry, 1977, p. 71). The majority of students still come from middle- or upper-income homes. This means that a policy ostensibly designed to assist those students who would otherwise be denied access to higher education on financial ground is, in fact, allocating a large proportion of its budget to the sons and daughters of the relatively well-off. Admittedly there is a grants means test which places restrictions on the amounts higher-income families may receive, but the dominant picture is still one of a large number of low-income tax payers – who do not use higher education facilities – subsidising those who are better off.

Critics of the grant system maintain that if the aim of the policy is really to provide equality of access, then the financial assistance is being given at the wrong stage of the education process. Most students who are at risk 'drop out' before the point of entry into higher education; thus the proportion of students from 'manual' backgrounds in full-time education between 16 and 18 years of age is approximately the same as that in higher education. This is clearly a crucial period for the low-income family, for it is at this stage that the student starts to forgo income if he or she remains at school without receiving any general financial assistance. If grants are to be awarded it is likely that they would make a greater contribution towards the establishment of equality of access if they were given at this stage. However, the education budget is obviously limited and so if this reform were implemented savings would be necessary elsewhere. Advocates of this view suggests that these could be achieved by replacing grants by loans in further and higher education.

Unlike a grants system, which redistributes the costs of education between people (i.e. from taxpayers who do not receive higher education to students), a loan system requires the recipient of education to bear its cost but allows him or her to redistribute the burden over time. As we have seen, education expenditure is an investment which can be expected to yield returns in the form of increased future earnings, and a loan scheme requires some of these earnings to be used to repay the costs of education. Supporters of a loan scheme claim it will be both more equitable and efficient than the present grants system. It would be more equitable, they claim, because it would reduce lifetime income inequality by requiring students who receive higher future incomes as a result of education to bear its costs. It would not discriminate against students from low-income backgrounds because they, in common with all students, would earn extra income in the future with which they could repay their debts. Moreover, the proposal is often combined with the suggestion that the grant budget should be redistributed to the 16–18 years age group which, as we have seen, is the one in which inequality of access to higher education seems to start. Increases in efficiency would result, they claim, from encouraging a more responsible attitude among students who would be expected to make better use of their time if they were incurring private costs, and by freeing higher education from constraints on expansion resulting from dependence on general government revenues.

As one would expect, vociferous arguments have been advanced against these claims, especially by the National Union of Students. Opponents of loan schemes argue (i) that it would exacerbate existing inequalities of access because it would deter students from low-income backgrounds, whereas in higher-income families parents would tend to look upon education as a consumption expenditure which they would finance, thereby releasing their children from the burden of debt repayments; (ii) that it would fail to release government expenditure for other uses for many years because the government would have to provide loan finance – as private banks would be unwilling to offer loans to students with little collateral – and these loans, like mortgage loans on housing, would only be repaid in the distant future; (iii) that the efficiency of higher education in Britain is already high as evidenced by the 'drop-out' rate, which is very low by international standards; much of this is because students, freed by the grant system from financial concerns, can devote their full attention to their studies; (iv) that it would deter people from entering relatively low-paid, but nevertheless socially useful jobs; and (v) that it would discriminate against women or others who left the workforce for childrearing purposes (some people have even argued that an educated woman's prospects would be affected adversely because she would be carrying a 'negative dowry'!).

To what extent is it possible to resolve these conflicting claims? On the question of equality of access it is certainly true that the replacement of grants by loans, *in itself*, is likely to penalise students from low-income homes more heavily. However, if the proposal is combined with one for redistributing the funds to the 16–18 years age group this will probably more than offset any regressive effects within higher education. Whether or not government revenue is actually available for redistribution in the short or medium term depends upon the loan finance arrangements. Current proposals envisage loans being provided by the private banking sector but being underwritten (guaranteed against default) by the government. This would free the existing grant budget for use elsewhere in the education system. On the issue of 'drop-out' rates and efficiency it is certainly true that wastage rates in Britain are low by international standards, but this is hardly surprising when one considers the demanding selection procedures applied to applicants and the rationing of places. In countries such as the United States entry to college or university is open to nearly all applicants with basic qualifications. In consequence over 40 per cent of the relevant age groups are in full-time education. Inevitably this means that many more marginal students with high 'drop-out' risk are admitted to college in the US than in Britain. This is almost certainly a more important determinant of relative wastage rates than the grant system.

Problems posed by the likelihood of students seeking high-paid jobs in preference to lower-paid, but socially useful, jobs have been countered by suggested modifications to the basic loan system. One such proposal is for a graduate tax in which repayments would be related to earnings. Under such a scheme students *as a group* would repay the costs of their education, although individual students would not repay the invidual costs they incurred. Thus a student who went into a low-paying occupation would have some of his costs paid by a colleague entering a more highly paid job. Such a scheme would embody a risk-pooling insurance principle where all students agreed to protect any one of their members from the adverse consequences of low future earnings. It would also, of course, overcome the problem of discrimination against women who may want to leave the workforce temporarily or permanently, although the need for protection from the burden of a negative dowry probably belongs more to the world of Jane Austen than the 1980s.

Summary

The education system has both *efficiency* and *equity* objectives. Efficiency requires the adoption of a system that maximizes net social benefits – that is, the greatest possible excess of benefits over costs. These benefits take two main forms: there are *production* benefits concerned with training the future work force, and there are a more diffuse range of *social* benefits. The equity objective requires the establishment of *equality of access* or the guarantee of a *minimum standard* in education.

Although a market system in education allows the expression of consumer freedom of choice and has certain other advantages, there are strong reasons for believing that it will not achieve either of these objectives. The attainment of efficiency is likely to be impeded because of *capital market imperfections*, consumer *imperfect information, externalities*, and spatial *monopoly* elements in the supply of education. At the same time, equity is unlikely to be achieved when access to education is determined by *ability to pay* and income is distributed unequally. For these reasons some form of state intervention in education is necessary, but this does not establish the form it should take.

Dissatisfaction with existing forms of direct provision and subsidy have led some economists to propose various changes. One suggestion is for the introduction of education *vouchers*. Schemes based on vouchers would, it is claimed, retain the advantages of a market system while guaranteeing everyone at least a minimum standard of education – thereby overcoming problems facing low-income families. Disputes about the relative merits of a voucher scheme have been based on two main issues: the *diversity* of the school system it would produce and the fears that it would lead to *segregation* and vastly different *standards of schooling*. Another proposal aims to reduce subsidisation by replacing *grants* to students with *loans*. This, it is argued, would produce a more equitable and efficient higher education system. Opponents argue that this would increase inequality, increase drop-out rates and deter women and others who would have difficulty repaying loans.

Further Reading

Blaug (1972) is still probably the best general text on the economics of education. Baxter, O'Leary and Westoby (1977) contains twenty papers on different aspects of economics and education policy including ones on vouchers, student loans and the distribution of benefits from education. Kent County Council (1978) describes a feasibility study on an education voucher scheme. Crew and Young (1977) put the case for student loans, while Verry (1977) considers the equity aspects of the student loans debate.

Questions for Discussion

1. 'The private rates of return on investment in higher education are sufficiently large for students from both poor and rich households to suggest that the abolition of student grants would not affect the social composition of students entering colleges and universities.' Discuss this claim.
2. Do you think that the education system would be more equitable if grants to 16–18 year olds replaced student grants?
3. Examine the case for using different levels of student grant to encourage students to follow courses which the government deems socially desirable.
4. 'As the production benefits of education are more tangible than the social benefits, the latter tend to be undervalued in discussions of education planning.' Discuss.
5. Explain how you would use cost-benefit analysis to estimate the social rate of return on investment in medical education.
6. The Education Act (1980) provides parents with freedom of choice among schools within their education authority, although if some schools are over-subscribed authorities typically employ place of residence as a criterion for allocation to schools. Analyse this procedure.
7. How would the operation and the consequences of a non-supplementable voucher scheme differ from a supplementable scheme?
8. Private market provision of education emphasises private benefits whereas state provision is concerned with social benefits. Discuss this claim.
9. What do you understand by the term 'equality of opportunity' within the education sector?

10. Do you think that education is a means of promoting social mobility or a means of preparing certain social groups for a predetermined place in the socio-economic system?

Housing 4

Although successive British governments have pursued the traditional aim of providing 'a decent home for every family at a price within their means', official figures show that in 1977 there were still one and a quarter million households (that is, about 8 per cent of the total) living in dwellings that either lacked basic amenities or were deemed unfit for habitation. Moreover over one million other households were living in dwellings which were officially designated as in a state of serious disrepair (i.e. requiring repairs costing more than £1000 at 1971 prices). In addition to substandard dwelling conditions, approximately 600 000 households were either sharing accommodation unwillingly or living in overcrowded conditions. In total, official figures suggest that in 1977 approximately two million households were living in unsatisfactory housing conditions; this represented over one in ten households. (In fact, unofficial estimates suggest that housing conditions are even worse than this, and that over three million households live in unsatisfactory conditions. See Lansley, 1980.) So much for a decent home for every family!

Why is it that these problems have persisted despite innumerable housing policy initiatives? What are the reasons for the discrepancy between the government's declared objectives and its achievements in the housing area? In this chapter we shall try to suggest some answers to these questions. In particular, we shall argue that there are certain special features (or failings) of the market system in housing that can be expected to lead to an inefficient and inequitable allocation of resources. Given these special features, we shall go on to discuss some of the major government policies that have been designed to overcome them. These will include rent control, the provision of council housing and the tax incentives offered to owner-occupiers. But first we need to look at housing objectives rather more closely.

Objectives

As in other social problem areas, society's main objectives can be specified in terms of efficiency and equity. However, in practice, the formulation of housing goals has tended to emphasise the equity objective, albeit in an indirect form. To appreciate this, consider the often-made claim that housing is a *necessity*. Now while it is undoubtedly correct that some form of shelter is necessary to sustain life, it is by no means clear that this establishes the necessity for luxury penthouse flats in Mayfair or the mock-Tudor residences of Esher or Cheadle. What people usually mean when they speak of housing as a necessity is that there is some *minimum standard* of accommodation that is a necessity of life as we have come to expect it in 20th century Britain. This is undoubtedly the official view implicit in the concept of 'a decent home'; that is, there is a minimum standard of housing below which no family should be allowed to fall. In our terms this is one interpretation of the equity objective.

Similarly, the equity objective can be shown to be behind the formulation of housing construction targets. For most of this century the overall shortage of dwellings in relation to the number of households seeking accommodation has been viewed as *the* dominant housing problem. Accordingly successive Governments have set building targets and judged their performance in terms of the number of dwellings constructed each year. This pursuit of housing targets has resulted in the conversion of a national shortage of 750 000 dwellings in 1951 into a crude surplus of approximately one million dwellings by the end of 1979 (see Robinson, 1982). At first sight this concern with the size of the total stock might appear to be an example of the pursuit of an efficient level of housing production. But in fact it is not. Rather, building more houses has been the method chosen to try to achieve a minimum standard of provision for everyone. In the drive to encourage housing construction, little attention was paid to increases in the amount of housing consumed by those families above the minimum standard who were already adequately housed, with the result that many writers now feel there has been overinvestment in housing at the expense of other forms of investment. Some have even attributed Britain's poor economic performance of recent years to a diversion of industrial investment funds to housing. Clearly the neglect of the efficiency objective can lead to adverse consequences. Accordingly our discussion of government policies in the final section of this chapter will consider some of the current proposals designed to rectify this failing.

The Market System and Housing

The market system is the main means of allocating housing in Britain. Even today when the level of government provision is higher than ever before, nearly 70 per cent of dwellings have been produced and are allocated by the market system. Of course, there are numerous forms of government intervention within the private market, including regulation and tax/subsidy policies, and different types of private property ownership but, in essence, most housing is provided through the market system. As we saw in Chapter 1, this system has several distinct advantages, but it also has a number of serious shortcomings. In the case of housing these shortcomings have often manifested themselves in the failure to meet society's minimum standards and the failure to produce an efficient quantity of housing. In this section we shall examine some of the reasons for this failure.

Equity: Income and Access to Housing

There is no reason to expect a market system to achieve the aim of a guaranteed minimum standard. This is because many families simply do not have sufficient purchasing power to buy, or even rent, good quality accommodation. Thus one of the main reasons for the persistence of substandard dwellings is the poverty of the families that occupy them. Recognition of this correlation between poor housing conditions and low-income households has led some economists to argue that the problem is not really a *housing* problem at all. For them it is just one other manifestation of general poverty; just as, without assistance, the poor would not be able to afford adequate food or clothing so they cannot afford adequate housing.

According to this view, slum housing may be inequitable but it is not necessarily inefficient. Indeed, some writers have argued that, given low-income demand for housing, slum housing represents an efficient supply response. But is this claim correct? Can a market system in housing be expected to produce efficiency? Other economists have argued that while general poverty is certainly an important contributory factor towards the persistence of substandard housing, it is not the only one. They point, in addition, to certain special features that can be expected to produce an inefficient allocation of resources. These are *capital market imperfections, imperfect information* and *discrimination*, and the existence of *externalities*. In addition, the housing market displays adjustment problems because of short run *supply inelasticity*.

Capital Market Imperfections

Housing is an expensive commodity. In 1980 the average price of a house in the United Kingdom was over £24 000 – more than three and a half times average annual earnings. This means that very few people are in a position to buy a house outright from their income and accumulated savings. Most people will need to borrow money. Moreover, because the size of the loan will be large in relation to the borrower's income, repayments will have to be spread over a long enough period of time to permit each monthly repayment to be small enough to be paid from the buyer's monthly wage or salary. To meet this demand, a number of institutions – the Building Societies – have grown up, specialising in long-term mortgage loans to

house buyers. In 1980 over five million housholds held
mortgage loans from 273 societies. In addition, in recent years,
the commercial banks have started to offer long-term loans for
house purchase on a wider scale, although by 1980 the value of
their loans accounted for only about 10 per cent of the Building
Societies total.

One feature that distinguishes the societies from other financial institutions is that they borrow short-term and lend long-
term – the reverse of normal practice. Thus while loans are
offered for up to thirty-five years, depositors and shareholders
are free to withdraw their money within days or weeks. This
highly liquid nature of their liabilities, and the illiquidity of
their assets (houses on which they have advanced loans cannot
be readily converted into cash) makes the societies very
cautious and unwilling to take risks that might lead to a loss of
confidence on the part of shareholders. This risk aversion is
particularly noticeable in their lending policies, where they
operate a stringent set of rules governing the types of property
on which they are willing to lend money, the amounts they are
willing to lend and the individuals to whom they will lend.
These criteria have been criticised on the grounds that they
reflect excessive caution, or even discrimination against certain
groups and housing areas, rather than the real risks associated
with different types of loan. For example, it has been argued
that building societies discriminate against manual workers
because their requirements about prospective borrower's
incomes favour those in occupations with stable incremental
scales at the expense of those in jobs where the earnings profile
is more uneven and/or includes substantial overtime payments.
Similarly, the traditional unwillingness of the societies to lend
on older properties, particularly the practice of 'redlining'
which designates certain areas as 'no-loan' areas, has been
cited as a reason for the accelerated decay of certain inner city
districts.

Imperfect Information

When people go to buy food they have a general idea of the
prices they will need to pay for eggs, butter, tea, and so on.

They will not necessarily shop at the cheapest shop because there may be other factors they take into account. For example, the shop's location, service, and the quality of its goods may also be important. But on the basis of these factors, most people develop shopping habits and tend to use the same shop regularly. However, if the level of service provided by a shop deteriorates drastically, or its prices rise substantially in relation to other shops, we may expect some shoppers to switch their custom elsewhere. This possibility prevents any one shop from getting seriously out of line with its competitors. The system exists because people go shopping frequently and are able to assess relative price levels continuously. As a result, they are well informed.

Well-informed buyers are essential if a market is to operate efficiently. If buyers do not possess adequate information on the goods and prices available throughout the market, some sellers may charge excessive prices and make abnormal profits. Unfortunately, imperfect information is widespread in the housing market. Nor is it confined to any particular income group; even middle-class owner-occupiers generally possess imperfect information. The transaction costs of buying and selling a home and moving to a new residence are sufficiently large to prevent people from changing homes as casually as they may change foodshops. Hence they enter the market only infrequently. Any change in housing will normally result from some extraneous factor, such as the need for a larger house or a change of job location. For most of the time, a household will remain in a house for which the price was determined some time in the past. If the need to change homes arises and, as is often the case, the change involves moving to a new neighbourhood or town, variations in prices between areas may mean that the area with which the household is familiar provides a poor guide to the prices it will find in the new area.

Of course, when a family decides to move it can spend time acquiring information about housing in the area in which it wants to live. But the costs of search in terms of time, money, and inconvenience can be high, especially if there is some urgency about housing requirements. The growth of an industry devoted to the dissemination of information on property for sale – estate agents – has reduced these costs somewhat, but they still remain formidable.

So far we have been discussing the problems faced by owner-occupiers. However, imperfect information presents low-income families in rented accommodation with even more acute problems. And among them, recent migrants to urban areas are at a particular disadvantage. This may be because they have only recently arrived in a city and have not had sufficient time to acquire the necessary information; or it may be that their lack of education or familiarity with the housing system prevents them from knowing how to acquire it. Moreover the disadvantages suffered by these families are often made worse by the presence of racial or other forms of discrimination that prevent them from obtaining housing outside their existing neighbourhoods. With their mobility reduced in this way, these families often find themselves confined to low-income areas and susceptible to unscrupulous landlords. Often they end up paying a higher price per unit for slum housing than other families pay for good quality housing in suburban areas.

Externalities

If one family on a street allows the state of its house to deteriorate so that it becomes an eyesore to their neighbours, the level of benefit the neighbours obtain from their own housing will be reduced. For they will be concerned with the visual appearance of their neighbourhood as well as with the characteristics of their own homes. Similarly, if one resident persists in holding noisy, late-night parties that disturb others in the vicinity, the benefit these neighbours derive from living in the area will be reduced. Both these examples indicate that the level of benefit a family derives from consuming the services offered by its own house is affected by its neighbours' activities – that is, there are externalities. If a market system is used to allocate housing, we cannot be confident that individuals will take externalities into account when deciding upon their actions. The result could be widespread external costs (or benefits) and an inefficient system.

Let us return to the first example involving the neglect of

maintenance and repair work to illustrate the significance of externalities in the housing market. In fact, the example we have chosen is a particularly important one because it plays a key role in the creation and spread of slum housing. To see how this works, consider a typical slum neighbourhood. Most of the housing will be substandard, with low-income families living at high densities in multioccupied, overcrowded buildings. Interspersed with this housing will be various abandoned buildings that have become uninhabitable and hence are subject to vandalism. The local environment will also be poor, suffering from an absence of decent recreational and leisure facilities and the proximity of industrial and commercial activities with their associated pollution.

Now consider a landlord who owns a building in such an area. Why doesn't he invest in maintenance and repair work to improve the quality of his property? Would not an improved building attract tenants who are willing to pay rents that offer him an adequate return for his investment? It does not take much imagination to work out the answers to these questions. The landlord will be only too aware that any investment he might make is almost certain to yield a poor return because the slum neighbourhood conditions will dominate any improvements that he might make on a single building. That is, the neighbourhood external costs would deter prospective tenants who would be willing and able to pay the rents that would make improvement worthwhile. Consequently the landlord is likely to decide against spending money on his property and thereby contributes to the decline of the neighbourhood.

Only if the landlord could be confident that other landlords in the neighbourhood were also going to improve their property would he be willing to consider investing. In this case the level of external cost imposed on his building by adjoining ones might be reduced sufficiently to make improvement worthwhile. However, mutual uncertainty among landlords about their neighbours' actions will usually mean that no one is willing to take the initiative. The essence of this problem (which is an application of what is sometimes known as the 'prisoner's dilemma') can be demonstrated in terms of the following simple example.

Suppose there are two landlords, Bert and Ernie, who own

two adjoining buildings in a certain street. Both buildings have become rather run-down and they are each trying to decide how much to spend on repairing them. For purposes of illustration, let us assume that they have both decided to spend £1000 and that they are each trying to decide whether to spend an extra £1000 on top of this sum. Let us start by looking at the problem from Bert's point of view. He cannot be sure what Ernie is going to do and yet he knows that because of externalities the return he receives will depend to a certain extent on Ernie's actions. The considerations that will enter into his decision can be summarised in the 'pay-off matrix' shown in Figure 4.1. The matrix shows that if Bert decides not to invest the extra £1000 and Ernie decides likewise, he will receive a 4 per cent return on his original investment. If, however, Ernie does invest while Bert does not, Ernie's improved building will bestow an external benefit on his property and raise his return to 6 per cent. So if Bert *does not invest* he will receive either a 4 or a 6 per cent return. On the other hand, if he decides to invest while Ernie decides not to, Ernie's less well-kept building will impose an external cost on his property and reduce his return to 2 per cent. But if Ernie did invest at the same time, Bert would receive some external benefit and his return would rise to 5 per cent. Thus if Bert decides *to invest* he will receive either a 2 or a 5 per cent return. But which option will he choose?

FIGURE 4.1
Bert's Rates of Return

	Ernie does not invest	Ernie does invest
Bert does not invest	4%	6%
Bert does invest	2%	5%

It is likely that Bert will approach the problem in the following manner. First, he will ask himself what is the best strategy to adopt if he thinks Ernie is not going to invest; the first column of the matrix shows that he would do better *not* to invest in these circumstances because then he would make a 4 per cent instead of a 2 per cent return. Second, he will ask himself what is the best strategy if he thinks Ernie is going to invest; the second column shows once again that he would do better *not* to invest in this situation. In this way he would make a 6 per cent instead of a 5 per cent return. Thus in both cases he will make a larger return by *not* investing. Now, because Ernie is faced with exactly the same uncertainties concerning Bert's behaviour, he can be expected to go through the same decision-making process. If he does, he will reach exactly the same conclusion: his best strategy is *not* to invest. Therefore neither Bert nor Ernie will invest and they will both make a 4 per cent return. Notice, however, that if they had both invested the extra £1000 they would both have been better off because they would each have made a 5 per cent return! This is the essence of the 'prisoner's dilemma'. By acting independently in situations where they are unsure of each other's behaviour, the decision-makers reach an outcome that is less desirable to both of them than one they could have reached if they had collaborated. But collaboration between slum landlords is unlikely to take place, especially as it is in any one landlord's interests to appear to collaborate – in order to get his neighbour to invest – and then to renege on the deal. Of course, whether external effects will be strong enough to bring about this state of affairs cannot be stated with certainty – but we can say that the existence of externalities does cast considerable doubt on the efficiency of the market system.

Finally in this discussion of external effects we should mention a more general set of external costs that are usually associated with poor housing conditions. For example poor health, fire risks, crime, and vandalism are just some of the ways in which these costs may manifest themselves. When health, fire, and crime prevention services are financed from taxation revenues, taxpayers in general will find themselves bearing these costs of slum housing.

Supply Inelasticity

In Chapter 1 we described the way in which the market system copes with changes in demand. We showed that if the demand for a commodity increases there will be a rise in its price, which can be expected to encourage some firms to produce more. This increase in supply will satisfy some of the additional demand. Moreover, as supply increases, there will be a tendency for the price to fall gradually from its immediate post-change level until a new equilibrium price is established. However, in some circumstances there is very little opportunity for increasing output as demand increases. Consequently demand remains unsatisfied while prices rise to – and remain at – the immediate post-change level. If these conditions apply we say that supply is *inelastic*.

The difference between a situation of inelastic supply and one in which the supply response is more flexible (elastic) is demonstrated in Figure 4.2. In both parts of the diagram the vertical axis measures the price of housing (in terms of £'s per week) while the horizontal axis records the number of dwellings demanded and supplied in this particular local market. In the first panel the point of intersection between the demand schedule (*DD*) and the supply schedule (*SS*) indicates an equilibrium price of £30 per week, at which 1000 dwellings are demanded/ supplied. Now suppose there is an increase in demand following the migration of additional families into the area. This is depicted by a second demand schedule (*D'D'*). This change in demand conditions leads to a new equilibrium at which the price has risen to £33 per week and the supply has increased by 20 dwellings. Note that a substantial increase in price (10 per cent) leads to only a small increase in the supply of housing (2 per cent).

In contrast, the second panel of the diagram shows how an identical equilibrium position followed by the same change in demand conditions results in a far smaller price increase and a much larger increase in the supply of housing. Here the equilibrium price only rises to £31 per week (3 per cent) whereas 50 more dwellings are supplied (5 per cent). Thus we can see that when supply is inelastic, the bulk of the adjustment to a change

FIGURE 4.2
Housing Price and Output with Different Supply Conditions

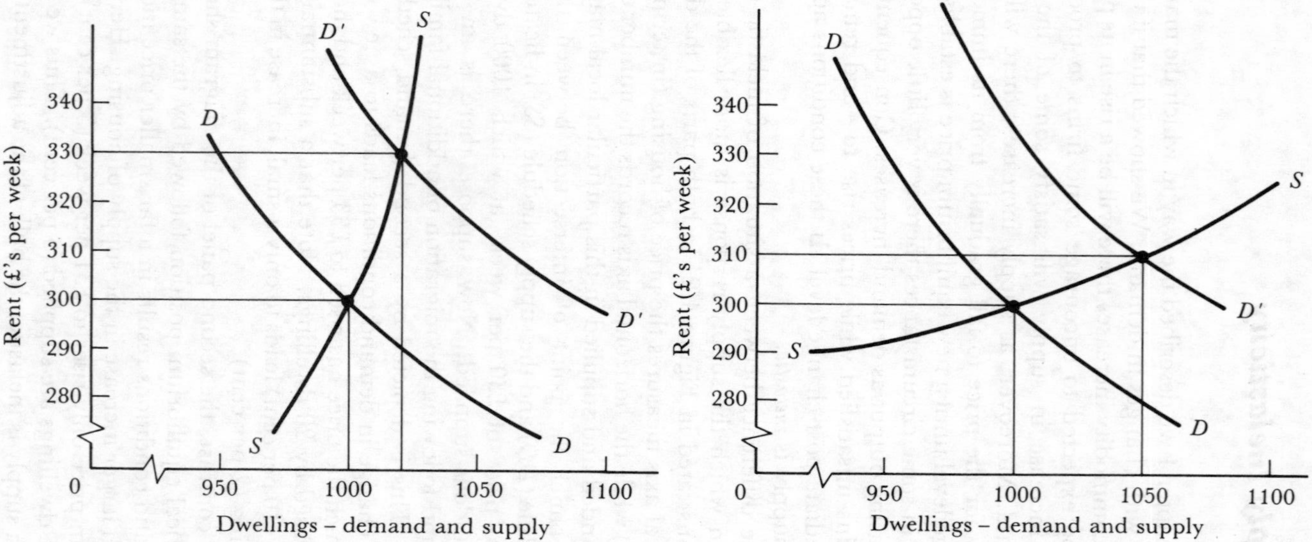

(a) Inelastic Supply

(b) Elastic Supply

in demand conditions will take place through a change in price instead of a change in the quantity of the commodity offered for sale.

Note that although we have not chosen to discuss supply inelasticity under the heading of equity, it does have important implications for the equity of the housing system. This is because when rents rise the owners of existing housing receive an increase in their incomes at the expense of their tenants. As long as it is impossible to increase the supply of a commodity for which demand has risen, the owners of existing stocks of the commodity have a supplier's monopoly and receive monopoly profits. Let us look at some of the factors that cause supply inelasticity.

Fixed Housing Locations

We have so far spoken of the housing market as if there was a *single* market. In reality it is probably more accurate to speak of a *series of local* markets. Because housing is fixed and cannot be moved from one location to another (with a few exceptions in the case of caravans, boats and tents!) the supply of housing will be specific to a particular area. If there is a shortage of cars in Leeds but they are plentiful in Liverpool, then the shortage in Leeds can be alleviated by transporting cars from Liverpool to Leeds. Such mobility is not possible in the case of housing and so supply shortages may persist in some areas while there are surpluses elsewhere. Of course there will be linkages between individual local markets. For instance, if there is a shortage of housing in Leeds compared with Liverpool, we may expect house prices to be higher in Leeds than in Liverpool. The lower Liverpool prices may induce some people to move from Leeds to Liverpool, and thus mobility of people may overcome the problems presented by immobility of housing. However this type of mobility is likely to be low because the decision to move from one town to another would involve a range of costs including a change of jobs, separation from friends and other forms of domestic disruption (see Chapter 9). The gains resulting from lower house prices would have to be quite substantial to bring about such movements.

Land Shortages

Shortages of land have frequently placed limitations on the supply of housing. Apart from a few notable land-reclamation schemes, such as those involving the Polders of the Netherlands, the total supply of land in an area is fixed. The quantity cannot be increased year after year in the way that the number of machines used in production is increased. Therefore, in the limiting case, there simply may not be any further land available for building. More frequently, however, the problem is not one of a total lack of land, but rather a shortage of land available for house building in the areas in which it is required. These shortages often arise because of the land-use restrictions introduced through town planning legislation. Under this system, land is designated for particular uses; for example, it may be reserved for recreational or agricultural use, in which case no house building would be permitted. These restrictions on the supply of land for building purposes may be very important in the short run. For even though restrictions may be relaxed if acute shortages of building land occur, the planning authority may be unwilling to do so without extensive deliberation.

Clearly, therefore, the *location* of a plot of land is of importance. The availability of suburban or rural land may be of little use if it is central urban land that is in short supply. However, transport developments which increase the ease and/or lower the cost of travel will tend to increase the substitutability of land at different locations. Hence a suburban site may become an alternative to a central city one following the establishment of a fast commuting service. This is tantamount to increasing the available supply of land for uses that require a central location. One example of this phenomenon was provided when the Victoria underground railway line was opened in London. This immediately gave greater access to Central London for a number of sites in the vicinity of stations on this line, thereby increasing the range of sites involving short commuting trips.

Productivity in House Building

In recent years it has taken an average of between one and two years to build a house. Is this rather lengthy period of construction inevitable? One way in which dwellings can be constructed more quickly is by the use of industrialised building techniques. These involve the mass production of standard building units that are either produced on the site or transported to the site for erection. However the adoption of such processes has not been as widespread as was envisaged originally. One reason for this is that the production of parts on a site requires substantial investments in capital equipment that will be specific to that site. Only if the development is really large will such investments be worthwhile. In cases where large-scale comprehensive development is taking place, or where certain types of dwellings are being constructed (high-rise flats, for example), such methods will be appropriate. However in the majority of cases the size of the plot to be developed, and the type of housing, precludes the use of such techniques. The alternative to the production of units on the site is production in a factory and delivery to sites at which they are needed. Although this does have the advantage of enabling expensive capital equipment to be used for more than one development, high transport costs and the difficulty of building to the higher specifications that are necessary when on-site adjustments are not possible, have meant that it is generally uneconomical.

Another factor which has deterred the adoption of schemes using capital equipment, which might have speeded up the construction process, is the changeable nature of demand in the building industry. When large amounts have been invested in machinery it is necessary to make sure that it is used to its full capacity. If machines stand idle they have to be paid for even though they do not yield any income. It is not possible to lay off machines when the demand for construction work falls in the way that it is possible to lay off some of the labour force. Consequently the violent fluctuations in demand have made the building industry very cautious about investing heavily in machinery.

A final factor militating against the use of mass production techniques is the need for a great deal of skilled specialist work not suited to such techniques. For example, bricklayers, carpenters, plumbers and electricians all work on tasks where the skill of the man is the vital ingredient. There is little scope for increasing the speed of work by replacing these labour inputs by capital equipment.

Government Policies

In the previous section we argued that housing problems arise because families have insufficient income to buy or rent decent housing or because, even if they have sufficient income, there are various imperfections in the housing market that prevent it from functioning efficiently. Inadequate incomes lead to inequity, whereas the imperfections result in inefficiency. Now the distinction between these two explanations is of some importance for housing policy. The view that housing problems arise because some families have inadequate incomes suggests that the problems could be tackled most effectively by supplementing the purchasing power of these families. According to this view, no specific intervention in the housing market is called for. The market-imperfections view, on the other hand, suggests that specific policies aimed at removing the imperfections will be necessary.

Of course, we do not necessarily have to choose one theory and reject the other; it is quite possible that both factors have played a part in producing the problems described at the beginning of this chapter. In this case elements of both policies will be necessary to remove them. With this in mind, we shall look at three of the major policies that have been introduced in the United Kingdom. The three we have chosen provide examples of regulation (rent control), direct provision combined with subsidies (council housing) and subsidisation operated through the tax system (assistance to owner occupiers).

Rent Control

Rent control is a means of protecting tenants from the high market rents which would result from shortages in the supply of rented accommodation. It was introduced originally as a temporary measure during the First World War, but has been retained in a variety of modified forms for most of the time since then. In essence, all rent-control policies involve specifying a maximum rent that a landlord may charge for a dwelling, and so the tenant receives an implicit 'subsidy' equal to the difference between the controlled rent and the market

FIGURE 4.3
Rent Control and the Supply of Housing

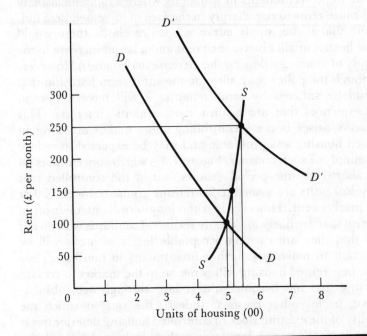

rent. A typical situation is depicted in Figure 4.3. Suppose that initially the market is in equilibrium when 500 units of housing are rented at £100 per month. However, following the in-migration of a large number of additional families there is a sudden increase in the demand for housing. This is shown by the demand schedule $D'D'$, which is to the right of the original one. If the market is left to operate freely, a new market equilibrium will be established when 550 units are rented at £250 per month. However the government may decide that rents of £250 per month are excessive and only attainable because it has not been possible to increase the supply of housing in the time available. Legislation may therefore be enacted to impose a maximum controlled rent of £150 per month. Thus tenants of controlled housing will receive a 'subsidy' of £100 per month, because the controlled rent is set £100 below the market rent.

Now the rationale for controlling rents in this way is the desire to protect tenants in situations where supply inelasticity will cause rents to rise sharply in the face of increased demand. (Note that if the supply curve was more elastic there would have been a smaller increase in rent and a larger increase in the supply of housing following the increase in demand.) However, although the policy may alleviate the short-term hardship that would be suffered by some tenants, it will have long-term consequences that are against most tenants' interests. This paradox arises because controlling rents makes investing in rented housing less profitable and may be expected to reduce the supply of such housing. Figure 4.3 – which concentrates on the short-run time period – shows that at the controlled rent only 520 units are available for renting compared with 550 at the market rent. However it is the long-term consequences of control that are likely to be more serious. Landlords who do not feel that they are earning acceptable levels of profit will be reluctant to make any further investments in housing. Thus little new rented housing will come on to the market to replace housing that has become substandard through age, obsolescence, or for other reasons. Indeed, the rate at which the quality of the existing stock of controlled housing deteriorates is likely to accelerate as landlords seek to reduce their costs by postponing maintenance and repair work. In terms of Figure 4.3, these medium- and long-term reductions in supply will cause leftward shifts in the supply schedule *SS*, indicating that less housing is available for renting at each rent level.

These theoretical expectations about the decline in the size and quality of the stock of rented accommodation have certainly been borne out by empirical evidence. For instance, at the time when rent control was first introduced there were over seven million rented dwellings in the UK; this represented about 90 per cent of all dwellings. Today there are less than three million privately rented dwellings and they account for only about 13 per cent of the total stock of housing. The lack of new investment in this sector is revealed when one considers that nearly 70 per cent of existing private rental dwellings were built before 1919. Furthermore, the deterioration in quality is evidenced by the fact that at the time of the last House Condition Survey (1976) nearly 40 per cent of rented dwellings lacked one or more of the basic amenities and nearly 15 per cent of them were classified as unfit for habitation (Department of the Environment, 1978).

The fact that a policy aimed primarily at tenant protection has had these adverse supply effects is due to the unusual nature of the 'subsidy' involved in rent control. In most cases when government decides that a particular group merits assistance it is the government that bears the cost, at least in the first instance. It usually does this by either paying the producer so that he can sell at a price below cost (as in education) or by assisting the consumer directly in cash or in kind (as in health care). In the case of rent control, however, government regulation specifies the size of the implicit subsidy but the cost is borne by the landlord. Not surprisingly this reduces the incentive to become a landlord.

The form of rent control that has operated since 1965 – that is, rent regulation – has attempted to overcome some of the disincentives experienced by landlords, through the use of a 'fair rent' formula. This specifies a rent level designed to provide the landlord with a 'reasonable' profit, but which protects the tenant by excluding from the rent any element attributable to extreme local shortages. However this has not stemmed the decline of the private rented sector. To a large extent this is the result of developments outside the private rented sector. Governments of both the major political parties have chosen to provide for future housing requirements through the provision of council housing and the encouragement of owner-occupation rather than the expansion of the private rented sector. Let us now consider some of these policies.

Local Authority Housing

Local Authority (LA) or council housing seeks to avoid the adverse supply effects of rent control by combining the direct provision of rented housing with below market, or subsidised, rents. The history of LA housing dates from 1919 when the Housing Act of that year placed the responsibility for dealing with the housing needs of their areas with LAs. The aspirations of the people who had lived through the First World War had prompted the government to act, although the need for some policy initiative had been apparent for some time. The massive rate of population growth and urbanisation experienced in the nineteenth century had produced health problems of a kind and on a scale not previously encountered. Public health legislation sought to tackle some of the major problems by specifying minimum housing standards, but these inevitably involved cost increases which placed the housing beyond the budgets of many working-class households. Thus the need for some additional policy had become clear; direct provision with subsidised rents was the result. By 1979 there were nearly 7 million LA dwellings which represented about 32 per cent of the total stock of dwellings in the UK. These are owned and managed by the individual LAs although most of the rent subsidy is provided by the central government.

In terms of the objectives identified in this book, the *direct provision* of LA housing is designed to overcome inefficiency – such as that resulting from supply inelasticity or 'prisoner's dilemma' type of externalities – whereas the *subsidy* element is designed primarily to deal with equity considerations. How successful has the policy been in the pursuit of these aims? In most discussions about council housing its equity aim tends to receive most attention and so we shall deal with this first.

At present tenants of LA housing receive two types of subsidy. All tenants receive a subsidy because rent levels are set below market rents, whereas some tenants on low incomes – approximately 45 per cent in 1979 – receive an additional means-tested subsidy in the form of rent rebates. Because these rent rebates are income related, and therefore primarily assist low-income LA tenants, they are broadly consistent with the equity objective. The general rent subsidy, on the other hand, is less clearly consistent with this aim. Certainly LA tenants as a group contain a large proportion of low-income households (8 per cent of LA households had incomes of less than £2500 per year in 1979), but there is substantial income variation within the group (17 per cent had incomes of more than £9000 per year). This suggests that a large proportion of the general subsidy budget is being received by middle- to high-income households. Some writers have suggested that the system would become more equitable if the general subsidy element was reduced – by raising rents – and the income-related component was expanded. And, in fact, current government policy is moving in this direction.

How does LA housing perform as far as improving efficiency is concerned? Certainly we would expect an LA to be able to overcome the deterrent to repair and improvement posed by negative externalities, and we might also expect LAs to increase supply elasticity through being willing to undertake building programmes that more risk-averse private developers might reject (although evidence on building times does suggest that private housing is built rather more quickly than council housing). But can we be confident that the public sector will produce the appropriate quantity of housing when it is provided in response to the preferences of politicians or bureaucrats, and is not subject to consumer market demand? Some writers have argued that the standards of LA housing (i.e. the *quantity* of resources embodied in each house) have been set too high and that LA tenants are therefore over-consuming housing. Such writers cite the lower standards prevailing in comparable newly constructed private housing as evidence in support of this assertion. However the very absence of consumer demand – and the complications presented by externalities and the interests of future generations of tenants – make it difficult to evaluate this claim. At best it must remain not proven until such time as suitable empirical evidence is collected enabling it to be tested properly.

Subsidies to Owner-Occupiers

Owner-occupiers now constitute the largest tenure group in Britain. By the end of 1980 over 55 per cent of dwellings were owner-occupied compared with only about 26 per cent in 1947. The rapid expansion of this sector of the housing market has undoubtedly been encouraged by the favourable tax treatment received by those households who choose to buy their homes in comparison with those who rent. To appreciate the nature of this favourable tax treatment, consider two individuals with identical incomes, family commitments and expenditures, one of whom decides to buy a house with the aid of a mortgage loan while the other decides to rent accommodation from a land-lord. Under present tax arrangements, the owner-occupier will pay less income tax than the renter although they have identical incomes. This is because the tax system does not levy tax on income earned to pay interest charges on a mortgage loan (as long as the loan is £30 000 or less) whereas no similar tax relief is offered to the renter.

A numerical example will illustrate the way in which tax relief is calculated. Suppose the owner-occupier borrows £20 000 from a building society at an interest rate of 10 per cent. Moreover assume he or she is liable to an income tax rate of 30p in the £ (30 per cent). The tax relief or 'subsidy' he receives will be as follows:

£20 000 × 10 per cent = £2000 pa interest payment
£2000 × 30 per cent tax rate = <u>£600 pa 'subsidy'</u>

Hence the owner-occupier is able to earn £2000 pa to pay interest charges and no tax is levied on this income – this is worth £600 pa; that is the amount of tax he or she would have paid on that income if it was not used to pay interest charges.

The sums that are allocated in this way are substantial: in the tax year 1978/79 nearly £1.3 thousand million was received in tax relief or subsidy by owner-occupiers. With sums of this size involved, it is obviously of major importance to ask whether these subsidies are consistent with the declared housing objectives of efficiency and equity. The answer, unfortunately, is that they are almost certainly not.

On the question of efficiency, it is likely that the subsidisation of house ownership has stimulated investment in housing at the expense of investment in other assets. As we mentioned earlier some writers have suggested that one of the reasons for Britain's poor economic performance in recent years has been the diversion of funds from investment in manufacturing industry to investment in housing. According to this view the aggregate quantity of housing is too great. Similarly, on the question of equity, a number of studies have shown that the amount of subsidy a household receives increases as the size of its loan, the value of its house and the tax rate it faces increase. This means that higher-income households within the owner-occupier tenure group receive far larger amounts of subsidy than lower-income households. In the numerical example quoted earlier, if the household was subject to a tax rate of 60 per cent, the tax relief would amount to £1200 per year (i.e. £2000 × 0.60). Thus the policy clearly fails to satisfy the full equality definition of equity, and even if it does realise the minimum standard condition – by assisting low-income owner-occupiers – substantial amounts of tax relief are misallocated because they accrue as subsidies to higher income groups.

The failure of existing subsidies to owner-occupiers to meet satisfactorily either the efficiency or equity aims set for housing policy has led to a series of proposals for reform. As in the case of LA tenants, such proposals have tended to favour a reduction in the subsidisation of owner-occupier housing in general and an extension of income-related housing benefits to this sector of the market. The first aim could be achieved by phasing out tax relief to owner-occupiers (if the existing loan ceiling of £30 000 is retained this will have the effect of phasing it out over time as inflation erodes the real value of loans and hence the tax relief on interest charges), while the second objective would involve the introduction of payments comparable to LA rent rebates to the owner-occupier sector. (For a more extensive discussion of these proposals see the further reading.)

Summary

With over one in ten families living in unsatisfactory housing conditions the aim of 'a decent home for every family' is a long way from being met. The private market cannot be relied upon to meet society's objectives. *Income limitations* prevent many families from obtaining adequate housing and thereby produce an *inequitable* distribution of housing resources, whereas *capital market imperfections, imperfect information, supply inelasticity* and *externalities* mean that the market will operate *inefficiently*. In an effort to overcome these problems a variety of government policies have been introduced, but some of them have produced undesirable side consequences of their own. *Rent control* keeps down housing costs for the tenant but has adverse supply effects. *Local Authority Housing* has augmented the supply of housing and provided rent subsidies for many low-income families. Part of its budget is, however, used to subsidise tenants who are relatively well off. Finally, considerable sums have been allocated to owner-occupiers in the form of *tax relief*; it is difficult to justify this policy on either efficiency or equity grounds.

Further Reading

A number of books on housing economics and policy have appeared in recent years. Lansley (1979) provides a good overview of the housing market and government policy towards it. Stafford (1978) deals with government economic policy as it affects the three main tenure groups and argues for greater reliance on private market mechanisms. Robinson (1979) applies techniques of economic analysis to both the housing market and selected government policies within it (including a chapter on rent control), while Maclennan (1982) provides the most recent, and probably most comprehensive, treatment of the economics of housing. From the non-economics literature, Cullingworth (1979) offers an excellent discussion of contemporary housing issues and the role of government within particular parts of the sector.

Questions for Discussion

1. Is there a case for subsidising housing, *per se*, or should assistance be confined to low-income households?
2. Discuss the consequences of selling council houses.
3. Discuss the probable consequences of removing mortgage interest payment tax relief from owner-occupiers.
4. If the problems of poor housing conditions result primarily from the inability of low-income households to afford anything better, would it not be preferable to provide cash assistance to those households directly instead of relying upon rent control, rent subsidies, etc.?
5. Consider the way information is disseminated within the housing market. Can you think of any institutional changes that would make the process more efficient?

6. 'The price of housing is high because the price of land is high.' Discuss.

7. Because the costs of council housing vary substantially between areas some people have recommended a system of national cost and rent 'pooling'. Why do you think costs vary? What would be the effect of rent pooling?

8. Rent regulation policy towards privately rented accommodation specifies a 'fair rent' level for each dwelling. This rent has been described as the rent which would be set in the market in the absence of scarcity. Comment on this idea.

9. What is 'gentrification'? How does it involve externalities?

10. Consider the effect a sustained increase in mortgage credit would have upon the housing market in (i) the short run and (ii) the long run.

Pollution 5

Pollution has been with us for a long time. In the fourteenth century a royal document complained about the 'abominable and most filthy stinks' generated by the activities of London butchers in Seacoal Lane. In the sixteenth century laws were passed prohibiting the use of coal fires in London, and in the 1850s perfumed sheets were hung over the House of Commons' windows to try and reduce the smell of the Thames. In the United States a magazine commented in 1881 that 'no dumping ground, no sewer, no vault contains more filth ... [than] the air in certain parts of [New York] City during the long season of drought'. Chicago's air was described by Rudyard Kipling in 1880 as 'dirt' and its river by another visitor as 'coated with grease so thick on its surface it seemed like a liquid rainbow' (quoted in Bettman, 1974).

More recently, however, concern over pollution has reached new peaks. This partly reflects a growing awareness of the impact of pollution on health and welfare (such as that of lead from car exhausts on children living in urban areas). But it also arises from aesthetic and ecological concerns. To fish or swim in unpolluted rivers; to walk in unspoiled countryside; to protect species endangered by indiscriminate dumping of waste: these and similar environmental considerations have acquired a more important place in society's scale of values in recent decades.

Corresponding to this increase in social concern, there has

been an expansion of interest among economists in pollution problems, and in this chapter we shall consider some of their contributions. As in previous chapters we shall begin by examining society's objectives with respect to pollution control. Should the aim be to eliminate pollution altogether, as some ecologists want? Should we ignore it as an overrated problem, as some industrialists imply? Or should we find some kind of balance? Obviously the answers to these questions are going to depend in part on basic value judgements concerning the quality of human life, the sanctity of animal life and so on; judgements about which economists – in their role as economists – have little to say. But the application of economics can help to formulate these judgements within a coherent framework that is useful for the formulation of social policy, and this is the subject of the first section.

The next section concerns the role of the market system with respect to pollution. Will the market achieve society's objectives concerning pollution control on its own? Or is some form of government intervention necessary? It will become apparent that pollution as a problem arises from the structure of property rights that underlie the operations of the market; accordingly the third section investigates property rights in more detail. Finally we examine government policies in relation to pollution control. We consider not the technological methods of controlling pollution – these lie in the engineer's province – but the various tools of legal and fiscal policy that can be used to cope with the problem. For simplicity the discussion is generally confined to air and water pollution; but most of the arguments apply directly to other pollution problems, such as noise, pesticides or the disposal of solid wastes.

Objectives

As in other chapters, society's objectives concerning pollution can be usefully summarised in terms of efficiency and equity. Economists have tended to concentrate on the efficiency objective and this bias will inevitably be reflected in what follows; but equity issues will not be ignored.

Efficiency

It may seem curious to apply the notion of 'efficiency' to some-thing as obviously 'inefficient' as pollution. Indeed many people feel that the efficient level of pollution is none at all. But those who think this way have usually only considered the benefits from controlling pollution; they have not considered its costs. In a world where resources are scarce, resources that are devoted to restricting pollution will not be available for ful-filling other goals. For instance, consider a chemical firm using a nearby river as a convenient place to dump untreated waste products. If it were forced to treat its waste it would have to install pollution control equipment – the manufacture and operation of which would use up resources that could have been employed in the production of other commodities. It would charge higher prices for its products, thus imposing greater costs on its customers and, except in most unlikely circumstances, reducing its profits. Indeed, if the treatment requirement were strict enough it might be forced out of busi-ness altogether, thus creating unemployment and personal hardship for its workers. This is not to say that it might none the less be socially desirable to prevent the firm polluting the river; the harm done by the pollution might greatly outweigh the beneficial effects of the lower prices and greater employment. It is merely to illustrate the more general point that pollution control has its costs: costs that cannot be ignored in any assessment of its overall desirability.

Nor are these costs trivial. The Department of the Environ-ment (1981) has estimated that in 1977/8 the total cost of existing methods of pollution control in the UK was nearly £2500 million. In the United States the Council of Environ-mental Quality estimated in its 1976 report that the total cost of meeting the requirements of the major federal environmental laws between 1975 and 1984 would be $250 000 million. Another study (discussed in Kneese, 1977, p. 214) estimated the costs of meeting the 1977 US automobile emission standards alone as $11 000 million.

So, although pollution control has benefits it also has con-siderable costs. How should these be taken into account when formulating the efficiency objective? To see how this might be done in a specific case, let us take the chemical firm mentioned above. Suppose that the principal effect of the pollution is to kill a large proportion of the river's otherwise thriving fish population; and suppose further that this is seriously affecting the business of a commercial fishery downstream. To simplify matters, let us make two other assumptions; first that no-one else is affected by the pollution, and second that the only way the chemical firm can reduce its pollution is by cutting back its (chemical) production.

TABLE 5.1
Costs of Chemical Production

Tons of chemical produced	Price per ton (£)	Cost of firm of producing an extra ton (£)	Pollution damage to fishery of an extra ton of production (£)	Social cost of producing an extra ton (£)
(1)	(2)	(3)	(4)	(5) = (4) + (3)
1	40	34	3	37
2	40	35	3	38
3	40	37	3	40
4	40	40	3	43
5	40	44	3	47

Table 5.1 puts flesh on the bones of the example by providing some hypothetical numbers. The first column shows the amount of chemical produced by the upstream firm. To keep the numbers manageable, this is given in units of a single ton. In practice the relevant numbers would be much larger; however, the principle will not be affected by the choice of units. The second column shows the price the firm receives for each ton it sells; we assume that it is in competition with other producers and therefore has to accept the going market price (£40). The third column shows the cost to the firm of producing each extra ton. This cost increases with each ton produced,

reflecting the fact that, say, the firm has to bring older machines into use as its scale of production increases (see the discussion of production costs in Chapter 1). The fourth column shows the damage to the downstream fishery's business that results from the extra waste dumped in the river every time the chemical firm increases its production by a ton; for simplicity, we assume this is constant although in practice it may well increase with each ton produced. The final column shows the combined cost to both the chemical firm and the fishery of producing an extra ton of chemical. Since no-one else is affected, this is the total cost to society of each ton: hence we shall call it the *social cost*.

What is the efficient level of chemical production? If we assume that the market price for the chemical (£40) reflects the value that the chemical's users place on it, then the social benefits – in terms of that value – derived from the production of the first ton exceeds its social cost (£37). The same is true for the second ton, despite the fact that the costs have increased slightly (to £38). The costs of producing the third ton (£40) equal the benefits from producing it; hence that ton is also (just) worth producing. However, the social costs of producing each of the fourth and fifth tons (£43 and £47 respectively) are greater than the social benefits from doing so. Hence the socially efficient level is three tons – the point where the extra social costs of further production begin to exceed the social benefits. Note that at this level there will still be some damage to the fishery; social efficiency does *not* require the total elimination of pollution, nor of the damage it creates.

In the example we have concentrated upon the increase in costs and benefits associated with each extra or *marginal* unit of production. In previous chapters we have called these marginal costs and benefits. Moreover, in the example there were two kinds of marginal cost – the cost of production to the factory, which we can term the marginal private cost (*mpc*), and the cost imposed on the fishery outside the factory, which we term the marginal external cost (*mec*). These combine to form the marginal social cost (*msc*) of production, or:

$$\text{marginal private cost} + \text{marginal external cost} = \text{marginal social cost}$$

On the benefits side, since there are no extra benefits accruing to third parties from the production of the chemical, we can assume that there is no difference between the marginal private benefit (*mpb*) and the marginal social benefit (*msb*): both are, in this case, equal to the price. Hence what the example has shown is that the *efficient level of a pollution-generating activity is at the point where the marginal social benefit of the activity equals its marginal social cost*.

A way of presenting the argument that we shall find useful later is in a diagram such as Figure 5.1. The horizontal axis shows different levels of a pollution-generating activity, and the vertical axis the marginal costs and benefits of the activity. The numbers used in constructing the diagram are taken from Table 5.1, but it should be emphasised that the diagram, and the point it illustrates, could refer to any activity that creates pollution, from private motoring to oil tankers flushing their tanks at sea. The *mpc* and *msc* curves show how marginal private and marginal social costs respectively increase with the scale of the activity; the difference between them at any point is equal to the marginal external cost at that level of the activity. The *msb* curve shows the marginal social benefit for each level of activity. In this case it is a straight line because in the example the marginal social benefit was equal to price and therefore constant; however, there is no reason to suppose it will be so in all cases.

Now the efficient level of activity will be that corresponding to the intersection of the *msb* and *msc* curves. For at any level below this the extra benefit from increasing the scale of the activity will be greater than the costs from doing so; and at any level above it, the extra costs will be greater than the benefits. Note, however, that there is a range of activity beyond the socially efficient point (from 3 to 4 in the diagram) where the *msb* curve lies above the *mpc* curve; this is an important point to which we shall return in the next section.

We have thus found a suitable definition for the efficient level of a pollution-generating activity – the point at which the sum of the marginal private and marginal external costs of the activity begin to exceed its marginal social benefits. Although we will see later that implementing this definition in practice presents some severe difficulties, it is none the less an impor-

FIGURE 5.1
Costs and Benefits of Chemical Production

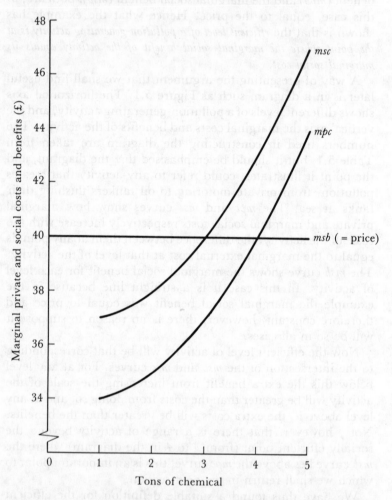

Tons of chemical

tant conceptual idea that is useful for clarifying discussion. But efficiency is not the only objective a society may have with respect to pollution control. Others, in particular the promotion of equity, may also be important.

Equity

Equity issues arise when the question of who should pay for pollution control is considered. At first sight this might seem simple; since it is the polluter who creates the problem, it should be the polluter who pays. But is this always the equitable solution? Suppose a factory making inexpensive clothes for the poor was polluting a particular river, and a group of rich boat owners wanted the river cleaned up so that they could sail their boats on it without offending their aesthetic sensibilities. Making the factory pay would raise the prices of the clothes it produces and make the poor who buy them even poorer; would this be fair? It might be more equitable to make the boat owners – who, after all, are going to be the ones who benefit – pay for the river to be cleaned. More generally, the question as to who should pay will depend on the situations of the parties involved. The equity of a particular system of pollution control cannot therefore be resolved by simple rules such as 'the polluter should always pay'; rather, the judgement will vary with the situation.

The Market System and Pollution

It is a demonstrable fact in our society that pollution and the market system coexist. But pollution in some form or other exists in almost all societies regardless of their economic organisation. No society has reduced pollution to zero, and it is unlikely that any ever will. So the question we must ask ourselves about the market system and pollution is whether pollution as a problem is inherent within the market system. An activity, almost by definition, becomes a problem when society's objectives with respect to it are not being attained. In this particular case we shall concentrate on efficiency and ask whether it is likely to be attained in the market. In the terms developed in the previous section, does the market system result in the marginal social benefit of a pollution-generating activity being equal to its marginal social cost?

The chief characteristic of a market system, as emphasised in Chapter 1, is that it consists of many individuals and firms, all making separate decisions on the basis of the costs and benefits to themselves of those decisions. Thus they are largely concerned with the private costs and benefits of undertaking certain activities and do not necessarily consider all the social costs and benefits. For instance, a mining company trying to decide whether to start operations in an area of outstanding natural beauty will consider only its own costs; it will not take account of the cost to those using the area for recreation. Similarly an airline, in considering whether to start a new night service, will only consider the costs and benefits accruing to it from this operation; it will not consider the cost to the people who live under the proposed flight path of the aircraft. Since social efficiency will only be achieved if social costs, private plus external, are taken into account, we can conclude the market system will not – on its own – achieve efficiency.

This can be illustrated by reference to our example. In making the decision about how much chemical to produce, the chemical firm will compare the marginal private cost from each ton with the extra revenue it can obtain by selling it. In this case the extra revenue – termed the *marginal revenue* – is equal to the price. So if the price is greater than the marginal private cost, then the firm will make a profit on that ton; if it is less, the firm will make a loss. Now for each of the first four tons, the price is greater than (or, in the case of the fourth, equal to) the marginal private cost; hence it will be profitable to the firm to produce up to that level. In terms of Figure 5.1, the firm will produce up to the point at which the *mpc* curve intersects the price line. However, as we saw in the last section, the efficient level of production is only three tons: the point at which the *msc* curve intersects the price line. Hence the actual level of production will be greater than the efficient level.

Now it could be argued that, in cases such as this where there are only two parties involved, this conclusion is incorrect. For it assumes that the party affected by the pollution will not react in any way to the fact its business is being damaged by the other party's activities. But it is equally plausible to suppose that the fishery will take steps to try to persuade the chemical firm to reduce its pollution. For instance, it might offer a bargain to the firm: reduce chemical output in return for some compensation for any loss in profits that would occur. Now the maximum compensation that the fishery would be prepared to offer would be £3 per ton of chemical output reduced; if it offered more than that, the gain it would make from the reduction in pollution would be more than offset by the amount it had to pay in compensation. Suppose it does in fact offer up to £3 per ton reduced. Then the chemical firm has to take account of the fact that for each ton of output it produces, it loses up to £3 worth of possible compensation from the fishery. In other words its 'costs' of producing each ton have risen by £3. Reference to Table 5.1 will quickly reveal that, when this extra cost is taken into account, production of the first three tons remains profitable but production of the fourth does not. Hence the firm will reduce its production to three tons – the efficient level. In terms of Figure 5.1, the effect of the compensation offer is to push up the *mpc* curve until it lies along the *msc* curve: so the new *mpc* curve intersects the *msb* curve at the efficient level.

Now this conclusion is at first sight rather remarkable. For it suggests that, if bargaining of this kind can take place between the parties involved, there will be no necessity for government intervention to control pollution, at least on efficiency grounds; the efficient level of a pollution-generating activity will be achieved by the market operating on its own. However, the key lies in the qualification. In practice most cases of pollution involve large numbers of firms or individuals. In that case the striking of private bargains involving each firm or individual affected seems impractical, to say the least. Put another way, the costs of private bargaining rise substantially as more people are involved; and as these costs increase it becomes less and less likely that such bargains will be struck. Hence it seems that cases where the market will achieve the efficient level of pollution control on its own are likely to be few and far between.

So in a world where external costs exist, the market system will not, in general, achieve efficiency. But our analysis cannot end here. For we have not yet determined why it is that there are divergencies between private and social costs; why it is that external costs of this kind exist. The answer to these questions lies in the structure of property ownership that is the foundation of a market-oriented society; and we must therefore digress a little to discuss the nature of this structure.

Property and Pollution

For an individual to 'own' a piece of property means simply tht he has certain rights over the use of that property. For instance if you own a car you have the right to drive it when you want, and the right to prevent other people driving it. If you own a house you have the right to live in it or to rent it out for someone else to live in. However, very rarely will you have the right to do anything you please with your property. In most societies, for instance, you will not have the right to knock people down with your car or to drive it at top speed through urban areas. Nor if you are a house owner are you likely to have the right to use your house for a brothel or bomb factory. Thus the owners of property have conferred on them, by virtue of their ownership, a carefully restricted set of rights as to the use of that property. Ownership of property means nothing more and nothing less than the ownership of certain rights.

Now one of the most important rights that property owners have in market economies is the right to sell their property. They can transfer all the rights they possess with reference to a particular piece of property to another person and obtain some compensation in return. Thus if you own a ton of steel, you have the right to sell this steel to a car firm and to receive a payment in return. In fact, given the structure of property rights, the only way the car firm can ensure that it has obtained the appropriate rights over the use of the steel is by buying it from you. It does not have the right, for example, simply to use the steel as if it were its own. The trading of property rights is the essential feature of a market economy.

However, there are some resources over which no private individual has any rights. Air is one and water (in most cases) is another. If motorists use the atmosphere as a dumping ground for the waste gases from their cars, they do not have to pay any compensation. If they did have to pay, then the cost would become an internal or private cost, and one they would have to take into account when making decisions about driving. Or consider the chemical firm and the fishery. Suppose there were fishing rights associated with the river and the fishery owned those rights. Then the chemical firm would have to pay the fishery for the use of the river, and the external cost would become a private one.

The difference between private and external costs or benefits thus derives from the existence or non-existence of certain property rights. Individuals or firms will incur private costs when they have to pay compensation in order to obtain rights over certain pieces of property; they will create external costs when they use pieces of property and are not required to compensate those adversely affected.

As a consequence of this kind of argument, a remedy for the pollution problem of a fundamental kind has been put forward by E. J. Mishan (1969). He suggests that property rights should be extended to cover environmental features. When someone purchases a piece of land, for example, the bundle of property rights obtained by virtue of the purchase should include a set of 'amenity' rights. These might include the rights that any air or water in the vicinity of the property should be of reasonable quality, that the owner should not be disturbed unduly by noise, and that the view should not be disfigured. If property owners did possess such rights, argues Mishan, then they could demand compensation when those rights were infringed. In that case, the hitherto external costs for the polluters would become internal ones (in that they would now be forced to pay for them) and they would have to make their production decisions accordingly. As a result, they would produce an efficient level of pollution.

This solution is ingenious and, since it goes right to the heart of the basic problem of pollution in a property-owning society, is also appealing. But it has its problems. First, litigation is a costly and time-consuming business. If all those affected by pollution were given amenity rights and were encouraged to sue in order to preserve these rights, the courts might be clogged for years, and in the meantime much of the pollution might continue apace. Further, to engage in civil action requires initial financial resources and a familiarity with the process of law which many people do not possess. Second, there is a question of equity. The assignment of compensation to the damaged party, although the equitable solution at first sight, might not always be so. Suppose, for instance, a hospital for poor families was located in a wealthy neighbourhood whose inhabitants were disturbed by the clanging of ambulance bells at night. Should these inhabitants automatically have the right to sue the hospital, thus raising the latter's costs? Allocating amenity rights to property owners means that whoever pollutes their property always pays – a solution that, as we saw earlier, is not necessarily the most equitable one.

Government Policies

The discussion so far should have convinced the reader that pollution as a problem has arisen directly from certain features of the market system, and the market, left on its own, will not solve the problem. Hence, in the absence of any radical reform of property rights, some government intervention is necessary. This can take any of four forms: *provision, regulation, taxation* or *subsidisation*.

State *provision* involves the state taking over pollution-generating activities and operating them at a level that is efficient and equitable. Although this is impractical in cases where private individuals generate pollution (such as motoring), it has more potential in situations where commercial enterprises are involved. All costs and benefits are internal to society as a whole, and if the government adequately represents everyone's interests, then state provision could result in decisions concerning pollution-generating activities that were socially efficient and equitable. However this would imply a massive extension of state ownership and control of the means of production, an implication that raises issues well beyond the narrower concern of pollution control.

In practice, *regulation* is the most common form of controlling pollution. Most countries have restrictions on the smoke emissions of private homes and manufacturing industry; they require vehicle exhausts to meet certain standards; and they (usually) regulate the waste that can be dumped into rivers or the sea. Now regulation of the right kind can produce an efficient level of pollution control. If the government has sufficient information concerning all pollution-generating activities, it can work out the efficient level of each activity (and hence the socially efficient level of pollution control) and pass laws compelling individuals and firms to operate at that level. But the amount of information required would be enormous. For instance, in Figure 5.1, the govement would need to know the exact positions of the *msb* and *msc* curves; to find these, it would need to know full details of chemical prices, of the chemical firm's private costs and of the external costs to the fishery. Multiply these requirements by the number of actual instances of pollution in modern society, and it will be apparent that the task of collecting the relevant information would be enormous. In practice, no government undertakes this task; instead, regulations are usually set in a fairly arbitrary, and hence inefficient, manner.

A method of achieving the same end that requires less information is through taxation or, as it is more commonly known in the pollution context, *charging*. A tax or charge could be levied on pollution-generating activities, designed to reduce those activities, and hence pollution, to a socially efficient level. Alternatively, a charge could be levied on the emission of pollution itself, again set in such a way as to achieve efficiency. The first is generally known as an *output* charge; the second as an *effluent* charge.

We shall illustrate how these kinds of taxes or charges could be used by considering the effect of imposing an output charge on the chemical firm in our example. Suppose a charge was levied on each ton of output equal to the value of the damage that was caused to the fishery in the production of that ton (£3 in the example). Then the costs to the firm of producing chemicals would rise; moreover, they would rise by exactly the amount of the external cost imposed by that production. The external costs would thus become internalised; that is, they would become part of the private costs that the firm considers when making its production decisions. In terms of Figure 5.1, the effect of the charge would be to shift up the *mpc* curve until it occupied the same position as the *msc* curve. The firm would now find that, at the old level of production, its marginal private costs including the charge were greater than the price. Hence it would reduce production to the point where they were equal to one another again. Since marginal private costs including the charge are equal to marginal social costs, this will also be the point where marginal social cost equals the price: the efficient level.

Now the significant feature of this result is that all the government has to know to impose the charge is the value of the damage done to the fishery. To achieve the same end by regulation, the government needs to know not only the value of the damage but also full details of the chemical firms' costs and revenues, a much more demanding requirement. Hence, in this case, to achieve a socially efficient level of pollution-generating activity by charging requires far less information than by regulation.

A similar outcome could have been achieved by levying a charge on the effluent, the pollution itself, instead of output. However the two are not equivalent in all case. If there are methods of pollution control other than reducing output (say, treating the effluent before it is discharged), then the effluent charge would be superior for it could not distort the choice of control method, unlike the output charge (which naturally favours output reduction).

Perhaps surprisingly, it is possible to devise a system of *subsidy* that has the same advantage over regulation as a system of charging. Suppose a subsidy is paid to the chemical firm to reduce its output below the level at which it would operate if there was no government intervention. Suppose further that the subsidy took the form of an amount for each unit of output reduced that was equal to the value of the damage caused by that unit to the fishery. In that case, for every extra ton of chemical produced by the firm, it would forgo a subsidy equal to £3. This foregoing of subsidy becomes part of the firm's costs of production, for the production of each ton of chemicals not only incurs the usual costs of raw materials, labour, etc., but also loses it £3. Hence the effect of the subsidy is to raise the firm's *mpc* curve in exactly the same way as the output charge did! (In effect the subsidy is operating in a similar fashion to the compensation offered by the fishery in our earlier discussion of bargaining.) The outcome will therefore be the same. The firm will produce at the point where the price it obtains for its product equals its marginal private cost of production, including the forgoing of subsidy, a point which, since the new *mpc* equals the *msc*, will be the socially efficient level. And again the only information required by the government will be the value of the damage to the fishery.

This is not to say that there are no differences between subsidies and charges. Profits are higher with subsidies than with charges. Hence, under a subsidy scheme, firms will be encouraged to enter the pollution-generating industry, while under a charging scheme they will be encouraged to leave it. Also there is a difference concerning equity. Under a subsidy system, the taxpayer pays to control pollution, while the polluters themselves do not; under a charging system, the polluters pay and taxpayers benefit. Which is the more equitable system will depend, as we saw in the first section of this chapter, on one's judgement concerning the relative positions of the polluters and those who either receive the revenue from the charge or pay the subsidy. If the former were rich and the latter poor, then charges might be considered more equitable; if *vice versa*, then subsidies might be preferred.

Either way, charging or subsidisation seem superior to regulation in achieving social efficiency, in that they require considerably less information for their implementation. However it might be objected that the amount of information required is still far too large to make their use practical. In most real world cases the value of the damage caused by a particular polluter is impossible to estimate. This is so for a variety of reasons. Certain types of pollution – that from motor vehicles, for example – come from an enormous number of separate sources; in such cases it is impossible to attribute one particular piece of damage to one particular polluter. Even where this can be done it is often very difficult, if not impossible, to place a monetary value on the damage caused. What is the cost to a child of a reduction in intelligence due to lead pollution? What is the value of a beautiful valley destroyed by strip mining? Or of a river poisoned by pesticides run off from adjacent farmland? Attempts have been made to place money values on these kinds of damage (usually based on how much people are prepared to pay to avoid them), but the methods involved are controversial and expensive. All in all, it seems as though even the more limited information requirements of the taxation or subsidy schemes designed to achieve social efficiency are not realistically attainable.

What can be done? One answer is to adopt a more modest objective. Instead of trying to specify the socially efficient levels of pollution-generating activities (and therefore of pollution), it is more practical simply to set, on a fairly arbitrary basis, pollution 'standards'. These can be either in terms of air and water quality (a common standard for water, for instance, is the level of cleanliness that supports fish life), or they can be in terms of the pollution emissions themselves (such as, for instance, the limits on the amounts of carbon monoxide that car exhausts may emit). Given these standards, the problem facing the economist becomes somewhat different; instead of determining the best method of achieving levels of pollution-generating activity that are efficient and equitable, it is now one of determining the most efficient and equitable methods of achieving these standards.

Again we shall concentrate primarily on efficiency. Efficiency in this context means 'least cost'; that is, the pollution standard should be achieved by methods that cost as little as possible in terms of resources. As before, the methods open to the government are provision, regulation, taxation or charges, and subsidy. To simplify matters, we shall confine the discussion to a comparison of regulation and charging.

As in the more general case, it is possible to imagine a system of regulation that would achieve a given pollution standard at minimum cost. If the government possessed information concerning the costs of pollution control for all the polluters concerned, it could identify those for whom such control was cheapest and legislate for them to be compelled to undertake the required amount of control. However, the information requirements to do this properly are again impossibly large. Hence, in practice, most governments using pollution regulation (and most governments do so most of the time) simply pass laws that are uniform in application, for example, that all polluters should cut back by a certain percentage, or that no polluter should emit more than a specific amount of untreated waste.

Now it is easy to see that uniform regulation of this kind will be inefficient relative to a properly organised charging system. If, say, an effluent charge is levied on untreated waste then those polluters for whom the charge is greater than the cost of treating their effluent will cut back; those who face expensive treatment costs will prefer to continue polluting and pay the charge. Setting the charge at a carefully chosen level will ensure that the 'right' amount of pollution control is undertaken, and this control will be undertaken by those who find it cheapest to do so. Hence, in contrast to the situation under uniform regulation, the pollution standard will be achieved at minimum cost.

An additional advantage of this kind of scheme is that it offers a continuing incentive for polluters to cut their pollution. Under regulation, once polluters have met the regulation, they have no incentive to reduce their discharge any further. Under a taxation scheme, however, each unit of untreated waste that they discharge carries a price tag – an inducement to engage in research to cut the costs of treatment.

Such schemes are not fantasy. Effluent charges have been used as a means of pollution control in Hungary, Czechoslovakia and France. In the Ruhr area of West Germany charges have been used as part of a water-management scheme to such good effect that one river carries a greater volume of effluent than its own natural flow and yet is clean enough to swim in. A study of the feasibility of introducing charges on emissions into the Delaware river in the United States found that it would create remarkable savings, achieving the same level of pollution control as direct regulation yet costing only half as much (Kneese, 1977, pp. 162–8).

There are, however, serious problems with charging schemes to which their advocates have perhaps not always given sufficient weight. First, in order to compute polluters' tax bills, it would be necessary to engage in continuous monitoring of their effluent, whereas with regulation occasional spot checks would probably be sufficient. Second, how does the authority responsible for levying the charge find the appropriate level at which to set it? If it has all the details of the relative costs of the polluters there is no problem; the authority can estimate the effect of the charge on the different polluters and calculate how much reduction in pollution would follow the levying of any particular charge. In the absence of this information, however, the authority is left with a trial-and-error procedure. This might work by initially setting a very low charge, observing the degree of reduction that was undertaken (if any), and then raising the charge in stages until the degree of reduction reached that which was desired. Such a procedure might eventualy work, but it would be slow, cumbersome and, for the polluters, costly and unsettling.

In an ingenious effort to overcome the second problem, Canadian economist J. H. Dales (1968) has suggested a variant of the charging scheme, which he terms 'pollution rights'. Under his proposal a board would sell to polluters a number of 'rights to pollute', the number of which would be limited by the level of air or water quality desired in the area. Potential polluters would have to bid for these rights, for the number of rights they owned would determine how much pollution they could undertake. Clearly, those who found pollution control expensive would be prepared to bid more to obtain these rights than those who found it cheap; hence the former would obtain the rights and the latter would not. The result would be that polluters with high treatment costs would continue to pollute, but would have had to pay the authority for the right to do so; while polluters with low costs would have to treat their discharge. The end effect, therefore, is exactly the same as in the case of charging, but with one important difference: the 'charge' has been set by the firms themselves by bidding against one another. Thus the authority need have no information concerning the firms' costs, nor does it need to engage in clumsy trial-and-error procedures. All it has to do is to issue the rights and arrange for their sale. This scheme has yet to be adopted anywhere in its entirety, but a limited version is currently being tried out by the US Environmental Protection Agency to control industrial air pollution.

Summary

Any assessment of the *efficient* level of pollution control must take account of the fact that it involves *costs* as well as benefits. Given the existence of such costs, we can define the socially efficient level of pollution-generating activity as the point at which the *marginal social benefit of the activity equals its marginal social cost*. In general the market system will not achieve this level because in such a system decisions are made on the basis of private costs and benefits which, in the absence of the relevant property rights, diverge from social costs and benefits.

Government intervention can take the form of *provision, regulation*, taxation or *charges*, and *subsidy*. Of these, provision raises issues well beyond the question of pollution control and is therefore rarely considered in that context. Regulation, charging and subsidy can all achieve efficient levels of pollution-generating activity, but regulation requires far more *information* than the other two. However the implementation even of an efficient charging or subsidy scheme requires more information than is generally available.

Given the information difficulties, governments generally do not try to achieve perfect social efficiency in practice but simply set pollution *standards* on a fairly arbitrary basis. These can be attained in a variety of ways; the two most commonly debated are *regulation* and *charges*. In principle *regulations* that are specific to individual polluters can achieve pollution standards at *minimum cost*, but in practice the lack of relevant information means that uniform regulations are applied. *Charging* schemes can generally achieve a given degree of pollution control at less cost than uniform regulation, but they face considerable practical problems of implementation. A method of overcoming these problems is to auction pollution 'rights' to potential polluters, the number of rights for sale being determined by the relevant pollution standard.

Further Reading

A comprehensive introduction to the economics of pollution is Baumol and Oates (1979). Burrows (1979) is a useful text that should be (just) within the grasp of someone who has mastered the material in this chapter. A stimulating but more advanced book is Dasgupta (1982). An important collection of readings, most of which are accessible to non-economists is Dorfman and Dorfman (1977).

On specific topics, the discussion of the relationship between pollution and property rights in Dales (1968) is excellent. Mishan (1969) contains chapters on the divergence between private and social costs and benefits and on various solutions (including 'amenity' rights). Pearce (1976) contains much useful material on the measurement of damage and control costs. The Minority Report of the Third Report of the Royal Commission on Environmental Pollution (1972), Anderson *et al.* (1977) and Marin (1979) discuss in detail the use of charging schemes as a means of pollution control in a non-technical manner.

Questions for Discussion

1. Many ecologists argue that the optimum level of pollution is zero. Do you agree?
2. Does the fact that many of the benefits from pollution control are intangible mean that it is impossible to place a money value on them?
3. 'If property rights were properly defined, there could be no pollution problem.' Discuss.
4. 'Externalities can always be internalised by bargaining between the affected parties.' Do you agree?
5. Should polluters always pay?
6. Smoking imposes costs on non-smokers. Does this imply that
   - non-smokers should pay smokers not to smoke?
   - smokers should carry on smoking but compensate non-smokers?
   - the government should ban smoking?
   - none of these?
7. Are output charges and effluent charges equally efficient?
8. 'The only difference between charges and subsidies as means of controlling pollution is in the long run.' Explain.
9. Why do you think governments generally favour direct regulation to control pollution, rather than charges or subsidies?
10. What are the practical problems involved in the use of charging systems to attain pollution standards? How might a system of 'pollution rights' overcome those problems?

Crime 6

Over three million serious criminal offences were recorded by the police in the United Kingdom in 1980. Of these, about 95 per cent involved fraud, theft or damage to property, and only about five per cent violence or sexual offences; violent offences however, have doubled in the last ten years. Crime control takes up considerable public resources; in 1980–1, for example, public expenditure on law and order in Great Britain cost over £3000 million – and press and politicians vie with each other to demand more. Yet until recently there was little analysis of the effectiveness of such expenditure or even of its aims, a gap that some economists and statisticians are now trying partly to fill.

As with other topics investigated in this book, there are three principal areas of interest to economists: the formulation of society's aims or objectives with respect to crime control; the use of the market system as a means of attaining those objectives; and the effectiveness of government and government policy. We shall look at these in turn. But before we do so, a word of warning. Crime – its definition, its causes and its effects – is a complex issue, involving psychological, sociological and political factors as well as economic ones. Inevitably, therefore, the contribution that economics can make to the area is a limited one, and this needs to be borne in mind in what follows.

Objectives

Three objectives are usually cited in the context of crime control: efficiency, equity and the preservation of civil liberties. That is, an ideal system of control would be one that reduces crime as far as possible, that spreads the benefits from that reduction as fairly as possible, but preserves those liberties that society deems essential. Let us examine these in more detail.

Efficiency

It might be thought that the most efficient level of crime control is that which brings about zero crime. Crime is socially undesirable; crime control reduces crime; therefore, the 'best' level of control must be that which reduces it to nothing.

But, as we saw in the case of pollution control, this reasoning ignores the fact that crime control not only has benefits, in terms of reducing crime, but also costs. There are costs of apprehending, convicting, and punishing criminals, and there are costs of engaging in preventive activities, such as police patrols. These costs are resource costs. Resources are consumed that could have been used to produce other goods or services: labour in the form of police officers, prison officials, judges and lawyers; buildings for courts and prisons; and capital equipment, such as cars and computers. The existence of these costs makes it extremely unlikely that the most efficient level of crime control will be that which produces no crime. Rather, it will be at a level that takes account of costs as well as benefits; more specifically, at a level where the costs of engaging in further control begin to outweigh the benefits.

This can be illustrated by a simple example. Suppose we were trying to decide on the efficient provision of daily police patrols in a particular area of a city. Suppose further that we could identify the benefits of these patrols in terms of, say, the number of crimes prevented during a year, and that we could attach a money value to these benefits. This is by no means as impractical as it might appear; ways of valuing the benefits of crime reduction will be discussed in a moment. In particular, suppose we know the money value of the extra reduction in crime per year resulting from one more patrol; that is, the marginal social benefit (*msb*) of police patrols. Assume, too, that we have similar information concerning the cost of an extra patrol, or the marginal social cost (*msc*). Then we could draw a diagram of the kind that by now should be familiar from earlier chapters. In Figure 6.1 we measure *msb* and *msc* on the vertical axis and the number of daily patrols on the horizontal axis. The *msb* curve slopes downwards, reflecting the reasonable assumption that the benefits from mounting an extra patrol decline the more patrols there are already; the *msc* curve slopes upwards, on the assumption that the costs of an extra patrol increase as more patrols are provided (because of the need for more overtime payments, for instance).

FIGURE 6.1
Costs and Benefits of Police Patrols

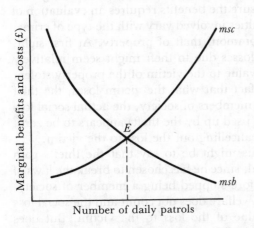

Figure 6.1 permits us to determine the efficient number of patrols. To the left of the point of intersection of the two curves, *E*, the *msb* is greater than the *msc*; to the right of the intersection, the *msc* is greater than the *msb*. That is, each patrol up to the intersection creates greater benefits than it costs, while each patrol after the intersection costs more than the benefits. Hence

the point of intersection determines the efficient level.

If we can measure the costs and benefits of different methods of crime control, we can use this analysis to determine the efficient level for each method – or, less ambitiously, to determine whether one method is more efficient than another. But can the relevant costs and benefits be measured? Let us look at some of the issues involved, beginning with *costs*. For some forms of crime control these are relatively easy to specify. The costs of police patrols, for instance, are simply the pay of the policemen involved, the price of buying and maintaining the vehicles they use, and so on. Others present more difficulty. For instance, the costs of a prison system should obviously include the direct costs of building and running prisons. But they should also include the contribution to (legitimate) production that prisoners might have made had they not been in prison (which may be greater in some cases than in others!).

Measurement of *benefits* also presents problems. These can be thought of as the reduction in the social losses resulting from crime. Hence to measure the benefits requires an evaluation of the losses. The difficulties involved vary with the type of crime. Consider the most common, theft of property. At first sight, measurement of the losses due to theft might seem relatively simple; just take the value to the victim of the property stolen. But this ignores the fact that what the victim loses, the thief gains. Since both are members of society, the actual social loss (that is, the resources used up by the theft) appears to be zero, the gain to the thief cancelling out the loss to the victim.

One reaction to this might be to say that the thief's gain should not be included, since he has chosen to break the laws of society and has therefore stopped being a member of society. Hence the gain in his welfare does not count and the social loss simply equals the value of the loss to the victim. But does everyone who breaks the law cease to be part of society? What about, for example, traffic offenders? Is someone who breaks the speed limit automatically deprived of citizenship? If not, then why does the breaking of some laws (such as those relating to property) lead to exclusion from society, whereas the breaking of others (which may be just as serious – speeding can kill) does not? Until questions such as these can be answered it is not easy to dismiss the zero-loss argument on the grounds that thieves should be excluded from society.

However, the same argument can be attacked from another direction. It ignores several costs that are important elements of the overall social loss due to theft. First, it does not take into account the psychological costs to the victim of being robbed – an experience that, as those who have suffered it will know, is far from pleasant. Second, and perhaps even more important, it does not consider the disincentive effects of dishonest activities on honest ones. For instance, peoples' incentive to work is likely to be seriously impaired if everything purchased out of the income from work can be simply abstracted by everyone else. Widespread theft would undoubtedly lead to a substantial fall in economic production; to the extent that any particular crime or crimes contribute to that fall, it should be counted as part of the overall social loss due to crime.

Third, the zero-loss argument does not include the cost of the thief's time and effort. The labour that goes into planning and carrying out a robbery could have been used in the production of other commodities, production that is lost due to the crime. If we are prepared to assume that the value of this lost production equals the amount that the thief could have earned through legitimate activity, then this production loss can be measured by his earnings loss. Moreover, if we assume that the thief is rational and will not take to burglary unless the returns are at least equal to what he could earn in legitimate activity, then the value of what is stolen must be at least as great as his earnings losses. Hence the value of the property stolen provides a lower-limit estimate of the cost of the thief's time. According to this argument, therefore, the value of the loss due to theft *can* be measured by the value of the stolen property, but only because it is a proxy for the cost of the thief's labour.

What of crimes other than theft? The losses due to crime involving the destruction of property (such as an act of vandalism or a car accident due to speeding) are relatively easy to measure; they are the value of the property destroyed. Crimes against the person (murder, rape, or again some car accidents) are less simple. One component of the cost – the loss of earnings or income due to the crime – may be relatively simple to assess, but the more important psychological cost of the induced pain and suffering is not. Here the methods developed for valuing the costs of ill-health discussed in Chapter 2 may be useful.

'Victimless' crimes – such as drug-taking or some sexual activities involving only consenting individuals – also present problems. Since those who commit such crimes are also those who 'suffer' from them, it could be argued that there is no loss involved, at least so far as they are concerned. The only damage resulting from these crimes would then be to the feelings of those who are not involved in the particular act being committed but who none the less object to it; again a psychological cost whose magnitude is difficult to estimate.

There has been no attempt to calculate the social losses due to crime in the United Kingdom, but there have been several in the United States. One was by the President's Commission on Law Enforcement (1967), in which it was estimated that in 1965 the total loss due to crimes against property (estimated as the value of property stolen) and crimes against the person (valued as loss of earnings), was nearly $6000 million – roughly $12 000 million in today's prices. Furthermore, since this estimate ignores all the psychological and disincentive costs to which we have alluded, the true loss is likely to be far greater.

Now that we have seen how some of the benefits and costs might be measured, let us return to the question of determining the efficient level of crime control. Can measures like these be used to determine whether a particular society has an efficient level? An attempt has been made to do so for the United States by Ehrlich (1973). He estimated that in 1965 an increase of 1 per cent in expenditure on police and courts would reduce the social losses due to crime by 3 per cent. The total expenditure on police and courts in 1965 was $3000 million and, as we saw above, the total social losses due to crime were $6000 million. Therefore the marginal social cost of increasing expenditure on courts and police was $30 million (1 per cent of $3000 million); and the marginal social benefit was $180 million (3 per cent of $6000 million). The marginal social benefit was thus six times as great as the marginal social cost; and it would therefore appear that the levels of police and court expenditures in the US were well below the most efficient level.

But studies concerned with more specific aspects of the criminal control system have come up with rather different conclusions. One by Carr-Hill and Stern (1973) of the use of police officers in England and Wales found no evidence that criminal offences were reduced by increasing expenditures on policemen. Indeed, the principal effect of increasing police expenditure was, in a sense, quite the reverse, for it generally led to an *increase* in the number of offences reported to the police (perhaps because the latter were more visible). This is an interesting example of how a systematic analysis based on an economic approach can lead to conclusions quite different from those based on popular beliefs and prejudices.

Equity

Efficiency is not the only objective that society might have in deciding on the allocation of resources toward crime control. An equitable allocation might also be a relevant consideration; that is, a distribution of resources between individuals or between areas that results in a fair distribution of benefits. If, for example, one district of a city has much more crime than another, it might be thought equitable to allocate more resources to it, so as to equalise crime rates throughout the city. Alternatively, it might be considered equitable to allocate resources so as to equalise the amount of crime reduced; this might involve allocating resources equally between districts.

It should be noted that it may not be possible to attain equity and efficiency at the same time. For example, it may be socially efficient to allocate resources to areas in which the marginal social benefit is greatest, which could mean allocating resources to the wealthier districts where the value of the property loss due to crime is much greater than in the poorer districts. But it is unlikely that such an allocation could be considered equitable, no matter how the latter is defined.

Liberty

Crime control should not be so extensive that it destroys civil liberties. Few would want to live in a police state, even if it produced very little crime. But, as with equity, preserving civil liberties may conflict with the attainment of efficiency. This possibility has been emphasised by Herbert Packer (1968). He described two stylised models of the procedure for bringing criminals to justice: the Crime Control Model and the Due Process Model. The Crime Control Model requires that there be a *high* probability of the *guilty* being convicted; this on the assumption that a high rate of conviction is an effective method of controlling crime and hence, in our terminology, of promoting efficiency. The Due Process Model requires that there be a *low* probability of the *innocent* being convicted, on the assumption that this will effectively preserve civil liberties. A system of justice based on the Crime Control Model is not too scrupulous about protecting the rights of defendants; it accepts the probability that as a result the innocent will at times be convicted, but will not be unduly disturbed by this (unless it happened so often that it began to interfere with the system's ability to control crime). A system based on the Due Process Model, on the other hand, requires extensive protection for defendants in an effort to minimise the possibility of people being punished for crimes they did not commit; it accepts that, as a result, many of the guilty will also escape.

Much of the law and order debate is over which of these two models should dominate the crime control system. For instance, in the wake of the riots in Brixton and elsewhere in 1981, many people suggested that police powers should be dramatically extended. Others argued that these powers were already too great; that their indiscriminate use – particularly of the notorious 'sus' laws – had in fact contributed to the riots. In essence this argument concerned whether the Crime Control Model should dominate the Due Process Model or, in other words, whether efficiency or civil liberty should take priority.

Another aspect of civil liberties concerns the relationship between the severity of the crime and the magnitude of the punishment. Most people believe that the two should match in some way. But meeting this objective may again conflict with attaining efficiency. For example, an efficient method of controlling parking offences might be to execute all offenders. In such circumstances very few people would continue to park illegally, and it could be argued that the loss to society of those who did and who then paid the penalty would be outweighed by the great savings in police resources and improvement in city traffic flow that would result. Yet (one hopes) there would be considerable resistance to introducing such a system. This is not only because most of us might want sometimes to park illegally, but also because most people would feel that somehow the punishment did not fit the crime – that the relatively trivial offence of illegal parking did not warrant such a drastic penalty.

As we have seen in other chapters, the existence of multiple objectives creates problems for policy makers, since all cannot be achieved simultaneously. They have to find some trade-off between them – more efficiency and less equity or civil liberty, or vice versa. Unfortunately social scientists and political philosophers have not found a way of specifying how such trade-offs should be made and, in practice, they are usually determined by political and social pressures. There is an interesting example of this in eighteenth century England. There, at the instigation of the big landowners, acts of Parliament were introduced making it a capital offence to poach fish or game. But juries, repelled at the magnitude of the punishment, began to refuse to convict, even in cases where the defendants were obviously guilty. As a result the laws had to be repealed. The loss in efficiency was 'traded-off' against the gain in civil liberty.

The Market System and Crime Control

There are many ways of controlling crime. Some are generally undertaken by the state – the provision of police forces, courts and prisons being the most obvious examples. But there is also much private activity directed towards crime control. Firms employ security guards and nightwatchmen. Individuals buy locks, bolts and burglar alarms to protect themselves and their property; in some countries they buy guns and other weapons. The cost of these activities is not trivial; one estimate for the United States (L. Friedman, 1976) put them at a level that was equivalent to about a third of total public expenditure on police services.

This raises a number of questions. Why are some forms of

crime control provided publicly and others privately? Would it be more efficient if the balance between public and private provision were altered? Many have answered yes – in particular, that there should be a greater reliance on private provision. From Sherlock Holmes to Philip Marlowe the private detective has been an established figure in crime fiction, usually far more efficient than his bumbling official counterpart. Firms, finding public law-enforcement agencies inadequate, often employ private security guards. There have even been proposals for private courts and private systems of law.

Again the issues involved can be illuminated by the use of the example of police patrols. Could we have a system of private police patrols? Why does it seem to be assumed automatically that this has to be provided by the state? If we can understand the reasons for public provision of this particular method of crime control, we shall be in a better position to appreciate why other methods are privately or publicly provided, and perhaps to decide on possible ways to improve the situation.

Imagine a private security agency that provides police patrols to any individual who is prepared to pay for it. If you wish your house to be protected by those patrols you pay an annual amount to the agency, which in return provides a certain number of patrols per day past your premises, the exact number depending on how much you are prepared to pay. (As we have already mentioned, arrangements of this kind are not uncommon in the commercial world; firms pay for nightwatchmen, banks for security guards.)

Now in these circumstances how many daily patrols would you buy? Presumably the answer will depend on how much benefit you derive from the patrols and how much they cost. More specifically you will buy patrols up to the point at which the extra cost to you from having one more patrol – the marginal private cost, or *mpc* – outweighs the extra benefit you would derive from that patrol – the marginal private benefit, or *mpb*. For example, suppose you had already arranged for two patrols a day and you were contemplating ordering a third. This would cost you, let us say, an extra £50 per year, and you value the extra protection it could offer at £100 per year. Then, if you were rational, you would arrange for that third patrol.

Now you consider a fourth daily patrol. Since the agency may have to pay more overtime or hire an extra constable, the annual cost could be greater than for the previous one, say, £70. Moreover, you estimate the benefit to you of this extra patrol to be less than the previous one because the risk of theft from your property is becoming progressively smaller, say £60. Then presumably you would not pay the extra subscription; you would settle for three daily patrols.

We can represent this in a diagram. In Figure 6.2 the *mpb* line shows that the marginal private benefit varies with the number of patrols already purchased; the *mpc* line shows how the marginal private cost varies (ignore for the moment the *msb* line). The number of patrols you purchase is determined by the intersection of the two curves, *F*. Each patrol purchased up to that amount benefits you more than it costs; every patrol purchased beyond that point costs more than it benefits. All this is exactly the same procedure that a rational person would use in purchasing any commodity that is offered for sale in the normal way. As we saw in Chapter 1, for many commodities this would result in the socially efficient level being purchased.

FIGURE 6.2
Private and Social Costs and Benefits of Police Patrols

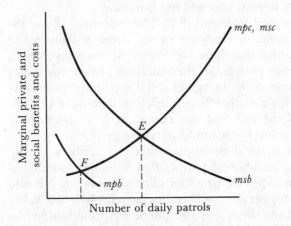

So why is it that police patrol services are not generally provided in this way? Is there something special about this 'commodity' that prevents private provision from leading to social efficiency?

It is generally thought that there is one very important feature of a police patrol that does make it different from other commodities. A policeman passing down a street does not just benefit one house; he also benefits every other house on the street. Potential criminals, knowing that a street is patrolled, will not know which house the patrols are supposed to be protecting; hence, to the extent they are deterred from robbing your house, they will be deterred from robbing all the other houses on the street. So your purchase of patrols has not only benefited you, it has also benefited your neighbours. Thus the patrols have not only generated private or internal benefits, they have also created *external* ones.

Now the existence of these external benefits implies that private provision will not lead to social efficiency being attained. Remember that in our example a fourth daily patrol would cost £70 and only generate private benefits of £60. But suppose there are three other houses in the street, the owners of which each benefit from the patrol by the same amount as you. In that case the total social benefits will be £240 – £170 greater than the cost – and it would be socially efficient if the patrol were purchased. However, since you only take into account the private benefits to you, you will not purchase it.

This is illustrated in Figure 6.2. The *msb* curve shows the sum of the benefits to everyone in the street of daily police patrols. We assume that there are no external costs involved in purchasing police patrols, so the marginal private cost (*mpc*) curve is the same as the marginal social cost (*msc*) curve. It is apparent that the socially efficient level, as determined by the intersection of the *msb* and *msc* curves at *E* is significantly greater than the level you would purchase privately.

Against this it could be argued that this analysis grossly understates the number of patrols that would be purchased under a system of private provision. For not only you but also everyone else on your street will be buying patrols; hence many more than just the three that you purchased would in fact be bought. But this ignores another problem – that of the *free rider*.

If your neighbours know that they are benefiting from your provision of police protection, they are not likely to buy their own. Instead, they will trust that you will provide enough to protect them; they will *free ride*. Hence, no extra patrols will be purchased.

In fact, there is a danger that the situation will be even worse than this. For, just as your purchase of police protection benefits your neighbours, if they were to buy some patrols you would benefit. Realising this in advance, you may wait and see whether anyone else purchases patrols, for you too would like to free ride. Therefore it may be that nobody in the street purchases protection – each waiting for the others – and as a result there could be no patrols at all (this is the same problem of the prisoner's dilemma that we encountered in the discussion of housing maintenance in Chapter 4).

Thus the services of police patrols do possess one important feature that makes them unsuitable for provision by the private market – the creation of substantial external benefits. Commodities such as these are often termed by economists *public goods*. The two characteristics that distinguish public goods are *nonrivalness* and *nonexcludability*. *Nonrivalness* means that one individual can consume a unit of a commodity without reducing the amount available for other consumers. As we have seen, police services have this characteristic; if you benefit from a police patrol, that does not prevent anyone else in the street from benefiting similarly. Contrast this with, say, the consumption of butter, as discussed in Chapter 1. If you consume a packet of butter, then no one else can consume it; your consumption is 'rival' with others' consumption. *Nonexcludability* means that it is impossible for an individual who is consuming a commodity to prevent anyone else from consuming it, that is, from free riding. Thus, with the police patrol it would be impossible for you to prevent your neighbours from benefiting; potential criminals will be deterred simply by the presence of the patrols, regardless of who actually pays for them. Contrast this again with butter. If you buy a packet of butter you can prevent others benefiting from it by simply hiding it away. Goods that have both these characteristics will not be efficiently supplied by a private market; hence the terminology 'public' goods.

We are now in a better position to understand why some crime control services are provided privately and some publicly. Locks and burglar alarms are both rival and excludable. If one individual fits a new lock to the front door, others cannot fit the same lock to theirs. One house being locked does not benefit others in any way (indeed perhaps the reverse: the burglar turned away from the locked house may try the others). On the other hand, law courts, prisons and the like confer benefits that are nonrival and nonexcludable. Suppose a criminal is convicted, imprisoned and, as a result, deterred from future crimes. Moreover, suppose other potential criminals, observing his fate, are also similarly deterred. Then every potential victim benefits; the benefits are nonrival and nonexcludable.

Finally a word concerning the other objectives mentioned: equity and liberty. As with most other commodities, market allocation of crime control would probably result in those with higher incomes having more protection. Whether this is equitable or not would depend on the definition of equity chosen; it would not be equitable under either of the two possible definitions mentioned previously. Nor would market allocation necessarily promote civil liberties. A private protection agency that arrested large numbers of people, and was not too scrupulous about determining their guilt or innocence before doing so, might be extremely effective in deterring crime against its clients; but it seems unlikely that this would produce an acceptable level of civil liberty.

Government Policies

The discussion in the previous section established the need for government intervention in the field of crime control. The next question is, what form should this take? As we have seen in earlier chapters, there are various ways in which governments can affect the production of a commodity, including the regulation of the market, tax/subsidy policies, or direct government provision. Which of these is most appropriate for the commodities whose function is to reduce crime?

Most economists would agree that the only feasible method

of allocating those methods of crime control that are public goods – such as police, courts and prisons – is by government provision. It is difficult to imagine any form of regulation, taxation or subsidy imposed on an otherwise private market that would enable those commodities to be allocated efficiently in that market. For this reason economists have generally not questioned the desirability of government provision, but rather have concentrated upon methods of improving it. In doing so they have relied upon a particular theory of criminal behaviour that we must outline before proceeding any further.

The theory postulates that most criminal behaviour is the result of rational decisions. More specifically an individual, when deciding whether to commit a crime, will weigh up the costs and benefits of doing so. If the potential costs are greater than the potential benefits of that crime, then he will not commit it; if the benefits are greater than the costs, then he will. Whether or not the crime is committed will therefore depend upon the relative magnitude of the crime's benefits and costs to the individual concerned.

The benefits of committing a crime are relatively simple to specify: the financial (and possibly psychological) gains from doing so. The costs are a little more complex. They will depend on a number of factors. One of these we have already discussed when we considered the social cost of crime: the opportunity cost of criminals' time, or the amount they could be earning in legitimate activities. The higher their legal earnings, the greater the amount they forgo in performing an illegal act and the greater the cost to themselves of doing so. Other factors affecting the cost are the probability of being caught and the severity of the punishment if caught. A crime with a high probability of getting caught and/or a long jail sentence will have higher potential costs than one with a low probability of apprehension and/or a small fine attached to it.

Although this method of analysis may seem simple – indeed almost tautological – it is quite powerful. For example, while it supports the 'common-sense' prediction that increasing penalties will reduce crime, it also yields the less obvious conclusion that increasing wage levels in an area might also be an effective form of crime control. For any increase in wages will increase the opportunity cost to an individual of spending time on criminal activities, and hence reduce his incentive to do so. Another possible method of government intervention is thus opened up; the government could reduce crime by expanding the economy or by reducing the incidence of poverty.

Despite its simplicity, this kind of analysis is by no means universally accepted. For it implies that, under the 'right' circumstances, anyone would commit a crime. That is, even the most law-abiding citizens might become criminals if they thought that the potential gains were large enough and that either the probability of getting caught or the punishment once caught was small enough. But some find this difficult to believe. Instead they argue most crime is undertaken by natural criminals – people who do not weigh up benefits and costs in the manner described, but whose psychology is such that they are inevitably drawn to criminal activity.

However, although there are doubtless a few individuals with this psychology, so-called 'psychopaths', it is difficult to accept the criminal psychology view as a total explanation of criminal behaviour. One difficulty with it is that, if it is correct, then nearly everyone has a criminal psychology. Most people have at some point in their lives broken a speed limit, fiddled their expenses, engaged in tax evasion or claimed more social security than they were entitled to. Over 90 per cent of adults questioned in a sample of 1700 in the USA had committed one or more acts for which they could have received a jail sentence, *excluding* traffic offences (L. Friedman, 1976, p. 7).

Another difficulty is that it does not seem to accord with the actual behaviour of most criminals. Several statistical studies show that increasing the severity of the penalties for certain crimes does have the effect of reducing them. Also, there is evidence to suggest that another prediction of the rational model mentioned above – that reducing the incidence of poverty would reduce crime – is also correct (Anderson, 1976, pp. 36–7). None of this is consistent with the view that criminals behave irrationally. For it implies that criminals do consider the costs of their activities (including 'opportunity' costs), something they would not do if their nature drove them to crime regardless of the consequences.

A further example of the usefulness of the economic

approach to crime for government policy concerns the penalties for criminal activity. As we mentioned earlier, a major part of the costs of crime control are costs of putting people in prison. These include not only the burden on the public purse at a time of financial stringency, but also the loss in production that results from taking people out of the legitimate labour force. (A broader interpretation of costs would also include the degradation and dehumanisation of prisoners that occurs in old, overcrowded prisons such as most British ones.)

Economists have concluded from this that it would be much less costly to punish people by fines rather than prison. For, unlike people in prison, people can carry on working while they pay off a fine; indeed they may work even harder in order to pay it off more quickly. A system of fines not only saves society the costs of actually maintaining prisoners in prison (food, shelter, warders etc.); it also has beneficial effects on the economy as a whole. Moreover, it does not bring criminals into close contact with one another in the way that prisons do, and is far less personally degrading; hence it may discourage recidivism.

Summary

Society has a number of possible objectives to consider when allocating resources to crime control: *efficiency, equity*, and *civil liberty*. An efficient level of crime control is one at which the *marginal social cost* of further control begins to exceed the *marginal social benefit*. If the market were to allocate all forms of crime control, then it is unlikely that any of the objectives would be achieved. In particular, efficient levels of some forms of control (police, courts, prisons) would not be attained because they are *public goods*. Public goods possess two characteristics that make them unsuitable for market provision: *nonrivalness* and *nonexcludability*. Nonrivalness means that the consumption of one unit of a commodity by an individual does not prevent another individual from consuming the same unit; nonexcludability means that it is impossible for the purchaser of one unit to prevent someone else consuming that unit. The existence of these characteristics impedes the efficient operation of the market.

The fact that private provision will not achieve efficiency does not necessarily mean that government intervention automatically will. However it is generally accepted that government provision of those methods of crime control that involve public goods is desirable. An economic or 'rational' approach to criminal behaviour can be used to suggest means of improving existing methods of prevention; such an approach is not universally accepted as an accurate description of the way criminals behave, but it does have some statistical evidence to support it.

Further Reading

Crime and its control are subjects of relatively recent interest to economists, and there is not much literature on the topic that is suitable for the non-specialist. Simple applications of economic analysis to various areas of criminal behaviour can be found in Pyle (1979), Williams and Anderson (1975) Chapter 10, and in Part IV of McKenzie and Tullock (1978). For an entertaining exposition of the arguments for private provision of all forms of crime control, including police, courts and legal systems, see D. Friedman (1978). For those with some economics, there is Becker's (1968) original article that stimulated economists' interest in the topic and Anderson (1976), which contains an excellent summary of the literature.

Questions for Discussion

1. Is the efficient level of crime zero?
2. How would you measure the efficiency of a police force? Of a prison system?
3. Evaluate the argument that the only cost of property theft is the opportunity cost of the thief's time.
4. The wealthier the area, the smaller the number of burglaries, but the greater the value of the property stolen each time. What does this imply about the desirable allocation of police resources between rich and poor areas?

5. Would it be efficient to execute all parking offenders?
6. 'If guns are outlawed, only outlaws have guns.' Discuss.
7. What are the implications of the existence of private firms offering security services for the argument that private law enforcement suffers from an intractable free-rider problem?
8. An American study has estimated that an average policeman on patrol comes across a street robbery once every fourteen years. In the light of this what is your attitude towards the popular view that there ought to be many more policeman out on the beat?
9. Are criminals born or made?
10. 'Large fines are likely to be a more efficient means of controlling crime than heavy prison sentences.' Do you agree?

Energy 7

Energy is a vital ingredient of every aspect of life. It is the source of the food, warmth and light that makes life itself possible; it powers the instruments and machines upon which our complex industrial economy depends; and by driving the means of modern transport it provides us with unprecedented levels of personal mobility and thereby exerts a fundamental influence upon our home, work and recreational locations. The quest to harness and transform energy has been a major source of technological and economic progress. At the same time, however, our very dependence upon particular sources has posed serious problems. The world's reliance upon Middle East oil and the disruption that results if these supplies are threatened, the sensitivity of successive British governments to strike threats by coalminers or power workers, and the controversy over the safety of nuclear power, are all examples of energy-related issues that have played a prominent part in policy debates during the 1970s and 80s. In short, energy both makes life possible and exerts a fundamental influence upon its form.

Energy can be derived from a variety of sources, but modern technology is particularly dependent on three main fossil fuels – oil, coal and natural gas. Together they account for over 90 per cent of the world's energy supplies. Now it is a feature of each of these fuels that they found naturally in the earth's crust. They are a legacy of the earth's earlier history, and a second crop will not be produced within the life span of any species. For this reason they are termed *non-renewable*. McInerney (1981) has defined a non-renewable resource as one of which:

> ... a definitive stock exists on the planet (not necessarily totally discovered by man), and for which the rate of stock creation over time is zero. 'Utilisation' of one unit of the resource necessarily implies its complete destruction; the useful resource services are totally and permanently lost during use, with the physical resource stock available for future use being thereby irreversibly depleted.

This definition highlights the crux of the energy problem. Because they are non-renewable, future supplies depend upon the size of existing resources and the rate at which they are being depleted.

Some commentators fear that at current rates of consumption certain energy resources will be exhausted in the near future with a consequent disruption in patterns of social and economic activity. For example, estimates of the use of oil – which is presently the world's most important energy source and one upon which much transport is almost totally dependent – suggest that at existing rates of consumption the world's reserves of crude oil will be exhausted in about 40 years. (The problems and pitfalls associated with predictions of this nature are discussed later in the chapter.) Indeed, according to some forecasters, the acute shortages of energy which are likely to occur in the not-too-distant future are just one aspect of the general shortage of natural resources that can be expected. This view of the future has been expressed most forcibly by Professor D. H. Meadows and his associates in their book *The Limits to Growth* (1972). They argue that if economic growth continues at the exponential (proportionate) rate that it has followed in the past, sometime within the next 100 years a crisis will occur as the absolute limits to growth placed by finite reserves of arable land, oil, coal, aluminium, copper, iron, and other minerals are encountered. At this point they predict 'the breakdown of society and the irreversible disruption of life-support systems on this planet'. To avoid this disruption they recommend a series of policy measures designed to conserve and/or reduce the rate of depletion of existing stocks of natural resources.

Whether or not one accepts these gloomy predictions (and we shall point out some crucial shortcomings that tend to cast doubt on their accuracy later on in this chapter), this work does highlight the problem facing a society with limited exhaustible resources. And, of course, it is a problem that confronts Britain most immediately in relation to the use it makes of its stocks of North Sea gas and oil. In this chapter we shall endeavour to make clear the nature of the available choices and the ways in which they may be made. To do this we shall follow the familiar sequence of analysis by asking (a) what are society's objectives in the use of energy, (b) to what extent can the price mechanism be used to meet these objectives, and (c) is there any need for government intervention?

Objectives

In most of the other chapters of this book we have been primarily concerned with the way in which society uses its scarce resources in the production and distribution of goods and services at the *present time*. This consideration is, of course, still important when dealing with energy. For example, consider a scarce natural resource such as oil: we still need to decide how it should be allocated between, say, industrial and domestic users, or between transport and electricity generation. But there is another dimension to the problem. Because eventually it is going to run out, we have to decide how it should be used *through time*. How much should we use in 1985, 1990, or the year 2000? This is the problem of choice that we shall concentrate on here – the problem of *intertemporal* choice.

Although it might appear at first sight that this intertemporal decision is a very different one from those we have been considering so far, we shall argue that the same considerations of *efficiency* and *equity* apply.

Efficiency

We can demonstrate the essence of the problem of intertemporal choice by using a simple example of a motorist who has ten gallons of petrol and wants to decide how it should be divided between this week and next week. (Later we shall show how the same principles apply to society over longer periods of time.) Now our motorist could use the total quota of ten gallons this week and have none next week. Alternatively he could save it all for a trip next week and do no driving this week. Or he could use five gallons each week. Clearly there are a number of options. To choose between them the motorist will need to consider the benefit derived from using different amounts of petrol in each week, or to be specific, the *marginal benefit* (*mb*). (At this stage costs are considered constant between the two weeks so we can just concentrate on the benefits.) This is shown in Figure 7.1.

In the diagram we measure week 1's consumption from left to right. The marginal benefit curve for week 1 (mb_1) slopes downwards from left to right indicating that as the motorist increases his use of petrol in week 1 so the *mb* derived from each

FIGURE 7.1
Inter-temporal Consumption of Petrol

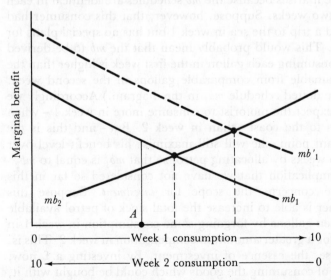

additional gallon gets less. For week 2, on the other hand, petrol consumption is measured from right to left. Thus the marginal benefit schedule for week 2 (mb_2) slopes downwards from right to left, but it also shows that the mb the motorist derives from consumption in week 2 falls as the level of consumption rises. Now it will be in this person's best interest to choose that combination of consumption over the two weeks in which mb_1 equals mb_2. This will ensure that the benefit level is maximised. To see why this must be so, consider a situation in which mb_1 is greater than mb_2. The motorist derives more benefit from the final gallon he uses in week 1 than he does from the final gallon in week 2. Clearly, therefore, if one of week 2's gallons was reallocated to week 1 it would add more to the benefit derived in week 1 than to the benefit lost in week 2. Such a possibility for increasing total benefit is shown in the diagram at point A. Only when mb_1 is equal to mb_2 is there no further opportunity for increasing benefits through such a reallocation.

In our example it appears that the motorist will choose to divide the total stock of petrol equally between the two weeks, but there is no reason why this must always be the case. In this instance it arises because the mb schedules are identical in each of the two weeks. Suppose, however, that this consumer had planned a trip to the sea in week 1 but has no special plans for week 2. This would probably mean that the mb to be derived from consuming each gallon in the first week is higher than the mb obtainable from comparable gallons in the second week. (See the dotted schedule mb_1 in the diagram.) Accordingly we would expect the motorist to consume more in week 1 – when he goes to the coast – than in week 2. But – and this is the important point – he will still maximise his benefit level over the two weeks by allocating petrol so that mb_1 is equal to mb_2.

A complication that we have not considered so far in this example concerns the scope for *investment*. Suppose this consumer is able to increase the total stock of petrol available above ten gallons by forgoing some consumption in week 1 in return for a greater amount in compensation in week 2. This is, of course, the essence of investment. By investing a £ now, instead of consuming the goods which could be bought with it, a person hopes to obtain the original £ plus some additional amount (an interest payment) in the future. In our example we have abstracted from this problem by assuming that a gallon forgone in week 1 makes available an equal amount in week 2. However, suppose each gallon forgone in week 1 produces, say, one and a quarter gallons in week 2. Hence total consumption in week 2 could be as high as twelve and a half gallons. This possibility requires us to modify our benefit-maximising formula. Instead of requiring mb_1 to equal mb_2 we now require mb_1 to equal $1.25\ mb_2$. That is, the mb of one gallon in week 1 must be equated with the mb derived from one and a quarter gallons in week 2 because this is the rate at which the consumer could convert week 1 gallons into week 2 gallons. This will tend to result in rather more consumption taking place in week 2 at the expense of week 1.

Another consideration that may affect the combination of petrol consumption between the two weeks is the motorist's subjective preferences regarding immediate consumption (in week 1) versus delayed consumption (in week 2). Economists usually assume that people prefer immediate consumption and that they require some compensation (an interest payment) for delaying consumption. Other things remaining equal, this means that each gallon of petrol will yield a higher mb in week 1 than in week 2. (Try to test your understanding of the investment and delayed consumption arguments by working out how they can be represented in Figure 7.1.)

By using this simple example of a person making a two-week intertemporal consumption decision, we have been able to demonstrate the essence of the search for an *efficient* allocation of resources through time. That is, resources should be allocated to maximise total (net) benefits over the period under consideration. The precise allocation that achieves this objective will depend on two factors: preferences for consumption in each period and the rate at which current consumption can be converted into future consumption.

Now these same considerations will apply equally to society's search for a *socially* efficient allocation of resources, although in this case we are dealing with maginal *social* benefits. Also the time periods under consideration will usually be considerably longer. Nevertheless, a socially efficient allocation of oil between the 1980s and the 1990s, for example, will still depend on preferences in the 1980s and 1990s, and the rate at which resources used to produce oil for consumption now could be used for investment purposes to produce goods (including oil substitutes) for consumption in the future. However, although the principles are the same, the need to consider a rather longer period of time does present some special difficulties when making social choices. As we have seen, an efficient allocation requires preferences for consumption now and in the future to be taken into account. However it is extremely likely that, when we are dealing with extended time periods of forty or fifty years or more, some of the people who will be consuming the goods in the future may not even be alive yet. How then can we know their preferences? In fact, we cannot know them and so the present generation must act as the custodian of future generations' interests. This brings us to the second main objective that society will probably wish to pursue in its allocation of resources through time – that of *equity*.

Equity

As in the case of efficiency, most of the discussion of equity found elsewhere in this book has been confined to the issue of fairness in treatment of different individuals or groups at a particular point in time. Such considerations are also of obvious importance in the case of energy. The plight of low- and fixed-income families facing soaring electricity and heating bills is one area of concern. Another is in the international arena where certain less-developed countries such as India, which are totally dependent on imported oil, have been particularly hard hit by oil price increases. But, just as in the case of efficiency, it is important to consider the way resources are allocated *through time*. As far as the equity objective is concerned, this leads to the desire to establish fairness of treatment between different generations. To be specific, it leads to a desire to ensure that the interests of future generations receive adequate consideration in the present generation's decisions about depletable energy-resource use and the stock of resources we bequeath to them. It also requires that their interests are borne in mind in the search for alternative or substitute energy sources, so that they do not inherit a world suffering from widespread contamination from nuclear or other waste products. Clearly these are objectives to which most people would subscribe but, as we shall see, the remoteness of the beneficiaries makes the specification of an equitable distribution through time especially problematic.

The Market System and Energy Resources

We saw in Chapter 1 how, under certain conditions, the price system will produce an efficient level of output. It is able to achieve this result because the actions of consumers and producers are co-ordinated through their responses to price 'signals'. So far we have been mainly concerned with the way in which the price mechanism is used to allocate resources at the present, but it can also be used to allocate resources over a period of time. However, in order for it to be able to perform this function it is necessary for future demand and supply conditions to be known. In some cases this information is actually recorded in formal markets; these are known as *futures* or *forward* markets. In a futures market, buyers and sellers enter into contractual agreements at the present that guarantee the terms of a sale or purchase at some date in the future. For example, a wholesaler may contract to buy fifty tons of coffee in two months' time at a price of £1500 per ton. In this way futures markets enable future demands to be registered alongside present demands. Hence a link between the present and the future is provided which enables producers and consumers to select the socially efficient 'time path' for their production and consumption.

To illustrate this point let us take a simple example. Suppose we are considering the consumption of a fixed stock of oil over a two-month period – say, July and August in a given year. Furthermore, suppose that we are at the beginning of July when oil is priced at £10 per barrel and that oil delivered in August is priced on the futures market at £11 per barrel. On the basis of these prices we may expect a particular pattern or 'time path' of oil usage over the two months. Now suppose some new information becomes available that indicates a substantial rise in the demand for oil during August. How could the futures market deal with this information? Just as in any other market, we would expect this additional demand to bid up the August price – to, let us say, £12 per barrel. However, if the futures price rises in this way, dealers will find it profitable to hold some of the oil, which was originally destined for July consumption, off the market until August, when they can realise the higher price. Thus we may expect a reallocation that will continue until the July price rises (as the July supply falls) and the August price falls (as supplies made available for August increase) sufficiently to make further reallocations unprofitable. Such is the way futures markets provide the mechanism for allocating resources over time.

Unfortunately, however, futures markets are in practice only confined to a few commodities and only extend over short periods of time. As such they can be quite useful in smoothing out short-term disturbances but they cannot really contribute toward the solution of long-term energy consumption problems. Instead, those people responsible for making decisions about energy usage have to rely on *expectations* about the future. Although this obviously introduces a great deal of uncertainty into the allocation problem (which we discuss further below), there is none the less still a potentially important role for the price mechanism. For although there might be no formal futures market, current prices are likely to respond to expectations about the future and thereby exert an influence on current activities.

To demonstrate this point let us consider the impact of the widely held expectation that oil is going to become increasingly scarce in the future. This may be expected to result in rises in current prices for two main reasons. First, higher extraction costs may be anticipated as the more easily land-based oil fields are exhausted and mining companies have to resort to more costly oil fields under the sea beds, or to shale and tar oils. Second, expectations of future scarcity and rising prices will increase the value of oil 'in the ground'. It will become a valuable asset that owners may wish to preserve in the hope of greater profits in the future. This will, of course, reduce the current supply available for consumption and lead to further price rises. However these price rises will set in motion a series of compensating activities. On the demand side higher prices will encourage conservation in the consumption of oil. There will be a strong incentive to drive smaller, more fuel-efficient cars, to improve home insulation standards, to set thermostat settings lower and so on. On the supply side the search for new oil fields can be expected to intensify as the gains to be made from successful discoveries increase. At the same time substitution between energy sources can be expected as oil becomes more expensive. Hence it will become economic to use some inferior and more costly energy sources that it was not worthwhile using when cheaper substitutes were available. (Some idea of the extent of this possibility is indicated by the fact that shale oil deposits in Colorado, USA, are estimated to contain more than three times the world's known reserves of liquid oil.) Overall, therefore, we can see how the expectation of a future scarcity – through the mechanism of price signals – will lead to reductions in current demand and/or the emergence of new sources of supply.

At this point it is worth recalling the work of Professor Meadows and his associates, which was described at the beginning of this chapter. It will be remembered that these researchers predicted a catastrophic breakdown in society and in life-support systems as natural resources are exhausted sometime within the next 100 years. However, one of the major criticisms that has been levelled at their work is that it fails to allow for the adaptive processes that can be expected to result from price signals. Critics of Meadows have argued that danger will be averted because both demand and supply responses of the type described above will come into operation as key nonrenewable resources become increasingly scarce. Moreover, it is argued, his predictions ignore the major contribution that can be expected to result from technical progress – which will itself be stimulated by the price mechanism. Thus research and development in mining, agriculture, manufacturing, transport, and many other fields can all be expected in response to rising resource prices. Unfortunately we are not able to predict the form of these changes with any confidence. After all, would a pundit living in the 1880s have been able to predict the technologies of the present – especially nuclear power? The answer is almost certainly not. But precedent does give us strong grounds for expecting progress in this direction. Of course, the fact that history has always provided examples of technological advance in the past does not establish that it will continue to do so in the future. Society's salvation is not assured. But the price mechanism does give us serious reasons to doubt the more extreme versions of the 'doom' school of thought.

From this account it might be supposed that the price system can be relied on to produce an efficient pattern of energy consumption through time. But this conclusion rests upon a number of crucial assumptions. We have concentrated on one – namely, that expectations about the future are accurate. If they are erroneous an efficient allocation will not be realised. Now a failure to anticipate the future correctly is really a special form of the information problem that we have come across before in connection with, for example, health care, education, and housing. That is, it is a possible source of market failure. Let us consider this and other types of possible market failure in more detail.

Imperfect Information

When lack of information refers to imperfect knowledge of the future, economists usually refer to it as *uncertainty*. Now there are several reasons to fear that uncertainty may result in an inefficient rate of energy resource depletion through time. For instance, consider the example we discussed earlier concerning an individual's decision about the present and future use of oil; but now, suppose that the time horizon is extended from two weeks to 10 or 20 years. In principle the same considerations apply in determining the efficient level of use in each period. But can we be confident that each individual is able to make rational decisions about the benefits they would derive from consumption now *vis-à-vis* the benefits they will derive in 10 or 20 years? And will the millions of decisions made by individuals privately produce a sum-total outcome that is in the present and future society's best interests? The Cambridge economist A. C. Pigou clearly though not when, in a celebrated phrase, he referred to individuals' attitudes towards the future as myopic – as a 'faulty telescopic faculty'. In his view individuals acting separately would attach less importance to the future than we, as a society, would want to attach to it. Thus a private market system would result in an excessive rate of resource depletion.

By the same token we may ask how decision makers within those industries dealing in energy resources will cope with uncertainty. Will it cause them to adopt an inefficient rate of depletion? To illustrate, consider the major oil companies. Uncertainty about future levels of demand, the possibility of the development or discovery of substitute energy sources, and fears of expropriation if sources of supply are located in politically unstable areas, will all provide a strong incentive for oil company executives to attach considerable importance to short-term profits at the expense of longer term considerations. Moreover the adoption of short-term time scales for policy purposes will almost certainly prevent the price mechanism from operating in the smooth fashion we described earlier. It will be recalled that if prices rise gradually in anticipation of future oil shortages this will set in motion a series of adaptive responses on both the demand and supply sides of the market. However if oil companies consider no more than one or two years ahead when formulating pricing policies, acute shortages are not likely to be given much thought until they are imminent. Consequently, instead of following a smooth adjustment path, prices are likely to remain too low for many years – thereby encouraging excessive oil use – and then rise violently as shortages become apparent.

Another problem associated with uncertainty concerns the amount of search that will take place for new energy sources. To be specific, there is reason to expect that, in the face of uncertainty, private market arrangements will result in too little search. For example, consider exploratory drilling for new oil fields. At present most companies undertake this drilling independently. The quantity of exploration they engage in depends on the private costs involved and the expected private benefits. Now while costs are bound to be incurred, benefits are not certain; they depend on the probability of finding oil and the size of the field discovered. Obviously this involves risk. And as most companies are risk averse, they try to avoid it. Thus, suppose – for purposes of illustration – that each exploratory bore hole costs £100 000, and that one in every 1000 bore holes reveals an oil field worth at least £100 million. Now if there were 100 prospecting companies operating independently, and each of them undertook ten borings, each would incur a certain cost of £1 million. However the benefits are far from certain; in fact the odds against any one company making a successful boring would be 100 to one. Faced with these odds, many companies may decide that the risk is too great to merit a £1 million expenditure and, therefore, decided not to go ahead. As a result fewer than 1000 drillings will be made and the oil field may well remain undiscovered. Notice, however, that the total benefit from discovering the field – at least £100 million – would cover the costs of 1000 borings. So it would be in the companies' joint interests (and society's) for 1000 drillings to be made. What is required, therefore, is an arrangement that will ensure that the optimal amount of drilling will take place.

One way in which the optimal amount of exploration could be achieved is through the co-ordination of activity. If there was an arrangement that reduced the risk faced by each company, this would probably be more attractive to most companies, even it it was achieved at the cost of removing the remote prospect of any one company 'striking it rich'. Such an arrangement would reduce risk by 'pooling'; that is, it would ensure that each company would share the benefits of the successful boring regardless of whether it actually made the discovery. Consequently the number of companies willing to carry out exploratory borings would be greater, and the chances of making a successful discovery would increase. Now while the private market has produced risk-sharing arrangements elsewhere – notably in the insurance industry, which bases its business on this principle – few such arrangements have been made in connection with energy exploration. As a result, it is probable that too little exploration takes place.

Externalities

The discussion in the first section of this chapter identified the societal objective of inter-generational equity. That is non-renewable resources should be used by the present generation in a way that shows due regard for the interests of future generations. But current market transactions will not necessarily register the impact of present day activities upon future generations. Because of this the costs and benefits borne in the future can be viewed as a form of inter-generational externality. And just as the failure to take account of external costs in a static context is likely to result in over production and consumption, so in the intergenerational context we can expect excessive current consumption because current prices will not reflect the external costs imposed on future generations.

Apart from inter-generational externalities, there are a number of conventional externalities associated with energy consumption which are not unique to it – but probably nowhere else are their consequences so alarming. Some examples will indicate why this is so. Consider a decision to mine for coal or uranium, or to drill for oil or natural gas. This will often involve the complete disruption of the affected area: the destruction of a scenic woodland or coastal area, the construction of unsightly buildings and drilling rigs, noise and air pollution, and so on. Before this took place the natural beauty of the environment is likely to have been a source of benefit to visitors and residents alike. This benefit is now lost. In many cases, however, unless there is a forceful public outcry, these losses will not have been given due consideration when the decision to devote the land to mining was made. This is because the landowner (whether it is privately or government owned) is unlikely to have received payment for the aesthetic benefits bestowed by the land. Thus they were *external* benefits. Moreover the problem is compounded because when such changes of land use are made they tend to be *non-reversible*; once an area of natural beauty has been destroyed it is almost impossible (at least, extremely expensive) to restore it.

Another case where externalities figure very prominently among the costs of the energy industry is that of accidents. Once again it should be emphasised that these are not specific to the energy sector, but the consequences are here quite dramatic. For example, an accident involving the oil super-tanker *Amoco Cadiz* resulted in the spillage of 1.3 million barrels of oil on the Brittany coast of France in 1978. In 1979 the worst supertanker collision in history between the *Atlantic Express* and the *Aegean Captain* left a ten-mile oil slick along the tourist beaches of the Caribbean island of Tobago. But both of these accidents were surpassed by the damage caused by a blow-out on the offshore oil rig *Ixtoc I* in the Gulf of Mexico in 1979: this produced an oil slick 500 miles long and 50 miles wide as thick as hot fudge in places! Finally there is no doubt that the potentialy most alarming externality is associated with nuclear power. As the anti-nuclear lobbies have pointed out, no other externality carries the same non-reversible, long-term danger as does radioactive contamination – a danger that was given frightening reality by the accident at the Three Mile Island nuclear reactor in Pennsylvania, USA.

Monopoly

When a firm has a monopoly, there is a danger that it will exploit the public by restricting output below the socially efficient level and charging prices that are higher than would prevail in a competitive market. In the case of certain key energy resources – most notably oil – the market is dominated by monopolies and producer cartels. Large multi-national oil companies whose activities extend from exploratory drilling and oil well operations, through transport and refining to retail distribution, rule the market. Their predominant position is maintained by the considerable barriers to entry that prospective competitors face in an industry where substantial economies of scale (i.e. costs per unit of output fall as the size of the firm increases) favour large, established firms.

In recent years, however, the behaviour of the Organisation of Petroleum Exporting Countries (OPEC) cartel has given cause for more concern. This group, which comprises the major Middle East oil exporting countries together with some other producers such as Nigeria and Venezuela, decides the price at which its member countries will sell oil on world markets. During the 1960s plentiful world supplies of oil meant that OPEC had little bargaining power and real oil prices (that is, the price of oil in relation to prices generally) actually fell. However, this era of cheap oil came to an end in 1973–4 when there was an Arab oil embargo and OPEC quadrupled its prices. Faced with this and subsequent price increases, some observers have claimed that OPEC members are exploiting their monopoly position by restricting output and raising prices. Indeed at the present time – faced with declining oil demand because of world recession – OPEC oil ministers' discussions are dominated by the quest to reach agreement over output restrictions to counteract possible falls in price.

However, we need to be careful in our analysis of the effect of organisations such as OPEC on the level of oil production and consumption. While it is undoubtedly true that OPEC members have restricted supply to maintain or raise price levels (and because they realise that oil left in the ground is a sound investment for the future when it is likely to become more scarce), this restriction is not necessarily a bad thing. Indeed, their actions may prevent (albeit sometimes unwittingly) the excessive present consumption of oil that would otherwise take place. One writer has argued that 'by exploiting their market power they have struck a resounding blow for conservation, and for the welfare of our successors' (Heal, 1981). Of course it would be preferable for this policy to evolve through international co-operation so that sudden oil price rises do not lead to world recession or have deleterious, international income-distributional consequences by hitting poor, oil dependent countries such as India. But it does mean that OPEC price rises, about which we all complain as consumers, are none the less in the interests of future generations. In fact some evidence suggests that the actual price increases that have been experienced since the 1960s, far from being too large, have not been large enough for conservation purposes.

In total, therefore, it seems that market failures in the form of imperfect information, externalities and monopoly power are sufficiently widespread in the energy sector to cast doubt upon the markets' ability to produce an efficient and equitable pattern of resource use through time. Accordingly we turn, in the next section, to government policies that have been adopted in the area of energy use to see if they have improved, or can be expected to improve, efficiency and equity.

Government Policies

Since the Middle East oil embargo at the time of the Arab-Israeli war in 1973 and the subsequent dramatic rise in oil prices, governments around the world have taken a far more active role in formulating national energy policies. In Britain this concern has been heightened by the desire to ensure optimal use of the domestic supplies of oil and gas discovered in the North Sea during the late 1960s and early 1970s. At the same time the use of these energy reserves has had to be reconciled with the use made of traditional domestic fuels, especially coal, in the light of not only the desire for a co-ordinated pattern of energy use but also the political constraints imposed by government sensitivity to the demands of coal miners and other power workers following, particularly, the miners' strike of 1974.

The response of successive governments to these sometimes conflicting requirements has produced a series of energy policy instruments: these may be classified in terms of the categories used in other chapters of this book as (i) taxation or subsidisation, (ii) regulation and (iii) direct provision. In fact all of these instruments have been used in policy towards North Sea oil and so – given its considerable topical interest – we shall first of all concentrate upon their application within this context. This will be followed by a more general consideration of government policy instruments in the light of the market imperfections discussed in the previous section.

North Sea Oil Policy

British Petroleum announced the discovery of the first British sector oilfield in the North Sea – the Forties field – in 1970. Subsequent discoveries such as the Brent and Ninian fields followed rapidly. Initially the policy objective of successive governments was to make sure that the benefits were realised by the fastest possible exploitation of the reserves. Subsequently, however, concern about uncertain overseas supplies, rising future prices and the recognition of a strictly limited supply (present estimates suggest that North Sea stocks will be exhausted towards the end of the 1990s) led to greater emphasis being placed upon the need for a depletion policy. In addition to this concern over the rate of depletion, it has been recognised from the outset that oil discoveries provide the scope for large monopoly profits for producers. As we saw in Chapter 4 – when discussing housing – an increase in the demand for a commodity in inelastic supply will produce price increases which benefit the owners of the existing stock of the commodity. The same considerations apply in the case of North Sea oil, where a few companies control the oil stocks. Clearly some mechanism is necessary to ensure that the benefits of oil discoveries are distributed equitably and not confined to a few companies and their shareholders. Hence government policy has sought efficiency and equity in two areas: the rate of resource depletion and the distribution of benefits.

A policy of levying *taxes* on oil companies in the form of a 'barrelage tax' (a tax per barrel of oil produced) or through 'royalty' charges (a tax on the value of oil produced), could be used to achieve both of these objectives. The tax would reduce the profitability of present sales in relation to future sales (because tax payments in the present are valued more highly by the firm than future tax payments, in the same way that consumption in the present is valued more highly than consumption in the future), and hence encourage conservation. At the same time income in the form of tax revenues would be diverted from oil companies to the government, which could use it for subsequent re-distribution.

At present the main tax that is applied to oil company operations in the North Sea is the Petroleum Revenue Tax (PRT). This is a levy on the assessed profits of each oil field, which is payable in addition to normal corporation tax. To what extent does the PRT operate in the manner described above? While it has undoubtedly had some effect, the government's desire also to encourage exploration in the North Sea has reduced its impact. For, recognising that such exploration is very expensive – because of the uncertainty and technically demanding nature of the work – the government has placed a number of limitations on PRT in order to avoid discouraging oil company investments. For example, a maximum annual limit has been placed upon the amount payable. Clearly such limitations have reduced the scope for redistributing current income although they may be justified in terms of future discoveries and greater longer-term aggregate income. Similarly, the incentive to conserve oil stocks will have been reduced by limiting taxation, especially in periods when current consumer demand has been buoyant. As such, taxes on consumer expenditure on oil, particularly excise taxes on petrol, must be seen as an essential accompaniment of producer taxes even though they clearly have had a longer and wider role than North Sea oil policy.

From the time North Sea drilling began the government has controlled activity through a system of *regulation*. Oil companies are not free to operate wherever they choose but must obtain a licence from the government. Licences are issued for 'blocks' of sea, each of which is about 100 square miles in area. Clearly this system could be used to divert monopoly profit to the government if the licences were sold to the highest bidder. For each company would have an incentive to offer a slightly higher price than its nearest competitor, and a process of competitive bidding would continue until the price offered by the successful company was equal to the excess profit it would otherwise make. (This process is similar to the one which operates in a perfect market economy where newcomers or potential newcomers to an industry prevent existing firms charging prices which would yield monopoly profits).

However, apart from a limited experiment, governments have not sold licences in this way. Rather they have preferred to offer them at a nominal charge to established companies on the grounds that these companies can be relied upon to operate in a 'responsible' manner. In fact this does not offer as much freedom to the oil companies as it might appear because government regulation extends beyond the granting of licences. The Petroleum and Submarine Pipelines Act, 1975, gives the Secretary of State for Energy very wide powers over oil company operations in the North Sea, including the power to specify maximum and minimum rates of annual production. Moreover, through the formation of the state-owned British National Oil Corporation (BNOC), the government established a means of both regulation and direct state intervention (*provision*). Through BNOC the government currently acquires 51 per cent ownership of each licence awarded to an oil company and thereby has a claim to oil profits and, in principle, a direct mechanism for influencing policy.

Clearly the entire North Sea oil industry is a complex

mixture of private market operations constrained by government tax/subsidy policies (PRT), regulation (licensing) and regulation/direct provision (BNOC). As such it would appear that the policy instruments necessary to achieve an efficient rate of resource depletion and an equitable distribution of its benefits are available. Whether current policies actually do so is the subject of a great deal of debate and we cannot hope to resolve the issue here. However it is worth noting that one authority on energy economics – Professor Colin Robinson (Robinson, 1982) – has claimed recently that government intervention is likely to lead to a less efficient pattern of oil use through time than would be achieved by the companies operating in an unconstrained way. He bases his argument upon, among other things, the claim that politicians tend to be over-concerned with short-term considerations and will therefore attach less importance to the future than our 'ideal' government would do.

Energy Plans for the Future

Despite the dissent of such critics, most governments take the view that they are better placed to decide upon the optimal pattern of energy use through time than is the private market. Accordingly they devise energy plans which specify targets for the production and consumption of alternative energy sources. We have seen already some of the policy instruments that are available to implement these plans for North Sea oil, but these are just industry-specific examples of a far more general range of policies.

Conservation – that is, slowing down the rate at which non-renewable resources are used up – has been a major concern of energy policy during the 1970s and 1980s. To a certain extent the price mechanism has encouraged this process, as rising energy prices have led to a fall in the current demand for energy. However, the government has supplemented the private market response through the use of a range of consumer *taxes* and *subsidies*. Examples include the active use of petrol and diesel oil excise taxes as a means of controlling demand and the offer of home insulation grants to increase the technical efficiency of energy use and, once again, thereby reduce demand. At the same time the relative prices of energy sources produced by nationalised industries, particularly electricity and gas, have been harmonised to avoid the excessive use of one at the expense of the other.

While the government has certainly introducd policies aimed at conservation, some people would argue that it has not gone far enough. Certainly those who feel that a continuation of present long-term growth trends will have catastrophic consequences as key natural resources are exhausted would favour more active government control of the long-term rate of growth. Members of this school of thought have proposed policies of *zero economic growth* or a *stationary state*.

Advocates of zero economic growth, as the name implies, take the view that the quest for growth has gone too far, and that attention should be shifted towards non-material concerns, the quality of life and the environment. Critics point out, however, that while this view may appeal to those who are already affluent, it has little attraction for the majority of the world's population who presently exist at the subsistence level. For them economic growth is the main hope of bettering their lot. Stationary state proponents, on the other hand, take a less extreme position. They argue that growth is permissible as long as it does not lead to the exhaustion of non-renewable resources or the destruction of the environment. Ultimately, however, the exhaustion of some resources through growth seems inevitable; indeed, it is difficult to see why this is undesirable if substitutes are available. Overall it is probably accurate to say that while relatively few people subscribe fully to these views, they have none the less performed a useful role in alerting us to some of the dangers of present long-term growth trends.

Another area in which government has either supplemented (through subsidies) or replaced (through direct provision) the private market is in the search for new energy sources and methods of production through *research and development*. Much research is of such a risky and expensive nature that it is unlikely to be undertaken by private firms on their own. For example, the much quoted possibility of shale-oil production presently requires approximately 1.7 tons of rock and huge quantities of water to produce a single barrel of

oil. The present level of oil prices simply do not provide sufficient incentive for private firms to invest in the development of
such processes. Similarly the scale of operations and level of
funds required has meant that nuclear fuel development in
Britain has taken place either within government establish-
ments or through close collaboration between government and
private firms.

Finally, energy plans since the 1970s have tended to incorporate an important element which we have not so far dealt
with explicitly: this is the *strategic* dimension. The formation of
the OPEC cartel has been viewed by many international rela-
tions strategists as rather more than a straightforward producers' cartel with economic bargaining power. Rather, the
central dependence of every industrial economy on oil has conferred a degree of power on the producer nations which, it is
felt, may well be used for political purposes. Individual oil
consumers, whether they are firms or private families, may not
be concerned about this possibility when oil supplies are
flowing normally – after all, how may people care where the
petrol in their tank comes from as long as the tank is full? But
the government will need to take a longer and wider view. It
must concern itself with a host of strategic issues. The concentration of OPEC states in the politically unstable Middle East,
and the desire to be free from uncertainty of supply from this
source, has been a major determinant in the Government's
plans for the conservation of North Sea oil.

Summary

Energy is vital for life. The world's main sources of energy –
oil, coal and natural gas – are *nonrenewable*; consequently we
have to decide on the optimal rate at which to use up the fixed
stock. This is a problem of allocating resources through time.
However, the same objectives of *efficiency* and *equity* are shown
to be relevant here, as they are in the allocation of resources in
a single period of time. The price mechanism has an important
part to play in bringing about an efficient allocation through
time. Indeed the disregard of adaptive responses caused by
price signals is shown to be one of the major defects of those

forecasters predicting 'doom' within the next 100 years when, they argue, certain key natural resources will be exhausted. But there are a number of possible sources of market failure. In particular, there is *imperfect information* caused by *uncertainty* about the future, *external costs*, and *monopoly*. These provide reasons for government intervention.

In Britain, government policy towards North Sea oil provides examples of *tax/subsidisation policy, regulation* and *direct provision*. More generally, a range of policies towards all the major energy sources in the 1970s and 1980s has been concerned with *conservation*, encouraging *research and development* and the *strategic implications* of the OPEC cartel.

Further Reading

Lecomber (1979) contains an excellent analysis of the problems surrounding the use of all nonrenewable natural resources. Among other things, he examines the problem of intertemporal choice and the role of the price mechanism in making intertemporal decisions. Butlin (1981) assembles an excellent set of papers on economics and resources policy. Chapters 3 and 4 are particularly good on the analysis of intertemporal choices, while Chapter 2 provides a thorough economic critique of world 'doom' models. The original world 'doom' model is given in Meadows *et al.* (1972), and an extensive critique is provided in Freeman & Jahoda (1978). In the course of a more extensive study, Webb and Ricketts (1980) discuss government policies toward energy, including North Sea oil. Robinson (1982) puts forward a provocative counter view of the effects of government policy.

Questions for Discussion

1. What reasons are there for supposing that consumption in the present is valued more highly than consumption in the future?
2. Use a cost/benefit framework to illustrate the difference between an investment decision involving an irreversible

change in land use and one involving a reversible change.

3. Natural gas prices were raised recently far above their costs of production. Why?

4. What effect has the rise in oil prices had upon the coal industry?

5. Why should estimates of world energy reserves be treated with caution?

6. Compare the predictions of Professor Meadows and others who have forecast 'world doom' with the earlier predictions of the Reverend Thomas Malthus.

7. Why might the expectation of oil price rises lead to less oil being produced?

8. Supposed strategic considerations in the supply of energy are really economic concerns. Do you agree?

9. Explain how risk pooling arrangements may be used to reduce the risk faced by any one company or individual.

10. Consider the case for and against developing nuclear energy.

Urban Congestion 8

Britain is a predominantly urban society; nearly 80 per cent of the population live in urban areas with over 30 per cent living in the major conurbations of Greater London, West Midlands, S.E. Lancashire, Merseyside, West Yorkshire, Tyneside and Clydeside. Nearly 40 per cent of jobs are located in these conurbations. Not surprisingly these concentrations of population and economic activity give rise to numerous problems of traffic congestion. Delays and frustrations of traffic jams, infrequent and unpredictable bus services, overcrowded trains, traffic noise, air pollution and accident risks are all common features of urban life. To understand why this should be, let us look rather more closely at the phenomenon of 'congestion'.

Congestion may be defined as a situation in which 'some people are waiting for other people to be served'. The word *served* indicates an important point about congestion. That is, it is usually associated with the supply of *services* rather than *goods*. This is because it is not possible to hold a stock of services to meet fluctuations in demand in the same way as it is possible to hold stocks of cars, TV sets, clothing and so on. Thus each of the transport services mentioned above encounters congestion at some time or other when heavy demand exceeds the capacity of the system to supply the service. Of course sufficient capacity could be built to ensure that supply could meet even the most abnormal demands, but it would be very expensive to do this. Extra trains could be built to meet the exceptional demands that occur on the occasional bank-holiday weekend, but they would be seriously under-utilised for the remainder of the year. Similarly an extra lane of urban motorway could ensure that the periodic congestion resulting from rush-hour traffic accidents would be less disruptive, but it would be under-used for most of the time. Consequently most operators do not provide the maximum capacity that would be necessary to meet even the highest levels of demand placed on them, and so users of the service in times of peak demand often encounter congestion.

Because congestion arises when excess demand is placed on certain services during peak periods, it can be viewed as one result of the way in which society has chosen to allocate its scarce resources in these areas. For our purposes, however, we wish to know whether the existence of congestion is consistent with an efficient and equitable allocation of resources, and if it is not, what modifications to the allocation system are likely to make it so. To enable us to answer these questions we shall concentrate on one particular form of congestion – that is, urban road congestion. However this is only for purposes of illustration; similar considerations apply to most other forms of congestion.

Before starting on this examination, however, it is worth pointing out a difference in our approach to the social problem dealt with in this chapter. In most of the other chapters in this book we have looked at the way the market system allocates resources, noting its advantages and failings, and have then moved on to consider various forms of government intervention that either modify or replace the private market. However in the case of roads, nowhere is the market used as the primary means of allocation. Consequently, in this chapter, we look at the most commonly found non-market system of allocation to see whether it performs the role expected of it before considering the possible forms of intervention. But, as elsewhere, we start with a consideration of society's objectives in the use of road space.

Objectives

When deciding on the way it should use its road system, a society will need to consider all the benefits and costs that arise from its use. Accordingly we start by discussing briefly the nature of these benefits and costs; this enables us to define an efficient level of road use. However, as we have seen in other chapters, society will have other aims besides the efficiency objective. A concern to establish equity and to preserve as much freedom of choice as possible is also likely to be of some importance in the case of road use. Consequently, when we come to discuss the extent to which public policies realise their efficiency aims, we shall look at their implications for equity and freedom of choice as well.

Benefits of Road Use

Benefits arise from road use because transport is necessary to satisfy a wide range of work and leisure activities. Travel is rarely valued in its own right, but it is often necessary for satisfying other demands. Hence the demand for travel is often termed a *derived demand* – derived from the 'final' demand for particular activities. For instance, in the case of business and commercial traffic, it is necessary to move raw materials and semi-finished goods to the factories where they will be incorporated into finished products ready for consumption, and also to move these finished goods to the shops from which they will be sold to customers. The demand for this transport is therefore derived from consumers' demand for final goods and services. Similarly, in the case of private traffic, the demand is also a derived demand; a journey to work is necessary before one can earn income, watching a film requires a trip to the cinema, and so on. Probably only in the case of pure recreational travel is the journey valued for its own sake. This association of travel with different activities means that the benefit individuals derive from a trip, and hence their demand for the trip, will be related to the benefit they derive from the final activity. Thus trips along the same stretch of road involving commercial deliveries to shops, private shopping trips, commuting journeys to work, and so on, will all yield different levels of benefit. This will need to be borne in mind when deciding on the way that demands on limited road space are met.

A second factor that will affect the level of benefit that travellers obtain from a journey is the mode of transport they use. For example, if we look at the relative merits of car and bus travel we usually find that the car has the advantages of door-to-door travel, privacy, guarantee of a seat, a flexible route and, usually, a faster journey time; while the bus has the advantages of no parking problems, no frustrations of driving, and the option of undertaking other activities (for example reading) while travelling. The level of benefit travellers obtain from a journey will depend on their preferences regarding these characteristics. If they place a high value on door-to-door travel and hate depending on timetables, they will tend to value a car trip more highly; if, on the other hand, they enjoy reading a newspaper or magazine while travelling and become agitated by driving, they will prefer the bus.

Costs of Road Use

Once a road has been built the costs that arise from using it can be divided into four main categories according to who bears the costs. First, there are the *private* costs of road use that are paid directly by motorists or the firms employing them. These include petrol costs, vehicle depreciation and also some non-monetary costs, in particular the costs of time spent on journeys. This last item is particularly important in the case of transport for its represents a major portion of private travel costs. At first sight it may seem strange to speak of time 'costs' for time is not bought and sold on the market in the normal way. But it is a scarce resource (there are only twenty-four hours in a day!) with a distinct opportunity cost. For example, time spent on travel has an obvious cost as far as people travelling for business or commercial reasons are concerned, because time spent on a journey is usually far less productive than time spent in an office, factory, or shop. But time spent on travel also represents a cost to a person travelling for non-business reasons; most people can probably think of more pleasant ways to spend the time they now use for travelling. Certainly most of us would prefer (and would be willing to pay for) an extra half-hour in bed in the morning instead of fighting traffic on the way to work.

The second category of costs is the one of particular concern in this book – that is *congestion* costs. In the case of road users, these are the costs that one motorist imposes on another when the number of vehicles using a road reaches the point at which drivers start to impede each other's movement. This results in frequent stopping and starting and lower traffic speeds. The delays that occur cause higher journey costs both through higher vehicle operating costs (for example more brake and tyre wear, higher petrol consumption, and so on) and longer journey times.

The third category of costs can be termed *environmental* costs. These are imposed by users of the road system on non road users, such as pedestrians and residents who live in the vicinity of the roads. They include a range of non-monetary items such as noise and air pollution, unattractive visual appearance and increased risk of accidents. Not all of these costs will vary with the level of road use and congestion; some arise as soon as a road is built, but others – such as noise – tend to increase as the level of congestion grows. Notice, however, that a crucial feature of both congestion and environmental costs is that although they result from an indvidual's journey, the individual does not bear them himself. He imposes them on other people. In the case of congestion costs they are imposed on other highway users, whereas in the case of environmental costs they are imposed primarily on non road users. Because these costs are borne by people other than the traveller we term them *external* costs.

Finally there is the category of costs that is borne, in the first instance, by the central or local government. Accordingly, we may call them *public-sector* costs; they cover road maintenance and repair work, traffic police services, street and traffic sign operations, and so on. Of course road users will pay for some of these costs indirectly through various tax payments, but they are different from private costs because there is no direct association between the costs incurred on an individual's behalf and the tax payment he makes.

The Efficient Level of Road Use

An efficient level of road use occurs when the net benefit obtained from using a road system (total benefits minus total costs) is maximised. Thus we need to take into account the level of benefit received by each traveller and all the costs, both private and external, that result from his journey. If we consider a group of road users, the sum of the individual benefits and costs associated with each one of them will indicate the total benefits and costs that arise for that particular volume of traffic. When the volume of traffic that maximises net benefit is achieved, we have an efficient level of road use. Let us now see whether this volume of traffic will be produced by the arrangements currently employed in Britain for the allocation of road space.

Traffic and Road Use in Britain

We shall demonstrate the level of road use that can be expected to occur under existing arrangements in Britain by using a simple example. Suppose we have a single stretch of urban motorway running from a suburban area to the city centre which is used by car commuters for their journey to and from work. Let us look at the costs and benefits that will result from their use of the road.

Costs

As we have seen there are a number of different categories of costs. In this instance we are particularly interested in the distinction between *private* and *external* costs. Moreover, to make our point as clear as possible, we shall restrict our consideration of external costs to *congestion* costs in the first instance, although we shall extend the analysis to include other externalities later on

Suppose, near the beginning of the road, we set up an observation point that enables us to count the number of vehicles passing per minute. We may express this as a *flow* of vehicles per minute. When the flow is low each vehicle will be able to travel freely at its chosen speed – subject to speed restrictions – without impeding other vehicles. However, as the flow increases a point will be reached at which vehicles begin to delay each other; the delays will tend to become greater as the flow continues to increase. The road becomes congested. As additional cars join the flow they slow it down and impose costs on others. Typically, time costs form a large part of congestion costs. The simple numerical example shown in Table 8.1 indicates the nature of the problem.

The first column shows the flow of vehicles per minute. To keep the arithmetic simple we have shown these in units of a single vehicle per minute. In practice such increases would probably have a negligible effect on costs; however, the principle is not affected by the unit of measurement adopted. The second column shows the time it takes for each vehicle to travel along the road at different levels of flow. This is the private time cost per vehicle for the journey. When there is no congestion, the journey time taken by each vehicle is ten minutes. This situation prevails up to a flow of four vehicles per minute; beyond this point congestion begins and journey times become longer. At five vehicles per minute the journey takes eleven minutes, at seven vehicles it takes sixteen minutes, and at ten vehicles it takes over thirty minutes. The important point to note is that when additional vehicles join the stream

TABLE 8.1
Vehicle Flows and Time Costs

Vehicle flow (cars per minute) (1)	Journey time per vehicle (minutes) (2)	Total journey time —all vehicles $[(1) \times (2)]$ (3)	Increase in total journey time as flow increases by one vehicle (4)	Cost *imposed* but not *borne* by last vehicle $[(4)-(2)]$ (5)
1	10	10		
2	10	20	10	0
3	10	30	10	0
4	10	40	10	0
5	11	55	15	4
6	13	78	23	10
7	16	112	34	18
8	20	160	48	28
9	26	234	74	48
10	34	340	106	72

they slow down *all* the traffic. It is not just the additional vehicle that travels at the new, lower speed, but also the traffic that was on the road before the increase in flow. For example, when the flow increases from four to five vehicles per minute the journey time for all motorists becomes eleven minutes each; the vehicle that did not originally travel takes eleven minutes while the four vehicles that previously took ten minutes now also take eleven minutes. Hence we may say that the additional motorist has imposed a *congestion* cost upon the original motorists.

If we look at columns (3), (4), and (5) in Table 8.1 we can see the extent of these costs. Column (3) shows the total journey time taken by all vehicles. For example, at a flow of four vehicles per minute total journey time is forty minutes (4 × 10); at five vehicles it is fifty five minutes (5 × 11), and so on. Column (4) shows the increase in total costs as the flow increases by one vehicle; for instance if we look at the row showing five vehicles per minute we see that the increase from four to five vehicles adds fifteen minutes to the total journey time (55–40). This sum of 15 minutes is attributable to the fifth vehicle that joins the flow. However, the fifth vehicle takes only eleven minutes to make the journey itself – see column (2), so the difference between eleven and fifteen minutes – four minutes – represents the congestion costs it imposes on other motorists. These congestion costs are shown in column (5).

In this example we have been concentrating on the way that costs change as *additional* vehicles join the flow; that is we have been looking at the costs attributable to the *marginal* vehicle. In previous chapters we have termed such costs *marginal* costs. Moreover, we have shown that at each level of flow the costs arising from the marginal vehicle can be broken down into two components: the private cost and the congestion (or external) cost. Together they comprise the social cost arising from the marginal motorist's journey, that is marginal private cost + marginal congestion cost = marginal social cost.

An alternative way of presenting this information, which shows the distinction between private and social costs very clearly, is to depict it in the form of a diagram. This has been done in Figure 8.1. The horizontal axis shows the flow of vehicles per minute on the road. The vertical axis measures the

FIGURE 8.1
Vehicle Flow and Journey Costs

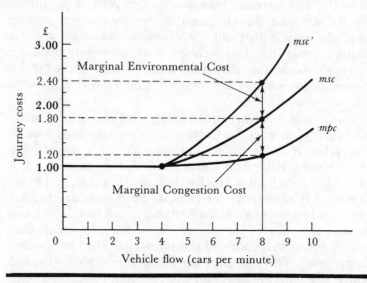

cost of using the road. In our numerical example we expressed these costs in minutes. However, a number of ways have been devised by economists for estimating the monetary values that motorists attach to their time. For example, situations in which travellers have the choice between fast-expensive and slow-cheap modes of transport, and hence have the opportunity to 'buy' time savings, have been used to estimate the value of time implicit in individuals' decisions. Thus we can express the costs in money terms. This will also enable us to combine a range of market priced and non-priced items later on.

The two curves in the diagram show the way marginal private costs (*mpc*) and marginal social costs (*msc*) change as the vehicle flow on the road increases. Up to a flow of four vehicles per minute there is no congestion, and therefore as traffic increases the cost per vehicle journey remains constant at £1.00. Because there is no congestion, marginal private cost equals marginal social cost. At a flow above four vehicles, congestion sets in and the marginal social cost associated with each vehicle becomes greater than the marginal private cost by an amount equal to the marginal congestion cost. For example, at a flow of eight vehicles, marginal private cost equals £1.20 whereas the marginal social cost equals £1.80; thus marginal congestion cost equals 60p. This means that the eighth vehicle to join the flow imposes a cost of 60p on all the other vehicles as well as incurring a cost of £1.20 itself. As can be seen from the figure, when the flow increases and congestion becomes more serious, the divergence between private and social costs becomes larger. Hence at a flow of ten vehicles per minute the marginal congestion cost equals 80p.

So far we have restricted our attention to congestion costs but we can quite easily introduce other forms of external costs. For example, suppose the noise and pollution suffered by residents adjoining the highway become more acute as the level of congestion increases. This will mean that *environmental* costs are being incurred. These can be represented in our diagram by constructing a second marginal social cost schedule such as the *msc'* curve above the previous one. Now the discrepancy between the marginal private cost and marginal social cost is greater than before because an additional category of externalities has been included. Thus at a flow of eight vehicles per minute *mpc* will remain at £1.20 but *msc'* will now be £2.40; marginal external costs will comprise 60p of marginal congestion costs plus 60p of marginal environmental costs.

Benefits

The benefit that each potential motorist will derive from using the road for his or her journey to work will depend on the importance placed upon the particular journey: some will derive considerable benefit while others, who have access to alternative means of transport or places of employment, or can make the journey at a different time or by a different route, will derive less benefit. If we rank road users according to the level of benefit they obtain from a journey we can see the extent of these variations. A typical pattern is portrayed in Figure 8.2.

The diagram shows the flow of vehicles per minute that may

FIGURE 8.2
Vehicle Flow and Journey Benefits

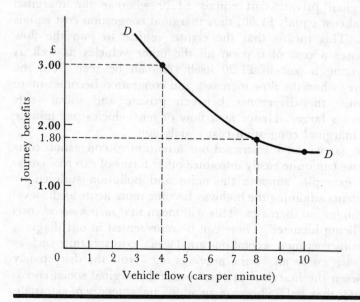

travel along the road, and the level of benefit that each motorist would derive from using the road. Once again we have assumed that each motorist is able to express his level of benefit in terms of money and that the economist will be able to infer these benefits from the cost the motorist is willing to incur to use the road. The curve *DD* expresses this information. For example *DD* shows that the fourth motorist to join the flow of traffic values the journey at £3.00 whereas the eighth road user attaches a value of only £1.80 to it. Thus each point on *DD* indicates the level of benefit received by the last car user to join the flow. Therefore we can say that it indicates the level of benefit obtained by the *marginal* vehicle user or, put alternatively, it is a *marginal benefit* curve. As we have confined our attention to the benefits received by individual motorists, it is of course a marginal *private* benefit curve. However, as the incidence of externalities is not as widespread in the case of benefits as it is in the case of costs, at least as far as road users are concerned (drivers who enjoy travelling in convoys provide an exception!), we may assume that marginal private benefits (*mpb*) equal marginal social benefits (*msb*). Thus the *msb* associated with the eighth motorist's journey along the road is £1.80.

Notice that if the cost of travelling along the road was in fact £1.80, eight motorists would make the journey. The first seven motorists would do so because they value a journey more highly than its cost to them, whereas the eighth motorist just finds it worthwhile to make the trip because its value to him is equal to the cost. The ninth potential motorist would not travel because he values the trip at less than its cost. Thus we can see that, as well as being a marginal benefit curve, *DD* is a travel demand curve; it shows the number of motorists that will travel at each level of cost.

The Level of Road Use

Having looked at the costs and benefits that arise from the use of roads for journeys to work, we are now in a position to see what the level of road use will be under existing allocation arrangements, and to compare it with the efficient level. This may be done more easily by bringing the information contained in our two previous diagrams together in a single diagram as in Figure 8.3. Once again the diagram measures the flow of vehicles per minute and records costs and benefits in terms of £s. Under the present arrangements for allocating road space in Britain we may expect an equilibrium flow of ten vehicles per minute. The intersection of the *DD* and *mpc* curves at this traffic volume indicates that the tenth driver to join the flow attaches a value of £1.60 to his journey, which is equal to the private costs he is called on to incur. Hence this traveller will just find it worthwhile to make the trip. No further car users will join the flow because they do not value the journey as highly as the cost they would have to incur. However, we can see from the diagram that £1.60 is not the total addition to costs arising from the tenth vehicle's journey, since there are congestion and environmental costs that he imposes on others.

FIGURE 8.3
Costs, Benefits and Road Use

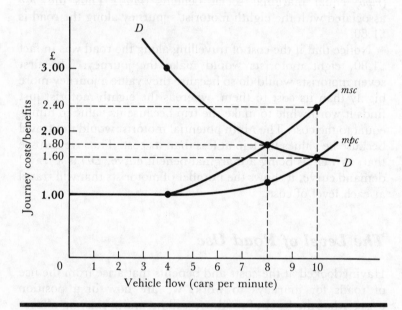

These are depicted by the difference between the *msc* and *mpc* curves, that is 80p. Thus the benefit that the tenth motorist obtains is less than the total costs (private plus external costs) of his journey. If the flow were reduced below ten vehicles the discrepancy between *mpb* (= *msb*) and *msc* would be reduced, until at a flow of eight vehicles per minute *msb* = *msc*. At this traffic volume the benefit derived by the last motorist to enter the flow, that is £1.80, is equal to the sum of the costs he imposes both on himself and others. This is the efficient level of road use.

It would appear, therefore, that a system of road use that does not require the car user to take account of the external costs of his actions will lead to an excessive number of vehicles using the roads. Indeed this is a feature of all congested resources whether they are roads or railways, beaches or airports. What is required is a mechanism for regulating use. In the next section we shall consider some of the responses to this problem that have been put forward in connection with the regulation of road use in Britain and elsewhere. (Before going on to to this however, you might like to test your understanding of the economics of congestion by considering why the socially efficient level of road use does not imply *zero* congestion.)

Government Policies

Schemes for controlling road use may be divided into two general categories: those employing taxes/subsidies and those using regulation. From the first group we shall discuss (i) proposals for levying congestion taxes on vehicles travelling on congested roads and (ii) the subsidisation of (typically publicly owned) mass transport services which create less congestion per passenger mile. The second group will include traffic management schemes which seek to reduce traffic congestion by regulating the way in which motorists may use the road system.

Congestion Taxes

Because road congestion arises as a result of excess demand for a scarce resource, a number of economists have suggested that the problem could be remedied by the extension of the price mechanism to road use. This, it has been argued, could be achieved by the introduction of congestion tolls or taxes. To see how these would work consider the example used in the previous section. It will be recalled that if motorists are left to their own devices they will ignore the external costs imposed through their use of the road. However, if a congestion tax was introduced that raised the marginal private cost of a journey to the marginal social cost, this would ensure that only those drivers who valued their journey at or above its marginal social cost would use the road. In this way traffic could be reduced to produce an efficient level of road use. In terms of Figure 8.3 this would be achieved by levying a tax of 60p per vehicle if the flow were eight vehicles. This would mean that the private cost incurred by the eighth driver (that is, the one who, after ranking, is shown to value the journey least highly of the eight on the road) would be raised to its marginal social cost level of £1.80.

Hence through the introduction of congestion taxes road users would be made aware of the social costs of their actions. As rush-hour commuting became more expensive, traffic volumes would be reduced in a number of ways. Some drivers might form car pools. Others might shift to public transport where the tax per passenger on a fifty-seat bus would be substantially less. In the longer term, commuters might look for employment in less congested areas where they would not have to pay these taxes, while firms confronted by workers demanding higher wages to compensate for higher travel costs would also have an incentive to relocate in less congested areas.

Notice, however, that in a congested area taxes would only need to be applied where a discrepancy existed between *mpc* and *msc* (that is where congestion occurs). If the *DD* curve in Figure 8.3 intersected the cost schedule at a traffic volume of four vehicles or less, where *msc = mpc*, no toll would be necessary. This point is significant because fluctuations in traffic flow throughout the day often mean that taxes will need to be applied on the same stretch of road at some times but not at others. This brings us to the problem of deciding on exactly how congestion taxes could be implemented. In essence there is a choice between methods of involving *indirect charges* and those involving *direct charges*.

Indirect charges

Car owners are already subject to a number of indirect taxes on road use. These include value-added tax on car sales, road fund licences and petrol taxes. Consequently, it has been argued that it would be straightforward administratively to extend these taxes to deal with road congestion. Unfortunately, however, none of them is ideally suited for this purpose.

Value-added taxes and vehicle licences are taxes on ownership rather than use; that is they are payable in full even if the car is driven on public roads for only one mile per year. Thus the economist terms them *fixed* costs. However, what matters to the motorist when considering a particular journey, and to the traffic authority concerned with the social costs of that journey, is the extra cost the journey is going to incur – that is its *marginal* cost. These taxes do not affect marginal cost. So while they may make some contribution to rationing road use – by reducing the demand for car ownership – they are not really suited to this purpose because they do not vary according to how much a car is used and whether it travels in congested urban areas or in deserted rural areas.

Petrol taxes, on the other hand, are related to the amount of use made of the roads. They are also related to some extent to the level of congestion in an area, because journeys in congested conditions tend to increase petrol consumption. Also, larger vehicles that take up more road space than smaller cars also tend to be heavier on petrol consumption. For all these reasons there have been several proposals for using petrol taxes more widely as a means of increasing the costs of motoring in congested areas. The most common proposal is for an additional tax levy on petrol sold in the districts designated as 'congested'. Such an arrangement, however, is bound to encounter a number of serious problems. In particular, it is certain that many car users would try to avoid the tax by buying their petrol in low-tax areas for use in high-tax areas. The incidence of these 'ferrying' trips could be expected to increase with the number of tax boundaries and the size of the tax differentials.

A third option that has been tried in some cities is a parking tax. These taxes are levied on parked vehicles and are designed to deter vehicles from entering congested districts. (Notice, however, that a parking tax does not have the same objective as a normal parking fee. The tax is designed specifically to regulate the volume of traffic in an area, whereas fees are generally used to pay for the provision and maintenance of meters or car parks.) This device is not subject to the type of avoidance encountered in the petrol tax case; all those motorists who wish to park in the designated area are liable to the tax. It does, however, have the disadvantage that it is only levied on those vehicles that actually park; it would not deter traffic that travels through congested districts but does not stop there.

The arrangements described above suggest that the main

methods for levying indirect charges for road use are deficient in one way or another. In all cases there are theoretical or practical problems of relating them to the use made of the road system. What is required is a system that actually bases charges on the external costs that arise from the use made of particular sections of the road network. To achieve this objective we really need to consider *direct* charges.

Direct charges

One method of directly charging for road use that is used extensively in other countries, and was once commonplace in Britain, is to levy tolls. In fact, tolls are still used on certain bridges and tunnels in Britain. However, an important criticism of the way that a typical toll road pricing system operates is that it is rarely used to achieve an efficient level of use on the road. This is because tolls are generally levied to produce revenues to finance road construction and maintenance, or for general budgetary purposes, instead of regulating road use. Indeed, tolls are often used in a perverse fashion because they are levied on fast, uncongested routes that – for congestion purposes – do not require charges. By the economist's standards these roads are under-utilised and so the price should be reduced.

These comments are not criticisms of the principle of toll roads but of the way they are operated at the present time. However, when we consider the way toll roads could be used to bring about efficient traffic volumes a number of problems become evident. In particular, the large number of toll booths that would be necessary to operate a flexible system, with differential charges on different sections of the road network, would be very expensive to administer. It would also produce enormous delays with resultant time loss costs. In the face of these difficulties, most experts have abandoned this approach and switched their attention to alternative methods of collection which, it is thought, would involve less heavy costs in terms of both time and money.

This has led to the suggestion of applying recent technological developments to road pricing by means of direct metering devices. These could record the number of miles each car travels in designated zones of a city, or the amount of time spent in each zone, and thereby provide a basis for subsequent charging. The meters could be either attached to the car or located at some central metering station. They would be activated manually by the driver (with accompanying measures to avoid evasion) or triggered by electronic devices set in the roads. Once activated, they would record units at different rates depending upon the level of congestion prevailing at the time. Meter readings could then be used to charge motorists in the same way as telephone or electricity companies charge their customers. Although this scheme might seem rather futuristic it was, in fact, considered in some detail by the government's Smeed committee nearly twenty years ago (Smeed, 1964). They concluded that it was both technically and economically feasible. It certainly appears, therefore, that the means for achieving an efficient level of road use have been available for some time. And yet nowhere in the world has this option been adopted. (Although some cities, such as Singapore, have introduced a system of charges for entry to the most seriously congested central-city areas and similar proposals have been made for London.) Possibly this is because, while congestion taxes may produce efficiency, they may fail to meet other objectives, such as equity.

Equity and congestion taxes

The purpose of levying a congestion tax is to reduce the number of vehicles on the roads. As a result, those people who continue to use the roads after the imposition of the tax will gain through shorter and more pleasant journeys. This will apply both to those people who previously travelled by car and those who travelled by bus. However, the reduction in congestion will have been achieved by deterring some car users from making their original journeys. Some of them will now make the journey by bus (where the tax per person is lower) while others will reschedule their trips at different times or by different routes (where congestion and the tax are lower). Some may cease to make the trip altogether, and others may seek alternative, less-congested work or shopping destinations. On balance these people are likely to suffer a loss in benefit from the introduction of a congestion tax. (Note that here we are talking about the loss of benefit resulting from not making a trip that was previously made, *not* from the payment of congestion taxes. If congestion taxes are returned to road users *as a group* – through the provision of new road capacity, etc. – they will not be a source of lost benefit in their own right.) This immediately raises a question of equity. Will these people be from low-income groups? Will congestion taxes force low-income travellers off the roads? Will car travel become a monopoly of the rich?

To answer these questions we really need a detailed knowledge of the incomes and preferences of different road users; only then could we forecast how each group would react to congestion taxes. While a certain amount of information is available it is insufficient to reach firm conclusions, and so we must content ourselves with a few general observations. It seems likely that the main beneficiaries would be (1) high-income car users who would prefer to pay a tax and save some of their relatively more valuable time and (2) low-income bus users who would benefit from improved services in less-congested conditions. The main losers are likely to be lower-income car users who would prefer to spend time (through congestion) instead of more money. Even here it is possible that some travellers may gain if they transfer to public transport which is sufficiently improved in the post-congestion tax situation to represent an improvement for them over pre-congestion tax car travel. Thus it is difficult to conclude what the equity implications of a congestion tax are; those at the top and bottom of the income distribution are likely to gain whereas at least some of those in the middle are likely to lose.

Moreover, these are only the direct, short-term consequences of the tax. In the longer term it could be expected to affect the level of property prices in a city, as these will be dependent on the costs of transport. Land values would tend to rise at the centre and fall at the periphery. At the same time rural areas would face lower taxes than urban areas. Ultimately this would affect the whole price structure of goods produced in rural and urban locations. A complete evaluation of the long-term equity consequences of all these effects would clearly be a complex task. However, this brief discussion has identified some of the issues that would need to be resolved in order to assess whether the equity objective is likely to be met. It is, no doubt, partly a result of the uncertainty surrounding this question that alternative methods of traffic restraint have been favoured by politicians.

Subsidies to Public Transport

Most cities operate publicly owned bus and/or rail services which are able to carry passengers in a more fuel-efficient fashion, and with lower congestion and environmental costs per traveller, than private car transport. Would it not, therefore, be possible to reduce road congestion by subsidising public transport fares and thereby attracting car users from the roads? Moreover, would it not also directly benefit low-income public transport users and low-to-middle income car users (who would transfer to public transport), and therefore be more equitable and feasible politically? Clearly the large number of cities both in Britain and abroad which do subsidise public transport suggest that these views command widespread support. But are they valid?

On the question of efficiency, it has been argued that the marginal *social* cost of bus travel is below its marginal *private* cost; additional bus passengers who transfer from private cars produce a reduction in external congestion costs. (A bus is equivalent to three to four cars in terms of congestion generating capacity but will carry up to forty to fifty times the number of passengers.) This, it is argued, establishes the case for a public transport subsidy. However, available evidence suggests that the demand for bus travel has an extremely low price elasticity of demand; that is, demand increases by only a small amount in response to fare reductions. Hence even very large bus subsidies are unlikely to secure appreciable reductions in the level of congestion.

It may be, however, that the second-best policy of subsidising public transport is preferred because of its alleged equity advantages. But statistics on public transport usage show that a large proportion of passengers is drawn from higher-income groups (Le Grand, 1982, ch. 6). This is particularly true of certain services such as the London underground system. Thus subsidisation for reasons of equity will need to take account of the socio-economic composition of passengers on particular parts of the network. Moreover, questions of equity should also consider the source of the subsidy; benefits would clearly be received by the users of public transport but who would bear the costs? This is an issue which has attracted an enormous amount of attention recently, resulting in large part from the Greater London Council's decision to introduce a 'Fairs Fare' policy. This introduced substantial reductions in bus and underground fares in an attempt to attract passengers back to the declining public transport system. Under existing subsidy arrangements in Britain, however, public transport subsidies are financed primarily from local government revenues. This means that local ratepayers pay for fare reductions. In reasonably self contained towns and cities, such as Sheffield, subsidisation is paid for by ratepayers who are also, by and large, transport users. In London, however, much of the opposition to the 'Fairs Fare' policy arose because ratepayers were paying for fare reductions received by non-resident commuters, tourists etc. This, it was argued, was inequitable. Many argued that where such 'leakages' of subsidy are so widespread, subsidisation should be financed by central rather than local government. The political controversy surrounding the 'Fairs Fare' policy and the eventual declaration of its illegality attest to the complexity of the issues involved.

Even this brief discussion has indicated that the range of gainers and losers who need to be considered to establish the equity implications of public transport subsidies are not as clearly definable as it might seem at first sight.

Traffic Management

So far we have discussed schemes which seek to reduce congestion through the use of the price mechanism. In practice, however, most cities have tended to rely far more heavily on planning or traffic management methods. These include the use of one-way systems, bus lanes, parking restrictions, traffic free areas, and park-and-ride schemes. More recently, proposals for the issue to essential users of permits that would selectively restrict entry to congested areas have been suggested. To some extent the reliance upon such schemes reflects the dominance of transport planners and engineers – with their emphasis upon physical design solutions – within the policy decision-making process. Moreover it is probably felt that such schemes are more acceptable politically than road pricing or subsidy proposals. Most traffic management schemes tend to be accepted after some initial dissent from particular interest groups, whereas pricing proposals often encounter far more lasting opposition. However, economists argue that traffic management methods suffer from a major disadvantage: they restrict the expression of *freedom of choice* and thereby produce *inefficiency*.

A pricing system, it is argued, enables users to state their intensity of preference by the price they are willing to pay to use a road. It thereby gives a means of distingushing between essential and inessential traffic as determined by the users' preferences rather than by those of the traffic authorities. The flexibility of road pricing enables road users who value their journey at a price equal to, or greater than, the costs they impose on others to undertake the journey, whereas a traffic management restriction does not allow the expression of these personal tastes. (Note that there are strong similarities between the argument for preferring tax/subsidies to regulation in the transport case and the argument for preferring tax/subsidies to regulation in the case of pollution control – see Chapter 5). Against this view, others argue that this freedom of choice is so dependent on an individual's income, and the distribution of income is so unequal, that for all but a few people their preferences are dominated by income limitations. Supporters of this view would maintain that traffic management solutions are least equitable in the sense that everyone is treated equally.

Summary

Congestion arises when there is an excess demand for a scarce resource. Typically it is associated with service industries that experience peaks in demand. In this chapter we have concentrated on one manifestation of the problem – urban road congestion. Because it arises through competition for a scarce resource, we have treated it as part of the general economic problem; that is, how do we allocate scarce road space among those groups who wish to use it? Once again society's main objectives have been defined in terms of *efficiency* and *equity*. The efficient level of road use occurs when the maximum level of net benefit is derived from using the roads. Under existing road use arrangements in Britain, however, it is argued that this aim is unlikely to be met because there is no incentive for the individual road users to take into account the *external (congestion and environmental)* costs they impose on others. In consequence, there are too many vehicles travelling on certain stretches of congested roads. Accordingly a number of proposals for reducing traffic volumes to the efficient level have been put forward. These include wider use of *petrol and parking taxes*; the introduction of direct *congestion taxes*; the *subsidisation of public transport* and various *traffic management schemes*. Of these, direct congestion taxes command most support among economists on efficiency grounds, although the subsidisation of public transport may be preferable on equity grounds. At the moment, however, insufficient empirical evidence exists to make an unambiguous judgement on this issue.

Further Reading

There are a number of textbooks devoted to the economics of transport which discuss urban congestion: Gwilliam and Mackie (1975) and Button (1982) are two which are recommended for the student with a basic background in economics. For the non-specialist, Thomson (1974) is probably more suitable. The latter author has also written an interesting book which, after a general discussion of urban transport issues, considers the transport systems of some of the world's major cities, Thomson (1978). Walters (1968) is probably still the best – if not the most accessible – discussion of road pricing principles. Nash (1982) provides a good treatment of the economics of public transport.

Questions for Discussion

1. How might a system of road pricing be used to assist investment decisions on new road building?
2. Because the external congestion costs that one road user imposes upon another are borne, in total, by road users as a group and do not affect non road users, they do not imply an inefficient use of resources. Do you agree?
3. Consider the case for and against selling licences which would be necessary for a vehicle to gain entry to the presently congested central areas of large cities.
4. Is queuing a more equitable means of dealing with congestion than using a pricing policy?
5. If public transport in cities was free it would solve the problem of traffic congestion? Do you agree?
6. What is 'peak load' pricing? What is its relevance for the transport industry?
7. At present bus companies have a public service operator obligation to provide a comprehensive service including services on sparsely used routes and/or at times of low demand. Do you think that pricing policy, instead of charging standard fares per mile, should reflect these variations in demand and costs per passenger mile?
8. Consider the arguments for and against abolishing road fund taxation and replacing it by additional taxes on petrol and diesel oil.
9. Time savings are a major benefit of most transport improvements. How do you think economists might go about valuing these savings?
10. It is sometimes argued by anti-road-building campaigners that building new roads does not solve traffic congestion because new roads generate additional traffic. Show how this possibility would affect the analysis carried out in this chapter.

The Regional Problem

9

A regional problem exists when there are substantial inequalities in the standards of living experienced by people living in different regions of a country. The most obvious manifestation of regional inequality occurs in the labour market, where certain regions consistently experience below national average levels of income and above average rates of unemployment. Thus in 1979–80 average household income in Great Britain was £134 per week, but regionally it varied from £117 per week in Yorkshire and Humberside to £153 per week in the South East. Similarly the national unemployment rate in 1980 was 7.4 per cent but this varied from 10.9 per cent in the North to 4.8 per cent in the South East. (For the UK as a whole the most depressed region was Northern Ireland, with an average household income of £113 per week and an unemployment rate of 13.7 per cent: *Regional Trends*, Central Statistical Office, 1982.) Associated with a lack of job opportunities, depressed regions often experience the out-migration of young, mobile workers and, as a consequence, are left with a population containing an above average number of elderly and dependent individuals. In 1980 the North West, the North, and the Yorkshire and Humberside regions lost 36 000 persons through out-migration while, interestingly, the main regions to benefit from in-migration were the less urbanised areas of East Anglia and

194

the South West.

Apart from measures of economic welfare associated with employment conditions, there are other aspects of regional inequality which contribute towards differences in people's standards of living. Thus while some regions enjoy a pleasant environment and are well provided with parks, recreation space and leisure facilities, others still exhibit the legacy of earlier periods of industrial expansion which have left them despoiled and polluted. In other areas apparent rural tranquility often conceals a neglect of infrastructure and a lack of facilities associated with the long-run decline of agriculture. In both cases there is frequently an above average proportion of sub-standard housing and a lower standard of health care and education than is available in more prosperous regions. For example, the 1976 House Condition Survey shows that the three Northern regions referred to above had 7 per cent of their housing stock classified as unfit compared with only 3 per cent in the South East. Again only about 20 per cent of students in the Northern regions stay at school beyond the statutory minimum leaving age compared with over 30 per cent in the South East.

Of course, this emphasis upon *regional* inequality should not be taken to imply that regions do not display wide variations in prosperity within their boundaries. In fact the distribution of income between households within many regions is more unequal than the distribution of average incomes between regions. In particular, the dramatic decline of the inner-areas of the large conurbations within all regions, and the associated growth of employment in suburban, new town or previously rural locations, has posed a distinct *urban* problem where the inequalities described above are concentrated within much smaller areas. Nevertheless, despite these developments, the persistence of readily observable differences between regions continues to concern policy-makers and so we shall concentrate upon this level of analysis. The chapter is organised as follows: in the first section we consider why, given society's objectives, regional inequality is undesirable; this is followed by a discussion of the market system and regional inequality; finally, we analyse the various government policies that have been used to try to reduce regional inequality.

Objectives

As in other chapters we shall consider government aims in connection with regional policy in terms of the general categories of efficiency and equity.

Efficiency

The existence of regional inequality often means that a country is failing to use its resources efficiently. For example, consider a situation in which there is widespread unemployment in the north-east of England but labour shortages in the south-east. Clearly if the unemployed labour in the north was available for work in the south, firms would be able to fill their vacancies and increase output. In this way national output would increase. The simultaneous existence of unemployment and unfilled vacancies is the most extreme form of labour productivity differences between regions but they are also reflected, albeit to a lesser extent, in differences in earnings. For instance, consider two bricklayers, one working in the low-wage economy of the north and the other in the more prosperous south. If we know that their skills are identical and that they work equally hard, the higher earnings of the southern worker will reflect greater productivity resulting from factors such as the superior tools and equipment with which he works, the way management organises his time and the supply of materials which he uses, etc. If the less productive northern bricklayer was working in the south his skills would be put to better use and his productivity would increase. Thus an efficient allocation of labour would require marginal productivity to be equalised between regions; only then would it be impossible to increase national output by a (marginal) worker moving from one region to another.

The same arguments apply to the market for capital equipment. In this instance regional inequality will mean an excess supply of capital equipment in some regions and shortages elsewhere. Once again this is likely to result in productivity differences between units of capital equipment in different regions. Consequently national output would be increased if the excess capital equipment in depressed regions, with a low or zero productivity, was availble for use in areas where desired output exceeded the capacity of the existing stock of capital equipment to produce it. (Obviously the kinds of goods and services produced vary between regions, and much capital equipment is fixed in location and specific to a particular product. Consequently the scope for moving existing equipment is very limited. But the efficiency objective remains important for deciding upon the location of new investments in capital equipment).

Therefore we may conclude that an efficient allocation of resources between regions would be one in which the marginal product of capital and labour was equalised. This would mean that it would be impossible to increase national output by a reallocation of resources between regions. (See Chapter 1 for a general discussion of marginal conditions and efficiency.) At present the persistence of regional inequalities in the earnings of both labour and capital suggest that resources are allocated inefficiently. However, a word of caution is in order. Not all differences in earnings reflect inefficiency; within a market system some jobs command higher earnings than others because they require more skill, education and training, and regional inequality may simply reflect a higher proportion of highly skilled jobs in some regions. But despite this qualification, there is considerable evidence that much regional inequality is not of this type; this is the regional problem.

Equity

We have defined the regional problem as a state of inequality in the living standards of people living in different areas of the country. Just as general inequality in the distribution of income between rich and poor households may signify a failure to achieve an equitable distribution – especially if the inequality results from circumstances over which individuals have only limited control – so inequality between households living in different regions may also be unacceptable on equity grounds. This inequality is particularly apparent in terms of employment opportunities where workers, especially young workers, with comparable levels of skill and willingness to work find their prospects of employment crucially dependent upon where they live. Moreover, a persistent division between high-income areas and low-income depressed regions is likely to lead to a concentration of cultural and other facilities in the better-off regions thereby reinforcing feelings of regional deprivation. Considerations such as these suggest that the equity objective in regional policy requires a reduction in inequality or, put alternatively, the achievement of an acceptable degree of *regional balance*. (Opinions about what is acceptable may, of course, differ: however, the alternative definitions of equity between two individuals discussed in Chapter 1 can be applied, with a little modification, to specify equity between regions.)

The Market System and Regional Balance

How can regional balance be obtained? One theory is that just as the market system can be used to allocate resources between different firms and industries, so it can be used to bring about an efficient allocation between different regions. According to this theory, the fact that the market has not produced this result is due to the existence of specific market failures which, once identified, may be removed or overcome. Against this view, an alternative theory has been put forward by Professor Gunnar Myrdal. He claims that even a market system free of these failures cannot be expected to establish regional balance; indeed, it is the natural tendency of the market to produce a regional problem. We shall look at both of these theories.

A Spatial Market System

We shall continue with the example of bricklayers to see how the market will allocate their work between two regions; the prosperous south and the depressed north. In the south, economic prosperity leads to a high level of demand for new houses, factories, schools and other types of construction work that require bricklayers' services. On the other hand, there is far less demand for building work in the north. This state of affairs

FIGURE 9.1
The Allocation of Bricklayers between Two Regions

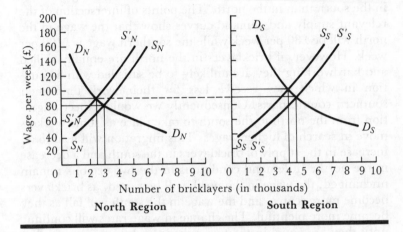

North Region   South Region

is depicted in Figure 9.1. The two diagrams show the demand for and supply of bricklayers' services in each region. The wages paid per week are recorded on the vertical axes and the number of bricklayers demanded by building firms, and the number offering themselves for work, are measured on the horizontal axes. A comparison of the two regional demand curves, $D_s D_s$ and $D_n D_n$, shows that at each wage rate the services of a greater number of bricklayers will be required in the south than in the north. For example, at a wage of £60 per week 7000 bricklayers will be demanded in the south but only 5000 in the north. The initial supply curves in each region, $S_n S_n$ and $S_s S_s$, are very similar. This indicates that there are no great differences in the number of bricklayers available for work at each wage rate in the north and south. Both curves are upward-sloping showing that as the wage rate rises more bricklayers will present themselves for work; conversely, as the wage rate drops, fewer are available. These changes in the supply of labour will result from bricklayers shifting into and out of the trade as employment opportunities and wages vary in relation

to competing trades and industries. (The scope for such movement will depend largely on the skills required in alternative
jobs. In reality, mobility in bricklaying will be less than in, say,
unskilled labouring.) Now initially, because the demand for
their services is greater, bricklayers will receive a higher wage
in the south than in the north. The points of intersection of the
relevant supply and demand curves show that the wage in the
north will be £80 per week while the southern wage is £100 per
week. However, if bricklayers in the north are equally skilled
and hardworking they are unlikely to be satisfied with a situation in which they receive less for their work than their
southern counterparts. Consequently we would expect migration from the north to the south to take place as some workers
move in search of higher wages. This migration will lead to an
increase in the supply of bricklayers in the south and a decrease
in the north. If demand conditions in the two regions remain
unchanged, the wage in the north will be raised, as bricklayers
become more scarce, and the wage in the south will fall as they
become more plentiful. The change in wage rates will continue
until they are equal in the two regions and there is no further
incentive for migration. The supply curves $S'_n S'_n$ and $S'_s S'_s$ in
Figure 9.1 represent the labour supply conditions in the two
regions after migration has taken place. At the new equilibrium
wage rage of £90 per week there will be 500 more bricklayers
than previously in the southern region and 500 fewer in the
north.

By a similar process, capital equipment can be expected to
be allocated between regions until there is no variation in the
earnings that it yields in different parts of the country. For an
investor is unlikely to be happy with a 10 per cent return from
an item of equipment, when the same equipment is earning
other investors 15 per cent elsewhere. However, as we pointed
out earlier, it is often impossible physically to move an item of
capital equipment from one region to another in the way that
labour can move. The scope for transporting existing power
stations or car plants is very limited! This means that decisions
on location are confined primarily to new investments, that is,
when new power stations or car plants are built. (This has a
bearing on the *mobility* of capital as we shall see in the next
section.)

Thus the market system may be expected to allocate factors of production between regions in a way that equalises their incomes, and in this way regional balance will be achieved. However, the discussion of the regional problem given at the beginning of this chapter suggests that it has not done so. One reason for this may be that there are specific market failures which have prevented it from operating efficiently.

Spatial Market Failures

It is possible to identify a number of possible sources of spatial market failure. In this section we have concentrated on two of these: factor immobility and externalities.

Factor immobility

A crucial feature of the spatial market system is factor mobility. Only if labour and capital can be induced to move between regions will the market be able to allocate resources in the way we have described. Without this mobility disparities between regions will persist. In reality there are a number of reasons why labour and capital may be immobile. First let us look at *labour* immobility.

The incentive for labour to migrate is provided by the prospect of higher earnings elsewhere. However the prospective migrant will also be concerned about the costs of movement. These will include travel costs and, more important, the resettlement costs – in terms of time and money – of changing homes. Most people live in houses they own themselves or in local authority dwellings, and in both cases resettlement costs may be considerable. The time and money involved in selling one house and buying another in a different part of the country can be substantial, while local authorities usually require households to qualify for housing by serving a period on their waiting lists. The private rented sector of the housing market, in which the costs of movement are relatively low, has for a variety of reasons (see Chapter 4) dwindled in size until it is now very small; this has had the incidental effect of reducing labour mobility.

In addition to these direct costs there are other, less tangible – but nevertheless real – costs of movement. Depending on their personal circumstances and how long they have lived in an area, most people will have built up a network of family ties and social contacts. If movement to another area means severing these ties most people will be averse to it. The further away from their original home people are required to move the greater will be the loss of contact with their old social environment and, therefore, the greater the compensation in terms of increased earnings they will require to overcome their dislike of moving. Overall, workers will require the increase in earnings obtained by migration to be at least equal to the sum of the direct and intangible costs of movement; if the increase is less they will not move. Consequently if the nature of regional migration required to establish regional balance involves movement over considerable distances, but individuals are well established in local communities and are averse to moving, then quite large earnings differences may persist. (Of course not all earnings differences signify market failure and inefficiency. A full specification of the costs of movement shows that inequality may persist because the benefits of movement are less than the costs.)

A second obstacle to full labour mobility may arise because the surplus labour in depressed or under-developed regions may not have the skills that are required by industry in the expanding regions. This problem is not specific to the regional case, as it may arise in any situation where the skills of the work force do not match the demands of the growing industries; however, it is often a particular problem in the case of those regions which have been heavily dependent on a few industries that are now in decline. If the work force comprises older workers who have spent many years learning skills that are now redundant, there is often great difficulty in equipping them for completely new employment. Even in less extreme cases, where regions are not dependent on just a few industries, the different employment structures between areas can act as an impediment to labour mobility; the labour requirements of high-technology, microprocessor-based industries, for example, are very different to those of much traditional manufacturing.

Capital immobility may arise for a number of reasons. To

start with changes in the allocation of capital equipment depend largely upon the rate at which new investment in plant and machinery takes place. As this usually represents only about 5 per cent per year of the existing stock of equipment in any year, any reallocation of equipment between regions necessitated by a change in demand or supply conditions will be subject to lengthy time lags. For the short-to-medium term, production will be dependent upon a capital stock built up in response to demand and supply conditions in the past. On the other hand, however, we should note that the funds which are used to finance spending on capital equipment can be moved around the country very easily, often requiring no more than the appropriate entries in bank ledger sheets. Hence capital has no 'home ties' of the type that inhibit labour mobility.

Uncertainty represents another reason why capital mobility may be restricted. Firms contemplating expansion often lack information about potential sites in unfamiliar areas. Acquiring information involves incurring certain costs in return for uncertain benefits, for a firm may search for some time without identifying a suitable site. Faced with this prospect many firms will choose to minimise uncertainty and invest in areas they know best – and because they are, by definition, expanding firms they are likely to be located in prosperous rather than declining regions. Even when information on the rates of return that can be expected in depressed or backward regions is obtained, there may be a tendency to associate a high level of risk with such investments. If these investments are genuinely more risky it is correct to reduce the expected return by an amount that compensates for the greater risk. However, it is often the case that a firm's views of a region are disproportionately affected by the poor performance of past investments which may in no way reflect the probable performance of future projects.

A final reason why capital may be immobile is its link with managerial or entrepreneurial immobility. This is primarily an instance of labour mobility but, because management makes the actual decisions about the location of capital equipment, it is probably best to include it alongside considerations of capital mobility. The theory of the spatial market system assumes that capital will be allocated to the areas where it yields the greatest rate of return. Even where this assumption is relaxed it is generally assumed that a firm strives after some financial target such as growth or sales maximisation. However, in recent years a number of investigators have questioned the validity of these assumptions. In particular, a large amount of work has concentrated on the actual decision-makers – the managers or entrepreneurs – and the way they make decisions in cases where their places of residence will be affected. Such work has suggested that decisions about changes in location will often reflect the decision-maker's personal preferences about living in a particular area of the country. If a region has an unattractive physical environment and a lack of recreational facilities, managers may feel that they or their colleagues would be unhappy living there. The troubles in Nothern Ireland have undoubtedly deterred a number of investment projects on these grounds. Conversely, a prosperous region with a well-developed range of leisure-time activities may well offer great attraction.

External costs and benefits

Under a market system the migration of labour and movement of capital will take place in response to private earnings differentials that exist between regions. However, there may be external costs and benefits associated with migration that firms and individuals do not take into account. If this is so, private costs and benefits will not coincide with social costs and benefits and an inefficient spatial allocation of resources will result.

For example, one of the outcomes of workers migrating to prosperous areas will be an increase in the demand placed upon the public facilities in these areas. If these facilities previously were being under-utilised then there will be little to worry about; but if they were operating at or close to full capacity problems will arise. Within the health sector the number of patients per doctor may be expected to increase, resulting in longer waiting times in surgeries; similarly increased demands upon hospital facilities will often lengthen queues for out-patient treatment or admissions. In education, class sizes will rise and the amount of attention able to be devoted to each child will fall commensurately. In housing, additional competition for council housing will increase waiting lists and exacerbate demand pressures in the private rental and owner-occupier sectors. Overall, a general deterioration in the quality of public services will occur. However, as it is unusual to give preferential treatment on the basis of length of residence in an area (with the possible exception of council house waiting lists), the lower level of service will not be confined to the new arrivals but will be common to everyone. For this reason we may say that the migrants have imposed external costs on the original users.

Of course the problem of deteriorating standards could be overcome by the provision of additional public service capacity. More doctors and teachers could be employed; in the longer run more schools, hospitals and houses could be built. However such a policy poses two problems. First, it may well be that there is not a shortage of capacity nationally, only in those regions gaining in population. This will mean that public services in the areas they leave are under-utilised. Clearly this will represent an inefficient use of the national stock of housing, hospitals etc. Second, the additional costs of providing extra facilities in congested areas are rarely levied directly upon those whose actions led to the expenditure – the migrants. Rather the costs are borne by the entire national or local population in the form of taxes or rates. So once again some of the costs of migration are borne by non-migrants. In circumstances where workers who migrate, and the firms who induce them to do so, fail to take account of these costs too much migration may result.

Conversely, if the movement of factors brings with it external benefits, there may well be too little transference under a market system. This situation sometimes arises in connection with a firm setting up in a depressed or under-developed area. The firm will be interested in its private returns but these may seriously underestimate the social benefits that its actions would produce. For example if a large, nationally known company establishes a factory in an under-developed area it may well act as a magnet for other, smaller firms, who would not have been confident enough to pioneer an untried location themselves. Thus the total benefit to an area in terms of increased incomes, reductions in unemployment, and so on will be far larger than the original firm's profits would suggest.

An Alternative View of the Market

In the previous section we identified two specific failures which, it was claimed, have prevented the market establishing regional balance. Against this view, Professor Gunnar Myrdal has put forward a completely different interpretation of the way the market operates (Myrdal, 1957). According to his theory the market, even when it is free from these failures, can be expected to lead to regional divergence instead of convergence.

Myrdal's account of the way the spatial market system operates stresses the cumulative nature of change. This leads to a tendency for richer areas to become progressively richer while poor regions become correspondingly poorer. He has argued that a region's initial advantage in terms of prosperity will act as a powerful source of attraction for subsequent capital investments which will, in turn, increase its prosperity even more. At the same time, the closure of a plant or factory in a depressed area will lead to a reduction in regional income and demand, to more closures and so to the onset of a downward spiral. Furthermore, according to this theory, the migration of workers from one region to another will lead to even greater discrepancies in earnings between areas than existed originally. The process works as follows. The inflow of workers into the prosperous regions will lead to an increase in the total demand for goods and services in the region and, as output expands to satisfy this demand, more incomes and jobs will be created which, in turn, will lead to further inflows of workers, and so on. On the other hand the departure of workers from the more backward regions will depress demand and output and lead to even greater stagnation. Myrdal's account differs from our earlier description of the market system by focusing on the *dynamic* process of total income change in a region which will either boost or depress the demand for its industries' products, and therefore change the demand for factors of production. In terms of the example dealing with bricklayers' earnings in

Figure 9.1, the demand curve in the southern region will shift to the right as migration into the region takes place, and regional income will increase (indicating that more bricklayers are required at each wage rate to satisfy the increased demand for building work), whereas the demand curve for bricklayers' services in the north will shift to the left. The changes in demand conditions will more than offset changes in supply conditions brought about by migration, and will lead to a greater disparity in regional wage rates.

Because of the tendency for a change in demand to set in motion further changes, which lead to even greater disparities between regions, this has been called a theory of cumulative or circular causation. It differs from the previous theory of market behaviour on the fundamental point that there will be no natural tendency for a country to move towards regional balance. In fact the tendency will be in the opposite direction, and as time passes disparities can be expected to become larger.

The empirical evidence which is available on patterns of comparative regional development does not enable us to say with any certainty which one of these theories offers the more convincing explanation of actual events. Within the United Kingdom regional disparities have persisted over many years but they have not tended to increase substantially. To some extent this is because Britain is a relatively highly developed and integrated economy in which developments in one region tend to spill over into other regions. A similar lack of cumulative divergence has been noted in the United States. Myrdal himself recognised these trends, but he attributed them to a greater tendency on the part of governments in more economically developed countries to intervene and counteract regional divergence. In many Third World economies of Africa and Asia the dynamic factors governing capital location and labour mobility tend to be far more pronounced.

Clearly the precise pattern of regional development observed in different countries is the result of both market forces and institutional arrangements, and it is difficult to establish empirically which theory provides the better explanation of regional disparities. However, the objective of regional balance requires some form of government intervention whichever theory one accepts. In one case it is required to remove or overcome factors which lead to market failure, whereas in the other case, policies are required to reverse the market process. Somewhat surprisingly the same main policy prescriptions may be relevant in both cases. In the next section we shall see why this is so.

Government Policies

Most countries have formulated some form of regional economic policy. We shall concentrate on the main issues that have arisen in the UK context. However, although the UK provides our examples, many of the problems and methods of analysis will be equally applicable to other countries. The formulation of policies designed to achieve regional balance can be divided into two stages. First it has to be decided whether surplus labour should be encouraged to move from depressed areas to regions where jobs are available, or whether capital should be invested in the depressed areas to provide jobs. That is, should policy aim to take work to the workers or workers to the work? Second, having made this decision, it remains to select policy instruments for the achievement of regional balance. As in other social policy areas, these may take the form of taxation/ subsidisation, direct provision or regulation.

Capital or Labour Movement?

The main argument usually advanced in favour of encouraging workers to move is that this policy does not interfere with firms' location decisions. The firm is left free to choose its most efficient location, bearing in mind its need for access to, for example, consumer markets, a suitable labour force and other firms making the components it uses. Critics of this view point out that firms' decisions are made for a variety of subjective reasons (as we mentioned in the context of managerial mobility) in which habit and inertia figure prominently. This means that some modification of private location decisions will not inevitably reduce efficiency. Indeed, efficiency may actually be increased if the information on which government decisions are based is better than that possessed by the firms themselves. This may well be the case when firms have highly imperfect information about such matters as labour availability or facilities in different regions. Furthermore, it is often argued that as industry becomes less dependent on specific sources of raw materials, such as coal or iron ore, and transport and tele-communications facilities become more sophisticated, there is greater flexibility in the choice of location – industry is more 'footloose' – and so arguments about inefficient locations, which result from a diversion from one site to another, become less important.

A second set of arguments favouring the movement of capital emphasises the greater difficulty and adverse consequences of encouraging labour mobility. On the first point, obstacles to labour mobility, particularly workers' attachment to their home environments, are likely to be more difficult to overcome than barriers to capital movement. Second, there are the external costs associated with labour migration. We have already discussed the external costs imposed through greater congestion in health, housing and education facilities in those areas receiving migrants, but there will also be costs borne by the remaining residents in the areas they leave. These arise because the costs of operating publicly financed services do not fall proportionally as the number of people using them declines. Thus the cost per non-migrating resident, in terms of charges or local government rate (i.e. tax) payments, will increase and/or the quantity and quality of these services will decline. This is particularly serious because the people who remain in the depressed areas are often the older residents who are less able to cope with these increased costs. Apart from these monetary external costs there will be another category of wider cultural external costs of migration. Many regions of the United Kingdom have distinctive characteristics of language, culture and environment that are a source of satisfaction to their residents and to visitors alike. A policy of labour migration that encourages the outflow of workers and the steady depopulation of these areas threatens the erosion of these distinctive regional features. Moreover, this tends to be an irreversible process: once a culture is destroyed it cannot be re-established.

Finally, supporters of the Myrdal thesis oppose policies of labour migration because, according to their interpretation of events, these will not establish regional balance. The process can only be expected to set off a cumulative chain which will lead to regional divergence.

Overall, therefore, although theories about the way the market operates – and hence the role of labour mobility – differ, there is some consensus about the broad lines of policy required to promote regional balance. In general, both schools of thought favour policies designed to encourage greater capital mobility, that is, policies which encourage industry to locate in areas in need of development. Not surprisingly, therefore, this has been the policy emphasis adopted by successive UK governments. However, although the general direction of policy has been agreed, the problem of selecting the appropriate instruments for the implementation of this policy remains.

A variety of policy instruments have been applied with the intention of encouraging industrial expansion in areas designated in need of development. These have sought to promote industrial growth that otherwise would not have taken place and/or divert industry from locations in more prosperous regions. As we mentioned above, three main categories of instruments may be identified: namely, tax/subsidy policies, direct provision and regulation.

Tax/Subsidy Policies

Subsidies have been used to influence firms' location decisions by altering the spatial structure of capital and labour costs. By reducing the costs of production below the market level in development areas, subsidies aim to attract firms to locations they would otherwise reject. Two main methods of subsidisation are open to policy-makers: they may choose to subsidise labour, so that the cost to the firm of each worker it employs is less the market wage rate, or they may subsidise capital so that its cost is below the market rate. (The cost of capital is the rate of interest the firm needs to pay on the funds it employs.) The preferred method of subsidy will depend on the government's precise policy objectives. If it is concerned with balance in employment opportunities, and wishes to eliminate large-scale regional unemployment in a short space of time, then a labour subsidy is likely to be more effective. Let us see why this should be the case.

To compare the relative impact of capital and labour subsidies on employment (and hence unemployment), we can look at the way a firm may be expected to react as it receives each type of subsidy. First let us consider a labour subsidy which reduces the cost of each worker to the firm. This will have two effects on employment: an *output* effect and a *substitution* effect. The output effect arises in the following manner. When the firm receives a subsidy the cost of producing its original output will be reduced and if it chooses to use these cost savings to increase its output, additional jobs will be created. The size of the output effect will depend upon the importance of labour in the production process; if labour costs form a large proportion of total costs (that is, the firm is 'labour-intensive'), then a labour subsidy will lead to large savings and a substantial increase in output and employment can be expected. Conversely, if the proportion is low (that is, the firm is 'capital-intensive'), a correspondingly smaller increase in employment will follow. The substitution effect will arise because a labour subsidy will make labour cheaper in relation to capital. Therefore there will be an incentive for the firm to substitute labour for capital where production techniques permit. This can also be expected to lead to an increase in employment. The size of the increase will depend on the size of the subsidy, the extent to which labour and machinery can be substituted in the production process and the length of time required to carry out this substitution. In some factories there will be considerable scope for employing workers on manual tasks that machines could be used to perform, whereas in other firms the methods of production are far more rigidly determined by technological considerations.

Now in the case of a capital subsidy the total costs of production will be reduced, and so some reduction in unemployment can be expected through the output effect. But the substitution effect will not work in the desired direction. The price of capital will fall relative to labour and so there will be an incentive to substitute capital for labour. If the substitution effect is strong enough it may more than offset the favourable output effect and lead to an overall reduction in employment. Therefore we may conclude that a labour subsidy can always be expected to lead to an increase in employment, but this will not inevitably be so in the case of a capital subsidy.

Given the theoretical expectation that a labour subsidy is likely to be more effective in reducing unemployment, it is somewhat surprising to find that this form of subsidy has not been applied very extensively in the United Kingdom. Indeed, prior to the introduction of the Regional Employment Premium in 1967 – which gave subsidies to manufacturing firms in the Development Areas according to the size of their labour force – subsidies had been almost totally related to capital expenditure. One argument that has been advanced to defend this bias concentrates on the long-term growth prospects of different firms. Our discussion above concentrated on short-term changes in the level of employment that may be expected to arise from the substitution and output effects. In the medium or long term it is likely that the output effect – the increase in employment that arises through growth in output – will be more important than substitution effects. This implies that policies aimed at securing a permanent reduction in unemployment should concentrate on assisting those industries which have long-term growth prospects and will provide a continuing impetus to the region, instead of simply aiding industries that mop up existing unemployment but are unlikely to survive competition from outside the region in the long run. Following this line of argument, it has been claimed that as technology progresses it is capital-intensive firms that will be more likely to grow and provide stable employment opportunities for the future. Thus capital subsidies are more likely to achieve long-run regional balance. However this view is not without its critics. Some regional economists claim that there is little evidence to suggest that capital-intensive firms grow more quickly (Brown, 1972). It is therefore open to question whether the most efficient policy has been adopted.

Nevertheless, as policy has favoured capital subsidisation and considerable sums have been spent in this way, we should look at the form it has taken in recent years. Basically, two metods of subsidisation have been employed: there have been a range of *grants* offered to assist building and the installation of capital equipment, and there have been *allowances* related to expenditure on capital equipment – which have been awarded through reduced tax demands made on firms' profits. The former set of inducements have generally been made outright at the beginning of a project, whereas the latter have accrued through time as annual tax payments become due. It has been argued that allowances are preferable to grants because they are only received when profits are made, and are therefore restricted to efficient firms rather than being allocated indiscriminately. However it has been pointed out that tax allowances discriminate in favour of multi-branch firms which may not make profits in their branches in development areas but are none the less able to claim tax concessions against their overall profits made in non-development areas. Such an opportunity is denied the single-branch firm setting up in a development area. Moreover, apart from assuming that private profit is necessarily an indicator of efficiency, the argument favouring allowances on efficiency grounds is open to the objection that certain firms that will be profitable in the long run may, nevertheless, fail to make profits initially. In such cases they will not receive assistance at the stage when it is vital to them, and may consequently fail to locate in the desired area. This is a special case of the 'infant-industry' argument which claims that some industries, like human infants, need nurturing in their early stages to enable them to flourish in later life.

Direct Provision

Direct provision in the case of regional economic policy does not usually involve the siting of nationalised industries or other public agencies within depressed regions (although it does sometimes take this form in the dispersal of certain civil service functions from London to South Wales and East Anglia) but rather the provision of facilities designed to make these regions more attractive to private firms. This policy has been pursued particularly in connection with 'growth pole' or 'growth point' strategies. These involve the selection of certain promising growth points within a region which then receive special assistance in the belief that they – through the mechanism of external benefits – will act as magnets for general expansion.

Direct provision has tended to take two main forms. On the one hand public agencies have prepared sites and built factories for incoming firms. These represent a form of direct capital subsidy which is given to the firm in kind in the belief that it will overcome some of the inertia towards movement that is considered to exist among industrialists. On the other hand, central and local government have financed investment in local transport and communications and other aspects of the infrastructure in a bid to make the environment more attractive to industry. These represent an attempt on the part of government to provide some of the external benefits that the firm would expect to reap if it located in one of the more prosperous regions.

The latter policy has been used quite extensively in Britain. In particular, substantial investments have been made in roads, as they were thought to be an essential precondition of regional growth. However, in recent years the wisdom of this view has been questioned. Doubts have arisen because of the small part of total costs of production that transport costs constitute. Also, a road may well have an adverse effect on an under-developed region. For example, a motorway linking a poorer region to a prosperous one will reduce the costs of transport from the poor to the prosperous area, but will also reduce costs in the reverse direction; this may open the previously protected regional market to the products of firms from outside the region, with a consequent decline in the domestic region's industries. At the same time doubts have been expressed about the cost-effectiveness of other infrastructure developments that improve the quality of the environment, questioning whether the budget could not have been spent more effectively through the use of direct subsidies to firms.

Regulation

Whereas the previous two sets of instruments have both tried to attract firms to development areas, direct controls have been used to prevent them from developing in areas not considered suitable for further expansion. This aim has been pursued by imposing specific bans on building in certain designated areas – notably London and the South-east. The policy has been operated through the system of Industrial Development Certificates (IDCs) introduced in the Town and Country Planning Act (1947), whereby a certificate has been required for any industrial development over a certain size. The scheme was extended to office development in 1964. Whereas certificates could usually be readily obtained for building in a development region, they have been far more rigidly rationed in other areas.

It is noticeable that direct controls differ from the previous instruments in that they do not seek to alter the spatial factor price structure facing firms. This could have been done by, for example, levying a tax on floor space or jobs in congested areas. Unlike subsidies they do not modify the market system; they replace it. Apart from the more general arguments that have been made in connection with government interference with firms' location decisions, it has been argued that the special danger of this more drastic policy is that firms denied the opportunity of developing in their chosen location – at any price – have either chosen not to invest at all or, alternatively, have chosen to locate abroad. The latter case has been claimed to be of special importance when multinational companies, whose location decisions span the whole world, are involved.

An Assessment of UK Regional Policy

The fact that regional inequality has stubbornly persisted despite the application of a wide range of regional economic policy instruments may be taken as evidence of the failure of this policy. Some of our comments which have been critical of various aspects of this policy may also suggest that we share this view. But such a conclusion would be incorrect. To assess properly the effect of regional policy it is necessary to compare existing regional inequalities with the pattern of inequality that would have existed in the absence of such a policy. Clearly, this is a difficult task for it involves establishing both (i) what *would* have happened as opposed to what *did* happen, and (ii) the impact upon this hypothetical situation of a complex set of policy instruments. Nevertheless, despite these formidable problems, the leading English regional economist, Professor A. J. Brown, feels that the regional policy of recent years has succeeded in diverting a substantial proportion of industrial investment to the development areas and has been responsible for generating an additional 70 000 – 100 000 jobs per year in those areas (Brown and Burrows, 1977).

Summary

A regional problem is said to exist where there are substantial and persistent inequalities in the standards of living experienced by people living in different regions of a country. Such inequality is undesirable on grounds of both *equity* and *efficiency*. Consequently society's objective may be defined as *regional balance*. Theories about the causes of regional inequality differ; one view maintains that a market system operating in a spatial sense would achieve regional balance but has not done so because of the existence of specific market failures, namely *factor immobility* and *externalities*. An alternative theory claims that a market has an inherent tendency to produce regional inequalities; this is known as the theory of *cumulative or circular causation*. Although theories about the way the market operates differ, there is some concensus on the broad lines of policy required to promote greater regional balance. In general, policies seeking to attract capital investment to regions in need of development are favoured. In the UK three sets of instruments have been used to pursue this aim, namely (i) subsidisation (of either *capital* or *labour*), (ii) *direct provision* of infrastructure and (iii) *regulation* governing the location of offices and industry. Despite the persistence of regional inequality, research suggests that regional policy has succeeded in reducing inequality substantially below the level it would have reached without such policy.

Further Reading

Brown and Burrows (1977) provide an excellent account of different types of regional problem, their causes and government policy instruments. Holland (1976, 1977) takes a rather different, political-economy perspective and argues that regional problems derive from particular features of the capitalist system. Manners *et al.* (1980) contains extensive empirical evidence on patterns of development in individual regions within Britain, while Maclennan and Parr (1979) present an interesting collection of papers on regional policy.

Questions for Discussion

1. How has the growth of multi-national corporations affected regional economic policy?
2. What effect has Britain's entry into the European Economic Community had upon its regional problems?
3. What theories of economic behaviour are growth pole strategies of regional policy based upon?
4. If 'bygones are bygones' can the capital costs of under-utilised infrastructure investments in depressed regions constitute a cost of migration?
5. The problems of depressed *regions* have often been likened to the problems of less developed *countries*. To what extent do you think this analogy is valid? What policy implications follow from your answer?
6. What political constraints do you think are likely to influence the formulation of regional economic policy?
7. The effectiveness of regional policy is often discussed in terms of the 'cost per job generated'. Do you think this is a satisfactory criterion for the evaluation of policy?
8. Suppose the government decided to build a car factory in a depressed region. How would you go about estimating the effect such an investment would have upon regional income?
9. What effect does the housing market have upon the operation of regional policy?
10. What factors do you think are important in explaining the recent growth of East Anglia and the South West Region?

The Distribution of Income and Wealth 10

Contrary to popular mythology, Britain is still an unequal society. The richest fifth of the population receives over 40 per cent of the national income, while the bottom fifth receives just 6 per cent. The top 10 per cent of wealth holders own over half the nation's marketable wealth. Official estimates indicate that over one-and-a-quarter million families were in poverty in 1977; poverty expert Peter Townsend, using a broader interpretation of poverty, suggests that nearly a quarter of all families in the United Kingdom are poor.

The economics of inequality and poverty were largely neglected during the boom years of the 1950s and 1960s, but have had a revival since then. The areas investigated include methods of measuring poverty and inequality; the objectives of redistribution policy; the role of the market; and the effectiveness of government policies. In this chapter and the next we examine these in turn. But before we do so, we must clarify our terminology. In particular, it is important accurately to distinguish between *income* and *wealth,* since the two are often confused. Both refer to an individual's purchasing power – his or her ability to buy goods and services. However, an individual's income is *the increase in purchasing power over a given time period;* whereas his or her wealth is the *amount of purchasing power at any given moment in time.* Income is what economists generally call a *flow* concept; wealth is what they term a *stock.* For example, an individual with £10 000 invested in a building society at an interest rate of 5 per cent, would have a *stock* of wealth of £10 000 and a *flow* of income from that wealth of £500 per year. This distinction is an important one and needs to be born in mind throughout what follows.

The Measurement of Poverty

The first problem involved in measuring poverty is to define what is meant by the term. This is not as easy it might appear. The official poverty line in the United States is over fifty times the *average* income in India. The American poor are thus extremely well off in comparison to the majority of Indians. Does this imply that poverty is not a problem in the United States – or indeed anywhere in the Western world including Britain?

The answer to this question will depend on whether one adopts an *absolute* or a *relative* definition of poverty. An absolute definition is one that could be applied at all times in all societies such as, for instance, the level of income necessary for bare subsistence. A relative definition relates the living standards of the poor to the standards that prevail elsewhere in the society in which they live. Thus, for instance, the poor could be defined as those whose incomes fall below, say, half the average income, or those who cannot afford to engage in the normal activities of individuals in the wider society.

Both interpretations have their problems. It turns out to be remarkably difficult to find an absolute definition of poverty that is quite independent of social norms; scientists from different cultures disagree on even basic nutritional requirements for subsistence, let alone on the requirements for warmth, shelter and so on. On the other hand, to adopt a strictly relative definition is to imply that the poor in India are no worse off than the poor in Britain, which is clearly absurd. Ideally poverty should be defined in some way that takes account of both considerations but no such definition has yet been found.

In practice most experts in the field define poverty relative to their own society. However even once this has been decided all problems have not been resolved. There remain two questions:

(a) what indicator of poverty should be used, and (b) what point on that indicator should be selected below which we shall regard people as poor. Possible candidates for indicators include household income, household expenditure, housing conditions, education attainment and employment status. In practice, because the data is easily available and because it generally correlates well with the other indicators, household income is preferred. There is less consensus on the cut-off point. Some use the minimum level as specified in government social security programmes, such as Supplementary Benefit. Others prefer a broader definition; an example is Townsend (1979) who tries to specify a level of income below which people cannot purchase the goods (such as meat) or engage in the activities (such as taking a holiday) that the majority take for granted.

Even when the indicator and the cut-off point have been selected there remains a further problem: should we measure simply the *numbers* of persons or families in poverty or should we try to get some measure of the *degree* to which they are poor? The first is often termed the *head-count* measure, and has the advantage of being relatively simple to put into practice. An example of the second is the *poverty-gap* measure, where the total amount of money necessary to fill up the gap between poor people's incomes and the poverty line is calculated. However, the question of degree is part of the broad question of measuring inequalities and raises deeper issues, some of which are taken up in the next section.

The Measurement of Inequality

Table 10.1 provides some figures showing the extent of income inequality in the United Kingdom for the years 1949 and 1980. Over that time the share of the top twenty per cent fell from 47 per cent to 41 per cent, while that of the next twenty per cent rose from 21 per cent to 25 per cent. As a result, the share of the bottom sixty per cent of the population remained virtually constant. So, contrary to received wisdom, there has been no great redistribution from rich to poor since the Second World War; such redistribution as has occurred has been from the very rich to the moderately well off.

TABLE 10.1
The Distribution of Income (UK)

Group	Share of income (%) 1949	Share of income (%) 1980
Top 20%	47	41
Next 20%	21	25
Middle 20% ⎫		18
Next 20% ⎬	32	11
Bottom 20% ⎭		5

Note: The 1949 and 1980 figures are from different sources and are not strictly comparable.
Sources: Royal Commission on the Distribution of Income and Wealth (1979); and Central Statistical Office (1982).

Tables such as 10.1 can be rather cumbersome and sometimes it is preferable to present the information they contain graphically. One method of doing this is to draw a *Lorenz curve*. Figure 10.1 shows the Lorenz curve for 1980. It was constructed by plotting the percentages of the national income received by different percentages of the population when the latter are cumulated from the bottom. That is, it plots the percentage of income received by the bottom twenty per cent, the percentage received by the bottom forty per cent, the bottom sixty per cent and so on. Now if there were full equality – such that the bottom sixty per cent of the population received sixty per cent of the national income, or the bottom eighty per cent received eighty per cent – then the Lorenz curve would lie along the diagonal of the diagram. Hence, the further the curve is away from the diagonal, the further is the distribution from full equality and therefore the greater the inequality. We can therefore obtain an indicator of the extent of inequality in a distribution by observing the position of the Lorenz curve.

A more precise measure of the amount of inequality implicit in a Lorenz curve, can be obtained by use of the *Gini coefficient*. This is calculated by dividing the area between the Lorenz curve and the diagonal by the area of the triangle formed by the

FIGURE 10.1
Lorenz Curve of Income Distribution (UK, 1980)

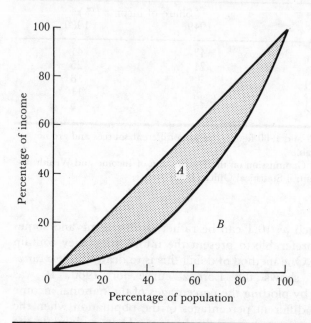

diagonal and the axes. In Figure 10.1, it is the area *A* divided by *A* plus *B* (the non-shaded area). As the Lorenz curve moves further from the diagonal, area *A* gets larger relative to *A* + *B*, and the Gini coefficient approaches 1, indicating greater inequality; as the Lorenz curve moves closer to the diagonal, *A* gets smaller relative to *A* + *B*, and the Gini coefficient approaches zero, indicating greater equality. If we calculate Gini coefficients for 1949 and 1980, we find them to be 0.41 and 0.36 respectively, suggesting some move towards greater equality, but only a small one.

However, one has to be careful in interpreting numbers such as these. The Gini coefficient is one of several 'summary statistics' that are used to measure inequality; others include the standard deviation, the coefficient of variation and Atkinson's index (the methods by which these can be calculated can be found in Cowell, 1977, pp. 152–4). All of these statistics are attempts to summarise a vast amount of information concerning differences in peoples' incomes by compressing that information into one number. In the process of this compression, inevitably, some pieces of information get emphasised while others get ignored. For instance, it is not apparent from the Gini coefficient (or indeed from Table 10.1) that the share of the top *one* per cent actually halved between 1949 and 1980. Another statistic – where the method of calculation 'weighted' the share of the top one per cent more heavily – might have shown a more dramatic change. Which statistic one prefers in this case will depend upon whether one believes the share of the bottom half remaining unchanged is more or less important than the share of the top one per cent being halved. More generally, the choice of summary statistic (or indeed of all methods of summarising information concerning inequality, such as tables or graphs) will depend on one's values; there is no objective method of measuring the extent of inequality.

Another set of problems that arise in measuring inequality concerns the data itself. Should income be defined as it is for income tax purposes; or should we use a broader conception that, for instance, takes account of capital gains or untaxed fringe benefits? Also, with whose income are we concerned – the individual, the 'tax unit' (the unit of assessment for the income tax) or the household? Are we interested only in differences in *annual* income, or ought we to concentrate more on differences in *life-time* income that people receive over the whole of their life? These are all important questions that have to be resolved before any serious attempt is made to measure inequality.

Objectives

The prime concern of any policy aimed at redistributing income and wealth is likely to be the promotion of equity or social justice. But what is an equitable distribution of income? Anyone trying to answer this question walks on dangerous ground. Most people have definite views as to what is just or unjust, fair or unfair, views usually held with a passion that brooks no argument. So we shall not come to any firm conclusion here about what society's objectives are, or should be, in this area. Instead we shall put forward four different kinds of objective and consider the arguments that can be put forward in their support. These we have entitled *minimum standards, equality, inequality* and *equality, but. . . . .*

Minimum Standards

The minimum standards approach concerns itself only with people at the bottom end of the income scale, the poor. Its advocates argue that the interests of equity would be adequately served if society ensured that no-one's incomes fell below a given minimum. The wealth of the rich, or the more general pattern of inequality, are of no concern; all that is required is the elimination of poverty.

Most would accept that a concern for poverty is an essential part of any policy for redistribution. However, to argue that it should be the only concern would be more controversial. We have seen that it is very difficult to say what we mean by poverty without some reference to the rest of the income distribution. Further, it seems a little odd to apply considerations of equity only to those at one end of the income scale and not to those at the other. If a principle of equity is to be applied to judge the amounts that people receive in income, should it not be applied throughout the income distribution, not just at one part of it? It is not clear that the problem of poverty can be so easily divorced that from that of inequality.

Equality

A more radical objective for redistribution policy is that of total equality. Every member of society, regardless of position or ability, should have the same income. To many this has a strong intuitive appeal. Our society cherishes equality of rights before the law and equal voting rights. Why should it not also be committed to economic equality: equality in economic resources?

The appeal of equality need not rest solely on intuition. An additional justification can be derived from the principle of *utilitarianism*. This requires 'the greatest happiness of the greatest number' or, more formally, that the sum of individuals' happinesses or *utilities* should be as large as possible. Suppose that, as utilitarianism requires, we can compare peoples' levels of happiness or utility. Suppose further that, as seems reasonable, an extra pound's worth of income offers less utility to the rich than to the poor. Then taking money away from the rich and giving it to the poor until their incomes are equal will raise the sum of utilities.

However, this conclusion can be challenged on several grounds. First, there are obvious difficulties in comparing peoples' levels of happiness or utility. Second, even if this can be done, it is not always obvious that an extra pound's worth of income is worth less to the rich than to the poor; as people's incomes rise they may develop more expensive tastes. Third, taxing the rich and giving money to the poor may make both rich and poor work less hard, thus reducing total production and hence total utility (this point will be discussed in greater detail below). Fourth, the argument does not take account of other conceptions of equity that might justify some degree of inequality; these we must now consider.

Inequality

Many believe there to be a strong case for some members of a society to receive more by way of economic advantage than others. For instance it is often argued that income should be distributed according to *need*. Equally often it is claimed that it should be distributed according to merit or *desert*. Precisely what constitutes a need or what makes one person more deserving than another will vary according to the values of whoever is putting forward the argument. As far as 'needs' are concerned, on different occasions it has been argued that the old need less than the young, the low-born less than the high-born (because the former have not been brought up with the latter's expensive tastes), the mentally ill less than the sane, the physically healthy less than the physically ill, the clerk less than the coalminer. On the 'desert' side, at various points in history it has been claimed that free people deserve more than slaves, aristocrats more than labourers, the hard worker more than the idler, the intelligent more than the unintelligent, men more than women, white more than black. In all these cases one or more of the features that distinguish one individual from another are isolated as the key factor or factors justifying an additional distinction in terms of a person's share in the distribution of economic resources.

In Western society, there has been more concentration on desert than on need. In particular, individuals are often considered to deserve any extra income they have acquired through their own efforts and sacrifices (from hard work, for example, or from savings). According to this view, income resulting from individuals' own efforts is justified; that which results from factors outside their control is not.

The desert view is implicit in another objective that often appears in discussions of redistribution: *equality of opportunity*. Under this conception a particular distribution of income is equitable if it is the outcome of a situation where everyone has the same opportunities open to them, the same chances of being rich or poor. A similar conception is that of *procedural justice*. If the income distribution is the result of a process, the rules of which everyone regards as fair, then the outcome is fair or just. An example might be a lottery; if everyone entering a lottery accepts the rules of the lottery, then the eventual distribution of the winnings from the lottery should be acceptable to all those participating losers as well as winners.

Equality, but . . .

There are those who would reject the idea that there are intrinsic moral reasons why one individual 'needs' or 'deserves' more than another, but who would none the less argue that some inequality is necessary if some of society's other objectives are to be attained. Measures aimed at reducing inequality might, for instance, interfere with individual liberty to an unacceptable extent. Also there may be substantial costs in terms of efficiency. For instance, equality of income would greatly reduce people's incentive to work, for they would receive the same income however hard they worked, and indeed if they did not work at all. Moreover, people would have a reduced incentive to save; people would not save to receive an extra income from their savings because it would all be taken away, and they would not save for their old age because their retirement income would always be adjusted to be the same as everyone else's. Thus the supply of labour and of capital investment, (financed out of people's savings) to the process of production would be severely reduced; and so, therefore, would production itself. The output of goods and services would fall heavily, and the net result of equalisation would be that everybody would be worse off.

This possibility can be illustrated by the diagram used in Chapter 1 to show the distribution of a commodity (butter) between two people (Adam and Eve). In Figure 10.2, the line *XY* shows all the possible distributions of a fixed quantity of butter between Adam and Eve. Now suppose that the initial distribution is a point such as *B*, where Adam receives considerably more butter than Eve. A benevolent government

FIGURE 10.2
The Efficiency–Equity Trade-off

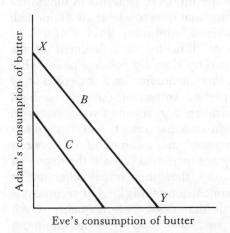

Eve's consumption of butter

(or God) observes this and decides to take some butter off Adam and give it to Eve. However as a result Adam, receiving less of the proceeds, begins to put less work into producing butter. The total amount of butter available therefore falls; the consumption frontier moves inwards, and they may end up at a position such as C where they are both worse off.

Now the force of this argument can be – and often is – exaggerated. People work for reasons other than money: enjoyment, self-esteem, status. However, it does seem likely that some disincentive effects of this kind exists and, that the greater the amount of redistribution the greater the disincentive – a fact that, if true, implies that there is a *trade-off* between achieving greater efficiency (in the sense of producing greater national output) and achieving greater equality.

With this in mind it has been suggested that an appropriate social goal might be the achievement of the maximum degree of income equality compatible with a given rate of economic growth. A practical problem with this approach is that no-one as yet really knows to what degree incentives are important and therefore to what degree inequality contributes to economic growth. This ignorance can lead people to use the growth argument to justify really staggering degrees of inequality. During the late 1960s, for instance, Brazil grew at the rate of 10 per cent a year, and paid some of its higher executives at US income levels. Yet the calorie intake of peasants in the north-east of the country fell during that time to a level about one-half the United Nations' prescribed 'minimum' level of nutrition.

To counter this kind of difficulty, a refinement of the approach has been suggested by Harvard political philosopher John Rawls. He argues that inequality in a society is only justified if it works to the advantage of the least well-off member. Thus if some difference in incomes is necessary to induce people to increase the national output, and if as a result of the overall output increase the incomes of the poorest sections of the community are increased (even if the degree of inequality remains the same), then then initial difference in incomes is justified. The conclusion of this kind of argument is that society should permit that degree of inequality which maximises the economic position of those with the minimum resources; hence it is often termed the *maximin* objective.

Adoption of this goal would have the advantage of enabling a society to avoid the kind of situation that existed in Brazil, for, under the maximin objective, the only inequality permitted would be that which maximised the welfare of the poorest peasant. A disadvantage of the objective is that it assumes society to be indifferent between varying degrees of inequality, all of which contribute to the same level of well-being for the least well-off, but which also contribute to considerable variations in well-being among other members of the community.

Such are some of the possible objectives that we might consider when deciding whether a given distribution of income is desirable. We must now examine the way in which incomes are determined in the market-place and, in the light of the above discussion, attempt to determine whether the resulting distribution could in any way be described as desirable.

The Market System and the Distribution of Income

In practice most governments intervene extensively in the market in order to redistribute income. But is such intervention really necessary? Could the market operating without government intervention meet any of the objectives discussed above? To answer these questions we must examine the way in which incomes are determined in the market-place.

Under a market system people derive incomes from selling the resources they own. Most people 'own' just one resource – their labour. This they sell to the productive system in return for wages. Some also own capital, with which they participate in production in return for interest payments and profits; others own land, the services of which they sell in return for rent. The income that individuals receive will therefore depend on two things: the amount (and type) of resources they own and the price they can get for them. People owning large quantities of resources of the kind that command a high price will have high incomes; people with few resources or with resources that can be sold for only a low price will have low incomes, and hence be in poverty. We need therefore to explain two phenomena: why some people own more resources than others, and why some resources command a higher price than others.

Difference in Resources

The available statistics concerning inequalities in resource ownership concern the distribution of *wealth;* that is, the value of peoples' holdings of land and capital. Some recent figures for the United Kingdom are summarised in Table 10.2. The first column shows the distribution of 'marketable' wealth; that is, the value of items that can be bought and sold (stocks, shares, property, etc.). The distribution is very unequal, with the top ten per cent owning well over half of all marketable wealth.

TABLE 10.2
The Distribution of Wealth (UK, 1979)

	Share of wealth (%)	
	Marketable	Marketable plus non-marketable
Wealthiest 1 per cent	24	13
Wealthiest 5 per cent	45	27
Wealthiest 10 per cent	59	37
Remaining 90 per cent	41	63

Source: Central Statistical Office (1981).

The second column shows the distribution of marketable and non-marketable wealth; it thus includes items such as private and state pension rights which, though arguably part of people's assets, are somewhat different from other items in that they cannot be marketed or sold by one person to another. Although more equal than the distribution of marketable wealth, the distribution is still quite unequal, with the top ten per cent owning well over a third of all wealth.

Why do some people own more wealth than others? Why do some 'own' more labour? There are basically two reasons: they may have *inherited* more or they may have *accumulated* more during their life-times. An individual may own wealth because he has accumulated it himself by, for instance, saving it out of his income; alternatively, he may have received it as an inheritance through a gift or legacy from someone else. The amount of labour an individual 'owns' will be dependent in part upon the physical strength and innate abilities that he inherited, and in part upon the skills he has accumulated during his life-time as a result of his education and experience. The amount of any resource owned by an individual will therefore be a result of inheritance, life-time accumulation, or both.

It is difficult to separate the different effects of accumulation and inheritance in practice. How much of an individual's labour resources depend on his genetic make-up and how much on his education and environment is a question that has yet to be resolved. Perhaps the major factor affecting the quality of the labour resources owned by an individual is intelligence; but there is enormous controversy as to whether intelligence, as measured by IQ (the intelligence quotient), is inherited or acquired through environmental influence. Even in the case of wealth, it is not easy to specify what proportion of the wealthy at any point in time gained their wealth because of their own efforts at accumulation or because of inheritance. However, such studies as have been done indicate that the role of inheritance is in many cases the major influence. Harbury and McMahon (1973) found that between one-half and two-thirds of all individuals owning wealth over £100 000 had fathers who left them £25 000 or more. Only around one-third could be described as 'self-made'; a fact which led the researchers to conclude that the importance of the latter in popular mythology derives more from the fact that they constitute exceptions to the rule rather than the rule itself.

Not only is it difficult to separate out the effects of inheritance and accumulation in practice, but it is also not always easy to separate them conceptually. For instance, consider the 'accumulation' of educational and other skills. Now it is commonplace in Western societies that the children of educated parents tend to do better in the educational system (and hence to accumulate more labour resources) than do the children from less-educated homes. This is because educated parents tend to introduce their children to reading and to other useful learning skills, and generally encourage a positive attitude towards school work in a way that less educated families do not. In a sense, the children of the former could therefore be said to have 'inherited' their superior skills from their parents – or at least to have inherited the ability to accumulate those skills.

A psychological determinist could extend this argument to rule out altogether accumulation as a source of difference in resource ownership as distinct from inheritance. He could claim that the ability to save out of one's income, to invent a new product, or to engage successfully in property speculation (all ways of accumulating wealth) were ultimately determined by one's up-bringing and/or one's genes. Hence the accumulation of any resource is inevitably a function of one's inherited abilities and therefore cannot be viewed separately from 'directly' inherited resources. This raises issues which are beyond our canvas here; suffice it to say that the ability to accumulate is to some extent dependent upon inheritance, and the importance of inheritance as a cause of differences in resource ownership must be thereby enhanced. At least it seems safe to assert that a substantial part of the inequalities in resource ownership in the present generation is the result of the inequalities in the previous one.

Differences in Prices

The second reason why people's incomes differ is because they receive different prices for the resources they own. To see how this comes about it is necessary to study in more detail the way in which the price of a resource is determined in a market system. Let us begin with a simple example.

Suppose that there are two firms, one making bicycles and one making cars. Both have roughly the same working conditions, and both are offering the same pay (say £100 a week). Now suppose there is a change in consumers' tastes due to, say, a rise in the price of petrol. They begin to demand more bicycles and fewer cars. The bicycle manufacturer will be able to raise his prices, and make more profits per bicycle; hence he will want to expand production. Accordingly, in order to increase his labour force, he will offer higher wages. Since working conditions are the same, the only reason a worker could have for preferring one factory to other would be the higher pay. Therefore workers would begin to move from the car firm to the bicycle firm. Now, so long as the wage differential remained, this movement would continue until the car firm had lost all its workers. In order to prevent this the car firm would have to raise its wages as well; and the bicycle manufacturer, with thousands of workers competing for his jobs, would be able to begin to lower his. Eventually a new equilibrium would be reached, where the differential between the firms was removed and the movement of workers ceased. At this point, more would be employed at the bicycle manufacturer's than before, but less at the car firm: the supply of bicycles would be increased and the supply of cars reduced, exactly in accordance with the original change in demand.

Although this example is confined to labour, the theory it illustrates is perfectly general. (Readers may note the resemblance between it and the examples provided in Chapter 9 on regional inequalities.) The demand for resources is *derived* from the demand for commodities. A change in the demand for one commodity will result in a change in demand for the resources employed in its production. This change will alter the price an employer is prepared to pay for those resources, and this will alter the amount of resources individuals are prepared to sell to the employer. Resources will thus be allocated in accordance with consumers' demands.

Now two implications of this example should be noted. First, and this is a general implication of the theory, it suggests that resources will in fact shift from one use to another in accordance with changes in demand and supply conditions. Second, it implies that, as a result of these shifts, the price of each resource (in this case, wages) will be equalised in all alternative uses. This second implication is less general; it results from the assumption that there was no difference between the work done in different plants, and hence that the only differences between the plants in the rewards from work were monetary ones. However, in the real world, there are many non-monetary considerations that affect the total advantages to be gained from employing a resource in one use rather than another. Consider the case of labour. Some jobs involve more pleasant tasks for the worker than others. Some have better working conditions; some, higher status or power; and many occupations require long periods of training, often at low pay.

Similarly, there are non-monetary considerations which affect the use of savings for investment purposes. Some investments are more risky than others; some more 'liquid' (that is, more easily converted into cash). Hence each use for a resource offers different advantages (such as monetary rewards, status and power) and disadvantages (such as discomfort, riskiness, and so forth). If we balance all these against one another, we obtain what might be termed the *net advantage:* the net gain to an individual owner of a resource from putting it to a particular use.

To see the implications of this, let us return to our example the bicycle and car factories; but this time we shall assume that the working conditions in the bicycle factory are less pleasant than in the car factory. Then, in order to encourage people to work in his factory, the bicycle manufacturer would have to increase the wage he offered beyond that of the car firm since, if he offered the same wage, the net advantages (wages plus working conditions) would be less and no-one would wish to be employed by him. He would not, however, be able to raise the wages to a point at which net advantages were greater than the car firm's, for in that case the car firm would simply follow suit. In other words, the wages would adjust so that there was no net advantage to working in one factory rather than the other.

The result is not confined to this example. Whatever resource (labour, land or capital) is concerned, no employer can offer a set of net advantages to the owner of the resource that is permanently greater than that offered of the resource employer. For the moment that the net advantages offered by one employer become greater than those offered by another, the latter will be forced to raise his; otherwise, no supplies will be forthcoming. We would therefore predict that the movement of resources between users in a competitive market will be such as to *equalise the net advantages* in each use.

Is this what happens in practice? Can we explain the differences in the prices that different resources (and hence their owners) can command by differences in non-monetary advantages? The markets for some resources do seem to operate in the way outlined. For example, risky investments often carry higher interest rates, so as to compensate investors for the disadvantages of taking risks. But the theory seems less satisfactory as a description of the way in which the market for labour operates. Jobs with high incomes, such as medicine or law, tend to be associated not with low non-monetary advantages, as theory would predict, but with quite the reverse – high status, good security, pleasant working conditions, considerable freedom in determining hours worked, and so on. On the other hand, low-paying jobs such as waitressing or farm work offer low status. little security, poor working conditions, and little choice as to working times.

Perhaps the only non-monetary 'advantage' that unskilled manual jobs have is the absence of training required; professional occupations generally require costly periods of training and their high salaries could be viewed as 'compensation' for this. But there is evidence to suggest that in fact professional salaries are often considerably higher than could be explained by the financial cost of training. Moreover, since most students seem to enjoy college, the actual personal sacrifice involved in having to go to a university or medical school may be substantially less than would be indicated by simple observation of the financial cost.

There are two principal explanations for this apparent failure of the theory to explain observed wage differentials. The *first* is that supply and demand do not in fact determine the price of labour. Rather, incomes and salaries are determined by social norms, which in turn are decided by largely non-economic factors. People have views concerning how much a job is 'worth' relative to other jobs, and these views are important determinants of how much they are actually paid.

Now it is true that feelings about differentials can be strong. But it is questionable how far these feelings can completely over-ride the forces of supply and demand. Many professionals regarded the erosion of the traditional difference between their earnings and those of manual workers as signs of society's imminent collapse, yet their concern has not stopped the phenomenon. On the other hand, some differentials have remained stable over remarkably long periods of time; periods when one might expect demand and supply conditions to have varied considerably. The role of social convention in determining the price of resources thus remains an open issue.

The *second* explanation for the theory's failure is that one of its crucial assumptions is not fulfilled in the real world – that of free mobility. The theory requires that resources can be shifted smoothly from one use to another. But in reality there are considerable barriers to such shifts. This applies particularly to labour. One of the reasons for the immobility of labour was noted in the previous chapter – the fact that a worker may have to move house in order to move jobs. Others include the following.

Differences in the innate ability required for different jobs

To become a coalminer requires more physical stamina than to be a clerk; to be a university professor requires more intellectual ability than to be a road-sweeper. Hence even if the net advantages of being a coalminer rise relative to those of being a clerk, or those of a university professor rise relative to those of a road-sweeper, there is unlikely to be a movement from one to the other to bring about equality.

Differences in the training required for different jobs

This should not be a factor leading to permanent differences between net advantages, but only one *delaying* their equalisation. For, so long as entry into a training scheme required to enter a particular occupation is open to all, then any increase in the net advantages of that occupation should bring about an increase in entry into training; and hence eventually, as the newly trained people emerge, an equalisation. However, in practice entry into training schemes is often heavily restricted. For example, children from low-income families have difficulties obtaining resources to enter medical school (despite the fact that they know the salaries they receive later may compensate them) and hence most doctors come from middle- and upper-income family backgrounds. If restrictions on entry of this kind exist, then we would not expect equalisation.

Professional associations and trade unions

Associations of professional people and trade unions act to raise the net advantages of their members. This they can do by closed-shop provisions, thus preventing non-members bidding down wages, or by extending training periods, with the effects described in the previous paragraph. It is worth noting that although it is usually trade unions who are attacked for their 'restrictive practices', it is often professional groups who have been major offenders in this respect; there is evidence that the training period of doctors, for instance, is longer than necessary for obtaining the required standards and the same is likely to be true of other professions. Indeed, for many professions the standards themselves – which also have the effect of restricting competition – have been criticised as being too high for the bulk of activities undertaken.

Discrimination

There are barriers to mobility resulting from the prejudice of employers against certain individuals because of their race or sex. For example, if a group of employers in an area prefers to employ only white males, then black males and women (of both races) could not compete for the jobs offered. As a result, net advantages for the white males would remain higher than those for the rest.

All of these barriers to competition operate so as to prevent the equalisation of net advantages. These are important factors explaining why people doing similar jobs can none the less be paid different wage rates; and , more generally, why wages for different occupations differ. Although our immediate concern here is not with economic efficiency, it is important to note that the existence of these barriers undoubtedly reduces efficiency, for the reduction in competition they create will prevent resources being allocated to their most productive uses.

The Market and Equity

Will the market achieve equity or justice in any of the interpretations discussed earlier? It is clear that, on its own, the market will not necessarily ensure that income remains above a *minimum standard* of living. Those with no resources (such as the property-less, disabled or very elderly) will not receive any income, and hence will not attain a minimum standard. On the other hand it is sometimes argued that, over time, the market will do better for the poor (at least in terms of their absolute standard of living) than systems with a greater degree of state intervention, for it generates higher rates of economic growth whose effects 'trickle down' to the benefit of the poor. However, the poor can only benefit from economic growth if there is some mechanism to direct at least some of the fruits of prosperity in their direction, so some form of state redistribution will be necessary if only to help those with no resources.

The market on its own is not likely to achieve full equality. A sufficient condition for this is equal resource ownership and the same price per unit for each resource; but while a perfectly competitive market (that is, one without the barriers to competition discussed earlier) might achieve the latter, there is no reason why it should create the former. Nor will it distribute according to *need* or *desert*. In particular, owing to the considerable role of inheritance, it would not be the same as a distribution on the basis of individual effort. Again, because of inheritance, it will not create *equality of opportunity*. Perhaps the only conception of equity to which a competitive market may conform is that of *procedural justice*, although even here there are many people who would not regard the rules of the market 'game' as fair or just.

Hence, under most interpretations of the term, there is a need for state intervention in the distribution of income in order to ensure a measure of equity or justice. The debate then becomes one of finding some form of intervention that can achieve this end, *without* seriously affecting the economy's ability to satisfy other objectives such as efficiency or liberty. In the next chapter we examine various government policies with such considerations in mind.

Summary

Poverty may be measured in *absolute* or in *relative* terms. The problem with absolute definitions is to find one that can be applied at all times in all societies; the problem with purely relative definitions is that they create difficulties for comparisons between different societies. Either way it is necessary also to select the indicator of poverty (income, expenditure, education levels etc.), to select the poverty cut-off point, and to decide whether poverty should be measured in terms of a *head-count* measure or by a more comprehensive measure as the *poverty gap*. Degrees of *inequality* may be indicated by the construction of the relevant *Lorenz* curves, and measured by summary statistics such as the *Gini coefficient*. However, the choice of inequality measure will depend on the values of the user.

The prime aim of distribution policy is likely to be justice or *equity*. But it is not easy to define an equitable distribution of income. Possible interpretations include one for which no-one falls below a *minimum standard*, where income is distributed *equally*, where it is distributed according to *need* or *desert*, and where it is the outcome of choices made under conditions of *equal opportunity* or *procedural justice*. Whatever interpretation is chosen, there is likely to be some trade-off between its attainment and that of efficiency; one possible 'combined' objective is for the economy to be organised in such a way as to maximise the welfare of the least well-off: the *maximin* objective.

Under a market system an individual's income depends on the *resources* he or she inherits and/or accumulates, and on the *price* he or she can obtain from selling those resources. The price for a resource is determined by the interaction of supply and demand. In the absence of any barriers to competition, this results in the *equalisation of net advantages* between occupations. However substantial barriers to competition do exist, particularly in the labour market. These include differences in *ability*, in *required training*, in *organisational strength*, and in the extent of *discrimination*. These, taken together with the unequal distribution of resources, imply that in practice any market-determined income distribution is unlikely to be equitable, however the term is interpreted.

Further Reading

The most comprehensive book on the economics of inequality and one well suited to non-economists is Atkinson (1975). Atkinson has also edited an immensely useful set of readings (1980), although some of these are too technical for those without any economics training.

On the measurement of poverty, and on its extent in the UK, see Townsend (1979) and Beckerman and Clark (1982). For a non-technical exposition of the ways of measuring inequality, see Atkinson (1980) pp. 40–3 and Gordon (1982), pp. 63–71. A detailed exposition, description and discussion of the figures on the distribution of income and wealth can be found in the many reports of the Royal Commission on the Distribution of Income and Wealth.

Weale (1978) discusses various interpretations of equity and justice and their implications for policy. The conventional theory of the market determination of resource (or factor) prices can be found in any elementary text-book such as Lipsey (1979); for an alternative view, see Routh (1980) Part 4 and Hunt and Sherman (1981), Ch. 17.

Questions for Discussion

1. In what sense, if any, can it be said that the lowest ten per cent of the income distribution in Britain are as poor as the lowest ten per cent in India?
2. Is there an objective way of measuring inequality?
3. Atkinson (1980, p. 40) gives the following figures for the income distribution in Britain and West Germany in 1964. Construct the Lorenz curve for each. Which is the more equal?

	Percentage of total income	
Group	*UK*	*West Germany*
Bottom 30 per cent	9	10
Middle 40 per cent	34	28
Top 30 per cent	57	62

4. Should we measure inequality in annual or in life-time incomes?

5. 'From each according to his ability; to each according to his need.' Do you think this is a sensible aim for distribution policy?

6. Discuss Rawls' proposal that the only justifiable inequalities in income and wealth are those which benefit the least well-off.

7. Should miners be paid more than doctors?

8. 'Under the market system, the net advantages of different occupations are equalised. Hence the distribution of income is not only efficient; it is also fair.' Do you agree?

9. Can the fact that high status, rewarding jobs are generally better paid than low status, boring ones be reconciled with the market theory of the determination of wages?

10. 'It is not in the long-run interest of employers to discriminate against women or blacks; hence discrimination in employment will eventually disappear.' Do you agree?

The Re-distribution of Income and Wealth 11

Most government policies concerning the redistribution of income and wealth fall into the categories of taxes, subsidies or regulation. Income and wealth taxes are obvious examples of the first, and the social security system of the second. The third includes legislative attempts to control the price that people receive for the sale of their resources; the classic case is the minimum wage. In this chapter we examine the implications for equity and efficiency of these kinds of policy, beginning with income taxes and the social security system, continuing with proposals for integrating the two through a 'negative' income tax or social dividend, and concluding with minimum wages and wealth taxation.

Income Tax

The UK income tax is often though to be highly progressive and hence to be an effective way of redistributing income. That is, it is supposed to take a much higher proportion of income from the rich in tax than from the rest of the population, and hence substantially to reduce the share of the former in the national income. In fact, neither belief is correct. The richest 20 per cent of the population pay about a fifth of their income in tax, almost the same proportion as the next 40 per cent. As a result, their share of the national income is not greatly affected by the tax, falling from 41 per cent before tax to 39 per cent after tax (Central Statistical Office, 1982).

Misconceptions about the redistributive power of the income tax system often arise because of a confusion between *average* and *marginal* tax rates. The average tax rate is the proportion of an individual's *total* income that goes in tax; the marginal rate is the proportion of any *extra* income that goes in tax. For instance consider an income tax system, not unlike the British one, where the first £1500 of income was exempt from tax and all income thereafter was taxed at a rate of 30 per cent. Then an individual with an income of £15 000 a year would pay £4050 in tax (30 per cent of £13 500), and hence would have an average tax rate of 27 per cent (£4050 as a percentage of £15 000). Any extra income, however, would be taxed not at 27 per cent but at 30 per cent: his or her marginal rate.

Marginal tax rates in Britain can be high; in 1982–3 they rose to 60 per cent on earned taxable income, and 75 per cent on any unearned income above £31 500. But a high marginal rate does not necessarily imply a high average rate. For the average rate will depend on the allowances claimed; that is, on the amounts that can be deducted from income before it is assessed for tax. Under the British tax system (and under those of most other countries) there are many such allowances, including payments made on life insurance premiums and the interest paid on mortgages. Judicious use of these allowances can often enable the better off substantially to reduce their burden. For instance, consider an individual earning £20 000 per year who has interest payments of £3000 on his mortgage, and who is subject to the income tax used in our earlier example. Including the personal allowance, he will be able to deduct £4500 from his income before it is taxed. His tax bill will therefore be £4650 (30 per cent of £15 500). He will thus have an average tax rate of 23 per cent; four percentage points *lower* than that faced by the £15 000 pa individual we considered earlier.

Another reason why income tax has a relatively small impact on the distribution of income is because some types of income are not taxed, or are taxed relatively lightly. These include many occupational 'fringe benefits', such as company cars or subsidised loans for house purchase. An even more important example is that of capital gains; that is, the profits made from the sale of assets – such as shares, property or works of art – that have risen in price since they were acquired. Such gains are a form of income, for they represent increases in the purchasing power of the individuals concerned – individuals who tend to be among the better off, since it is only they who have assets to sell. Yet, under the British tax system this type of income is taxed relatively lightly (specifically, all capital gains, however large, are taxed at the 'standard' rate, unlike other income where marginal tax rates increase as income increases).

Features such as this have led some economists to call for the introduction of a *comprehensive income tax;* one that taxes all income at the same rate regardless of source and that does not have an elaborate system of tax allowances. Others, despairing of the practical difficulties of introducing such a tax, have argued that the whole system should be replaced by an *expenditure tax:* – a tax on people's outgoings rather than their incomings. If introduced in their 'pure' form, either of these would undoubtedly be more equitable than the present income tax; however, they would create large transitional problems as well as provoking considerable political opposition from those who lost tax advantages.

We must now consider the effects of an income tax on efficiency – or, more specifically, on the incentive to work. An increase in the rate of income tax will affect people's desire to work in two ways. First, it will reduce the amount of income they receive from working an extra hour (from selling an extra unit of labour), and hence make working that extra hour, instead of using it for leisure, less attractive. Accordingly they might be inclined to reduce the number of hours they work; in other words, to substitute hours spent in leisure activities for hours spent working. Economists call this *the substitution effect*. On the other hand, the reduction in people's incomes due to the tax may make them want to work more hours in order to regain the income levels they would have had had there been tax. Such a response is likely if they have long standing expenditure plans, for example, a holiday abroad. This is called *the income effect* and, as can be seen, it works in the opposite direction from the substitution effect.

Now many people believe that high tax rates automatically deter people from working harder. But this may not be so. If the income effect is greater than the substitution effect, then the impact of increasing income tax rates will be to increase willingness to work, not reduce it. If the two are equal, then the net impact on work effort will be zero. Only if the substitution effect is greater than the income effect will the supply of labour be reduced. Thus we can make no statement *a priori* about the way income taxes might affect work; the matter can only be resolved by empirical investigation. A number of such investigations have been undertaken both in the UK and in the US (a useful summary can be found in Atkinson and Stiglitz, 1980, pp. 48–59). Interestingly, the principal results indicate that, at least for male earners, high income tax rates do *not* significantly reduce work effort.

Social Security

Most social security systems include both *means-tested* and *categorical* benefits. To receive a means-tested benefit, a family has to show that its income – its means – falls below a certain level. The principal benefit of this kind in Britain is Supplementary Benefit, paid to those on low incomes not in work. Categorical benefits on the other hand are paid to all those who fall within a particular social category (elderly, families with children, etc.), regardless of their income. In Britain they include child benefit, old age pensions and unemployment and sickness benefit.

Most categorical benefits (the exception in Britain is child benefit) take the form of *social insurance*. That is, they 'insure' against loss of income due to unforeseen or unavoidable events such as unemployment, sickness or old age. There are two possible kinds of social insurance: *funded* schemes, where individuals contribute to a fund that accumulates and is then used for payments to those same individuals when they become old, sick or unemployed, and *Pay-as-you-go* schemes (the kind used in Britain) where those in work contribute into a fund that makes payments to those currently not in work. In both cases individuals' records of past contributions to the fund affect what they receive when they need to claim benefit.

As with the income tax we ask, first, what are the effects of the different forms of social security on redistribution and, second, what are the consequences for the incentive to work. There is little doubt that the social security system *as a whole* reduces poverty. Although there are few figures showing the impact of the system on the income shares of different groups in the population, there have been estimates of its impact on the *poverty gap* (the total amount needed to raise all poor people's incomes above the poverty line). These show that in 1974–6, for instance, the effect of the system was to reduce the poverty gap from 3.5 per cent of GNP to 0.2 per cent (Beckerman and Clark, 1982, Chapter 5).

This would be sufficient to judge the system a success in terms of equity if our only interpretation of the term was one of minimum standards. However if the aim is to promote greater *equality,* then it is necessary to find out how much the system also benefits the better off; for if, in helping the poor, it simultaneously helps the better off as well, there might be little impact on overall inequalities. One test of this is to calculate what has been termed the *Vertical Expenditure Efficiency* (VEE) of the system; that is, the proportion of the benefits that accrue to households who would have been poor in the absence of benefits. Thus a system with, say, 95 per cent VEE would be extremely effective as a redistributive policy, since almost all its benefits would accrue to the poor; whereas one with, say, 5 per cent VEE would be likely to be ineffective, since most of its benefits accrue to the non-poor.

Beckerman and Clark (1982) showed that the system as a whole was on the effective side, with 57 per cent VEE in 1974–6; that is, 57 per cent of its benefits actually accrued to the poor. However, there was considerable variation by type of programme, ranging from 6 per cent VEE for sickness benefit and 13 per cent for child benefit and Family Income Supplement, to 60 per cent for Supplementary Benefit and 68 per cent for pensions. This is not surprising for the categorical benefits, such as sickness benefit and child benefit, since these go to all those in the relevant category regardless of income; although it is perhaps a little curious that a similar result does not hold for old age pensions. Supplementary benefit, on the other hand, being means-tested. might be expected to have considerable vertical efficiency; indeed, the surprise here is that it is not even more effective in this regard.

Since in general one might expect categorical benefits to have a lower VEE than means-tested ones, it might be expected that egalitarians and social security reformers would generally favour the latter over the former. However this is not so. Instead, many reformers argue for a 'Back-to-Beveridge' approach – called after the founder of modern social insurance, Sir William Beveridge. At the extreme, this would entail raising all categorical benefits to such a level that those in poverty who are in receipt of some form of categorical benefit (in fact, the vast majority of the poor) would be lifted out of poverty.

Those who espouse this view generally do so because of a major disadvantage of means tests; their relatively low take-up rates. People eligible for means-tested benefits often do not apply for them partly because of lack of knowledge, partly because of a reluctance to accept what may be perceived as charity, and partly because of the complexity of the administrative procedures involved. Categorical benefits, on the other hand, often have 100 per cent take-up.

Categorical benefits also have an advantage over means-tested benefits with respect to their effects on the incentive to work. All forms of social security create some disincentive to work. The payments mean that their recipients have to work less hard to obtain a given standard of living; in the terminology of the previous section, the income effect discourages work. Means-tested benefits, however, build in an additional disincentive, for they always involve a reduction in benefit if the individual concerned works harder (and thus raises his or her 'means'). The gain from 'substituting' work for leisure is reduced; hence there is a substitution effect as well as an income effect discouraging work effect. Put another way, individuals face a *positive marginal tax rate* on their earnings; any increase in earnings is partly 'taxed away' through a reduction in social security payments. In some cases this tax rate can go above 100 per cent: for every extra £1 earned, more than £1 is taken away in benefits. This state of affairs is often termed the *poverty trap;* that is, a situation where there is no net financial gain from working.

Thus, *a priori*, we might expect means-tested benefits to have a greater disincentive effect than categorical ones. In practice, however, things are not quite so simple, not least because some categorical benefits (most obviously, unemployment benefit) also involve a reduction in benefit if the individual works. Moreover, there is little evidence to suggest that *any* form of social security seriously discourages work effort. Despite the fact that everyone seems to know, or to have heard of, able-bodied men and women 'scrounging' off social security, no systematic survey has ever found them to be a significant problem. In fact most recipients of social security are generally found to be either unemployable (due to old age, sickness, single parent responsibilities etc.) or, if employable, unemployed through no fault – or desire – of their own.

Finally we must consider briefly the effects on the incentive to save. All forms of social security involve some disincentive to save. Pay-as-you-go insurance schemes are particularly vulnerable on this score; they are supposed to discourage people from saving for their old age or to cover spells of unemployment or sickness and, unlike funded schemes, they do not accumulate an investment fund that could replace the private savings.

The Negative Income Tax and Social Dividend

There have been a number of proposals for reforming the social security system. Of these, the most radical involves integrating the social security and income tax systems through a so-called 'negative' income tax or a 'social dividend'. In fact a form of negative income tax is already in operation in the United Kingdom – the Family Income Supplement – and types of social dividend have been advocated at various times by various political parties including, most recently, the Social Democrats.

The idea of a negative income tax to complement the existing positive tax originated with Professor Milton Friedman (1962). His reasoning was as follows. Under the existing income tax there is a basic income below which no one pays any tax (the 'allowance' level). If someone has income above the allowance level, then they pay a certain proportion of the difference between their actual income and that level in tax. It would seem logical, therefore, to make the arrangement symmetric; that is, if an individual has income below the allowance level, then he or she should receive a certain proportion of the difference between his income and the allowance level in the form of a 'negative' tax payment. Examples of how this might work for individuals at various levels of income are given in Table 11.1. The allowance level is £1500 and the proportion of the difference between this and the individual's income made up by the state (the negative 'tax rate') is 30 per cent. Column (a) gives each individual's income and column (b) his allowance (the same at all levels of income). Column (c) shows the difference between his allowance and his income, and column (e) shows the amount of this difference that is made up by payments from the state under the scheme. Column (f) gives his total income after he has received the state payment. Note that the individual with an income above the allowance level (at £2000) is in the normal tax system; he has a negative amount 'received from' the state, which is simply another way of saying that he has to pay tax.

The social dividend scheme originated with a proposal by Lady Rhys-Williams in 1942, was revived in the form of the tax-credit scheme proposed by the Conservative Government in 1972 and has recently been advocated by the Social Democrats. The basis for the scheme, in its most general form, is to pay every individual in society a flat amount (a 'social dividend') and then to tax all other income, regardless of source. The net change in the individual's income would thus equal the amount of the dividend minus any tax paid. For low-income individuals this amount would presumably be positive, and they would receive a net gain from the state. Others with larger incomes might have to pay more to the state in taxes than they received from the dividend. To see how this might operate, consider an example of two individuals earning £1000 pa and £2000 pa respectively. Suppose a social dividend scheme is introduced which pays £450 pa to both as a dividend and which taxed all their other income at 30 per cent. Then the lower-income individual would receive £450 and pay in tax 30 per cent of £1000, or £300: a net gain of £150. The higher-

TABLE 11.1
A Negative Income Tax

	Income (£) (a)	Allowance (£) (b)	Allowance *minus* Income (£) (c)	Tax rate (per cent) (d)	Amount received (c) × (d) (£) (e)	After-tax income (a) + (e) (£) (f)
	1000	1500	500	30	150	1150
NEGATIVE	1100	1500	400	30	120	1220
TAX	1200	1500	300	30	90	1290
	1500	1500	0	30	0	1500
POSITIVE TAX	2000	1500	− 500	30	− 150	1850

income individual would also receive £450, but pay in tax 30 per cent of £2000, or £600: a net loss of £150. Hence their after-tax and dividend income would be £1150 and £1850 respectively.

Now the reader may have noticed that this is precisely the same end result (in the sense that both individuals have the same incomes after the schemes are introduced) as for the negative income tax example given in Table 11.1. This is not a trick of the particular income levels chosen, as a selection of any others would show. In fact, any negative income tax scheme can be reformulated as a social dividend scheme by simply giving as a social dividend a sum equal to the product of the negative income tax rate and the 'allowance'. The two systems are in fact identical.

What are the advantages and disadvantages of replacing our present social security system with a negative income tax/social dividend scheme? Advocates of the negative income tax claim that it had three principal advantages over our present system. First, it is administratively simpler. By integrating the social security system into the tax system, considerable administrative savings could be made. Second, it would be a way of introducing more selectivity into the system, thus increasing its redistributive impact. But it would not suffer from the problem with other selective schemes; the low take-up of means-tested benefits. For every household in the country would fill out a tax return, and as their income was below or above the allowance level they would receive a payment from, or make a payment to, the state. Since everyone would be involved in the scheme, and no-one would have specially to apply, there would be less stigma attached to receiving payments. Third, the scheme preserves the incentive to work in a way that other social security schemes do not. Social security payments such as Supplementary Benefit or unemployment pay cease as soon as an individual enters work. But under a negative income tax scheme some of any extra earnings are retained, and income can thereby be increased by working. Consider the example of the negative income tax scheme with an allowance of £1500 and a 30 per cent tax rate. Now if an individual who was earning £1000 pa from work increased his or her work effort, so that he or she was now earning £1100 pa, it can be seen from Table 11.1 that his or her negative income tax payments from the state would go down from £150 to £120, but his or her after-tax income would go up from £1150 to £1220. By increasing his or her work effort he or she would therefore make a net gain, and he or she thus has an incentive to do so.

However the scheme also has its problems. First, the fact that it has lower tax rates than existing social security programmes might, while improving efficiency, result in less equity. In particular the scheme might not adequately provide for all those in need. For instance, in our example the amounts that even the poorest individuals received were not great; certainly not enough to lift them out of poverty. It would be possible to increase the amount received by the poor under the scheme by increasing the tax rate, say, to 75 per cent. However this would increase the disincentive effects of the scheme for, with every extra pound earned, the individual would lose 75p of negative income tax payment.

Another way of coping with this problem would be to raise the allowance level. But this would mean the scheme would provide substantial benefits to those not in need. For raising the allowance level sufficiently would take many people out of the positive income tax and into the negative one. As a result large numbers of people could become eligible for payments who were, by any criterion, far from poor. In short, the negative income tax/social dividend can create greater efficiency (by reducing work disincentives) only at the expense of equity; it has not resolved the problem of the equity-efficiency trade-off discussed in the previous chapter.

Minimum Wages

Many countries have a national minimum wage – the United States and France among them – and its institution has often been urged in the United Kingdom. We shall look at some of the economic consequences of introducing a minimum wage into a situation where there was none previously, and then use such conclusions as we might reach to evaluate its usefulness as a redistributive measure.

If a national minimum wage was to be introduced tomorrow,

the first immediate consequence would be a rise in costs to those employers employing individuals whose wages were below the new minimum. Now the employer might try to pass these increased costs directly on to the consumer by increasing his prices. But unless demand for his product is totally unresponsive to changes in price, it will fall as a result of the price increase. He will have to cut back production, reduce his labour force and accept a lower level of profit. Alternatively, he might try to maintain his level of production but lower his costs by replacing the now high-cost workers by previously uneconomic machines. These will be more expensive than the workers used to be, however, and hence his costs must still rise. Either way, therefore, there is likely to be a reduction in his work force, a rise in prices and a fall in his profits.

The extent of these effects, and their relative importance, will vary from industry to industry. In areas like the restaurant trade, which employ very low-paid labour and survive on low profit margins, the result might be a severe increase in unemployment and in the number of bankruptcies. In others such as agriculture which again employs a large proportion of the low paid, but the demand for whose products is relatively unresponsive to price changes (and whose employers – farmers – are often very prosperous), the result might be simply a rise in prices and little increased unemployment.

Whatever form the effects take, they will be compounded if higher-paid workers wish to maintain the differentials in pay between themselves and the low paid. For if they succeed in attaining their wish, the institution of a national minimum wage will result in *all* wages increasing so that the differentials are maintained. In that case, employment and/or inflationary effects are likely to be far more severe. In a study of the feasibility of introducing a national minimum wage, the Department of Employment (1969) estimated that if all costs were passed on to consumers, the increase in costs (and hence in prices) if differentials were largely maintained, would be up to three times as much as if they were not.

We are now in a position to examine the possible redistributive effects of the institution of a minimum wage. Since the minimum wage is likely to make some workers unemployed, and to cause some prices to rise and some profits to fall, it will transfer income *to* the low paid who remain in employment *from* (a) those low paid who were in employment, but are now unemployed, (b) the consumers of the products whose prices have risen, and/or (c) the profit-earners whose profits are reduced. Now whether this will significantly reduce inequality in incomes is debatable. It would only do so if in the three groups (a), (b) and (c) there are more people with higher incomes than those of the low paid still in employment. Since those unemployed are almost certainly worse off than those still employed; since products of industries employing a large proportion of low-paid workers (such as agriculture and textiles) form a large portion of poor people's budgets; and since many – although not all – profit-earners in low-paying industries have very low profit margins, it seems unlikely that this will be the case. Add to this the fact that the minimum wage only affects positively the incomes of those in work, and that, if differentials are maintained, even inequality within the labour force will not be reduced, it appears that the minimum wage will not be a very effective way of redistributing income.

In conclusion, so far as regulations of this kind are concerned, their principal advantage appears to lie in the fact that in some sense they tackle the root of the problem, and their principal disadvantage is their effects on the allocation of resources. Note that the latter are rather different from the effects of the tax and subsidy measures considered earlier. For the latter only affect the supply of resources, but legislative controls on the incomes that employers can offer will affect not only the supply but also the *demand* for those resources. Thus taxes and subsidies are not likely to cause 'involuntary' unemployment (although they may cause people to reduce their work effort voluntarily); whereas if legislative fixing of factor prices results in those prices being fixed above the demand and supply equilibrium price, the result might well be that some resources remain unused, despite the fact that their owners are willing to supply them to the productive process.

Wealth Taxation

The policies considered so far have all been designed to affect individuals' *flows* of income. It is also possible to achieve redistribution by affecting individuals' *stocks* of wealth. In particular, wealth can be taxed. There are two kinds of wealth taxation: that designed to affect the *holding* of wealth, and that designed to affect its *transfer* from one person to another. Into the first category fall what we normally term a wealth tax – an annual tax on the amount of wealth a person or household owns. The second category includes taxes on the transfer of wealth from one person to another, such as capital transfer tax.

Taxing the Holding of Wealth

Many countries, such as Sweden and West Germany, have a tax on the holding of wealth. The theoretical workings of the tax are easy to grasp: every year the net assets of each individual or household (depending upon what is taken as the operational unit for tax purposes) are valued, and a tax levied on that value at a proportional or, more usually, progressive rate.

There are two principal objections to a wealth tax: its *practicality* and its *effects on savings*. First, its practicality. It has been claimed that the problem of valuing households' assets on an annual basis would present enormous administrative difficulties. Many assets such as town houses or stocks and shares are bought or sold on the open market, and hence a valuation could be relatively easily obtained for these. But how would the authorities value assets which have not recently been placed on the market? What of a unique work of art or a country house? Or, on a more mundane level, how would a household's assets in the form of consumer durables or furniture be valued?

The fact that, as noted earlier, several countries do operate a wealth tax already must mean that these problems are not insuperable. One rather appealing method of overcoming them, for instance, is to allow each individual to set his own value on the asset concerned, and then to give the tax authorities the right to buy it if they wish at that value. Another alternative is to take insurance valuations. Either of these, or maybe both operating in conjunction, would seem to provide a reasonably satisfactory solution to the valuation problem.

Second, the question of savings. Many critics of a wealth tax have averred that its introduction would reduce savings. Now at first sight this might seem obvious. A wealth tax makes savings less attractive relative to spending money on consumption, since if it saved it is taxed, whereas if it is consumed it is not. This effect (similar to the 'substitution' effect discussed in the context of income taxes) would act to reduce savings. However, this is not the whole story. For the introduction of a tax would also reduce the post-tax amount of a given level of household savings. This might encourage households to save more in order to maintain their original levels of savings (in a manner similar to the 'income' effect in the income tax case). So we cannot say definitely without empirical investigation which of these two influences, operating in opposite directions, will predominate. There is no *a priori* case for the view that a wealth tax will automatically reduce savings.

Taxing the Transfer of Wealth

As we saw in the previous chapter, to have had a wealthy father is a considerable advantage in the game of getting rich. The inter-generational transfer of wealth appears to be particularly important in maintaining inequality in the distribution of wealth. So it has been argued that, as well as, or instead of, taxing wealth on an annual basis, it should be taxed when it is transferred from one person to another by means of a legacy or gift. Various types of such taxes exist or have been proposed, and we shall now consider a few of them.

The principal form of taxation on wealth transfers until fairly recently in the United Kingdom was *estate duty*. This taxed all estates according to their size, and included within each estate all gifts made up to seven years prior to the death of the estate's owner. Its principal disadvantage was that it offered considerable opportunities for tax avoidance. The biggest of these was that it did not tax gifts or transfers of wealth made seven years before death. Accordingly individuals could arrange to transfer their wealth to whoever they wished, and not pay any tax on the transfer so long as they managed to survive at least seven years after the transfer took place. The tax avoidance resulting from this and from other loopholes was so large that it prompted the comment that estate duty was paid only by 'the patriotic, the philanthropic and the downright unlucky'.

The failure to tax gifts has been rectified by the replacement of estate duty by the *capital transfer tax*. This taxes all transfers of wealth, including gifts as well as inheritances, and has the additional feature that it taxes at a rate which increases with the total amount of transfers the donor has made in his life-time.

Both estate duty and capital transfer tax are taxes on the *donor* of a gift or legacy. A different type of tax has been suggested which taxes the *recipient* of the transfer. The simplest form of this is the *inheritance tax,* under which the tax payment is assessed according to the size of an individual's inheritance; a more complicated version is the *life-time capital receipts tax* which taxes all inheritances and gifts according to the amount of such transfers the individual has received in the past.

One of the principal differences between taxes on the donor and taxes on the recipient is the incentive the latter gives for donors to spread their wealth. This can be illustrated by an example. Suppose a wealthy man has five children and £100 000 to give away to them either as a gift or as a legacy. Suppose further that one of the children (say the eldest) had already received a legacy of £50 000 from some other relative, whereas the other children have received none. Now if a tax on donors was in operation which taxed estates of £100 000 at, say 40 per cent, it would not matter to whom the father left his wealth; the tax would be the same (£40 000). But suppose a life-time capital receipts tax is introduced at the rates shown in Table 11.2. Now, if the father left all his £100 000 to the eldest child, who has already had a legacy of £50 000, then, including this new legacy, the child would have £150 000 and the total tax would be 60 per cent of £100 000, or £60 000. If he spread it among his other four children – who have had no gifts or legacies – giving them £25 000 each, then the tax on each legacy would be 10 per cent of £25 000, or £2500. The total tax bill on the estate would then be £10 000. Thus, by spreading his wealth among a larger number of people, each of whom have received little in the way of wealth transfers before, he can

---

TABLE 11.2
A Life-time Capital Receipts Tax

If accumulated total of all legacies and gifts received by individual is	Then the rate to be applied to a new legacy or gift is
£25 000	10 per cent
£100 000	40 per cent
£150 000	60 per cent

---

reduce the total tax to be paid from £60 000 to £10 000, a very sizeable reduction.

It might be objected that, in practice, this wealth-spreading effect might be relatively small, since individuals are not so eager to avoid tax that they will change their whole pattern of legacies or donations. However, experience of the operation of estate duty and capital transfer tax suggests that people are prepared to go to considerable lengths to avoid paying tax: from the complete giving over of wealth seven years before death to the setting up of elaborate tax-avoidance trusts. The desire to avoid taxation in any form is a powerful force. The attractive feature of taxes on beneficiaries is that this force is harnessed to achieve egalitarian ends.

Finally we should consider the effect on efficiency of taxing the transfer of wealth. As with taxing the holding of wealth, the principal question concerns the effect on savings. It is argued that many people save in order to have something to pass on to their children (or others close to them), and by imposing heavy taxation on transfers the incentive for them to save will be reduced. Now, as we saw in the case of the wealth tax, this argument is double-edged. For the fact that a certain amount of the transfer will be 'lost' in tax may encourage people to save *more* so as to compensate for the loss. As with the wealth tax, we cannot make any definite statement on the effects on savings of imposing a transfer tax.

By way of summarising this discussion of various fiscal measures, it is perhaps useful to compare the relative merits and demerits of taxes on wealth transfers versus taxes on wealth holdings. One of the principal advantages of the former is that when it takes the form of taxes on recipients it is actually redistributive, in the sense that it provides incentives to transfer wealth from the rich to the less rich. A wealth tax simply takes money from the rich; by itself it does nothing to increase the income or wealth holdings of the poor. Another advantage concerns the effects on savings. If, as seems plausible, the desire to save for your own future consumption is greater than the desire to save for others' consumption , and *if* there is a negative effect of wealth taxation on savings, then it is likely to be greater for a tax on wealth holdings than for a tax on transferring wealth (which does not tax your own future consumption but only that of those who will receive your wealth). However, a disadvantage of transfer taxation is that it does nothing to reduce large concentrations of wealth accumulated during an individual's life-time; if such concentrations are considered as socially undesirable in and of themselves, then (among tax measures) they can only be affected directly by a wealth tax on holdings.

Summary

The *income tax* is not as an effective instrument of redistribution as many suppose. Because of the system of *tax allowances,* the *average tax rate* (the proportion of income taken in tax) is generally much less than the *marginal tax rate* (the tax rate applied to increases in income). Also, important types of income, such as occupational fringe benefits or capital gains, are taxed at low rates. So far as efficiency is concerned, its effects on the incentive to work cannot be predicted from theory alone, for the tax has *substitution* and *income effects* that operate in opposite directions.

The *social security system* is an important redistributive tool. *Means-tested benefits,* such as Supplementary Benefit, have the advantage that they go to the needy; they often have the disadvantage of relatively low take-up due to the stigma and complexity they create. *Categorical benefits,* including child benefit and forms of *social insurance,* such as unemployment benefit and old age pensions, have the advantage of a higher take-up, but the disadvantage of often helping the better off as much as the poor. Both types create some disincentive to work due to the income effect; however, means-tested benefits also have a substitution effect.

A negative *income tax* or its equivalent a *social dividend,* could create greater administrative simplicity, greater redistribution and reduce work disincentives. However, it is difficult to devise such schemes that do all three simulaneously. A *minimum wage* can raise the wages of low-paid workers who remain in employment; however, it can also create unemployment, higher prices and lower profits. Its redistributive consequences are therefore not clear.

Wealth taxation can either take the form of taxes on the *holding* of wealth or taxes on *transfer* of wealth. The former have practical disadvantages; moreover, they may discourage savings, although this cannot be predicted from theory alone. Taxes on the transfer of wealth are of two types: *taxes on donors,* such as estate duty or capital transfer tax, and *inheritance taxes,* that tax the recipients of wealth transfers. There are various forms of the latter, including a *life-time capital receipts tax* and integration with the *income tax.* Both of these have the advantage that they encourage the spreading of wealth among the poorer sections of the population. The effects of transfer taxes on the incentive to save is uncertain, but is probably less than that of taxes on wealth holdings.

Further Reading

There is a good, though at points a little technical, discussion of redistribution policies in Culyer (1980, ch. 6), and a more elementary treatment in Atkinson (1975, ch. 11). Pond (1980) provides a useful short discussion of the problems of the UK tax system and possible reforms. A longer treatment of the relevant issues can be found in Kay and King (1980). A recent study of the effectiveness of the social security system is Beckerman and Clark (1982); old, but still relevant, is Atkinson (1969) A useful critique of back-to-Beveridge proposals for reform is Judge (1980). In the late 1960s there was an enormous literature on the negative income tax: see, for example, Lees (1967) and Christopher *et al.* (1970). An important recent contribution to the debate is Collard (1980). Minimum wages are discussed in Atkinson (1975, ch. 6) and Gordon (1982, ch. 10). Classic works on wealth taxation are Meade (1964) and Atkinson (1972).

Questions for Discussion

1. Does cutting income tax make people work harder?
2. The size of the substitution effect of the income tax depends on the marginal tax rate; the size of the income effect depends on the average tax rate. Explain this statement.
3. Discuss the case for a comprehensive income tax.
4. How would you measure the effectiveness of a poverty programme?
5. What are the arguments for and against relying on categorical benefits as the principal form of social security?
6. 'Replacement of the social security system by a comprehensive negative income tax would create both greater efficiency and greater equality.' Discuss.
7. 'Since wages are largely determined by convention, the introduction of a national minimum wage would have little effect on unemployment and hence would be a desirable redistributive measure.' Do you agree?
8. What are the problems of valuing individuals' wealth for taxation purposes?
9. 'An annual wealth tax is likely to be both inefficient and unfair.' Discuss.
10. Should taxes on wealth transfers be levied on donors or on recipients?

The Market
and the
State

12

In the first chapter we discussed a number of possible objectives that society might have with respect to allocating scarce resources among its members. In subsequent chapters we saw how market and non-market systems can be used to allocate resources in certain 'problem' areas and whether their use can meet the relevant objectives in the area concerned. Throughout, certain key issues emerged repeatedly. Many of the difficulties involved in allocating resources within these areas have strong links with one another; indeed many are simply aspects of the same conceptual problems. It is the purpose of this final chapter to try to isolate and to emphasise these links, and to draw out from the discussion some general lessons about different systems of resource allocation.

The Market and Efficiency

In Chapter 1 we saw that under certain conditions the market allocation of a commodity will provide the socially efficient quantity of that commodity. Let us recapitulate the argument. Under conditions to be discussed in a moment, the *market demand* curve will be identical to the *marginal social benefit*, or *msb*, curve. Also, market supply reflects social cost; that is, the *market supply* curve is identical to the *marginal social cost*, or *msc*, curve. Now the socially efficient level of provision is the point where the marginal social cost equals the marginal social benefit; that is, where the *msb* and *msc* curves intersect. Under market allocation, the quantity of the commodity that is actually provided will be the point where demand equals supply; that is, where the demand and supply curves intersect. Since these curves are identical with the *msb* and *msc* curves, the points of intersection will be the same. Hence the quantity provided in the market will be the socially efficient quantity – under certain conditions.

But what are these conditions? We can now be more specific than was possible in Chapter 1. First, consider the identity of the *msb* and market demand curves. This requires the fulfilment of two conditions: (a) that individuals are the best judges of their own wants and hence that their demand for a commodity accurately reflects the marginal private benefit to them of that commodity, and (b) that the marginal private benefit equals the marginal social benefit. If both these conditions hold, then the sum of the individual demands for a commodity (the market demand) will equal the sum of the marginal private benefits, which in turn will equal the sum of the marginal social benefits.

However, we have seen that for many of the commodities discussed in this book these conditions are not fulfilled. For instance, in the cases of health care, education, and housing, there exists *imperfect information*. Prospective patients are in a poor position to evaluate different methods of medical treatment; parents who have had only a limited education may lack the essential information necessary to choose the right school for their children; and the purchaser of a house may find it difficult to assess its faults before actually living in it. The existence of such ignorance means that consumers may not be able to assess accurately what will benefit them; if so, their demand for the commodity concerned will not reflect the benefit they actually derive from its consumption, and condition (a) will not be fulfilled.

Even if there is no obvious consumer ignorance, it is possible to doubt that individuals are always the best judges of their own wants. For instance, is a drug addict's demand for heroin really an expression of his own best interests? More generally, some would argue that many people are subject to such extensive social and economic conditioning that they cannot make 'proper' decisions concerning their consumption – that, for instance, advertising and other pressures induce them to 'waste' their money on cigarettes or alcohol instead of buying proper food or housing.

Others find this approach unacceptably paternalistic. They argue that people have a right to have their desires respected, regardless of the origin of those desires. The ultimate authority as to what benefits an individual wants should be himself; no one else is an appropriate judge.

The difference between the groups holding these two points of view is essentially a philosophical one concerning individual rights. However, both groups would probably agree that if there is substantial consumer ignorance then individuals are not necessarily the best judges of their own interests; and even the second group might be prepared to accept that there may be cases (such as the drug addict) where even a well-informed individual's demand for a commodity may not accurately reflect his long-term interests.

Condition (b) – that marginal private benefit equals marginal social benefit – is also unlikely to be met for many of the areas considered. For this requires that the commodity concerned has no *external benefits* associated with it; that individuals' consumption of the commodity benefits only themselves. But we have seen that health care, education, police patrols, courts, and prisons all generate external benefits. The existence of infectious diseases, and possibly also of a 'caring' concern by some for the health of others, means that the marginal private benefit of some forms of health care is less than the marginal social benefit. Education is not only of direct benefit to the person concerned but also can benefit those who work with him and the community generally. Private police patrols benefit everyone in the street regardless of who pays for them, and courts and prisons benefit potential as well as actual victims of crime. All in all therefore, for each of these commodities, market allocation is unlikely to result in an efficient level of provision.

Now let us look at the supply side. Two conditions are required to ensure that the market supply curve is identical with the *msc* curve: (c) that marginal private costs are identical with marginal social costs, and (d) that there are no monopolistic elements or barriers to competition in the relevant markets. If the first condition is not met, then individual production and consumption decisions will not accurately reflect their social costs. If the second condition is not met, then producers will be able to manipulate the prices their products receive to their own advantage.

Again these conditions are often not fulfilled in the areas discussed. The production and consumption of many commodities generate *external costs*, driving a wedge between marginal private and marginal social costs. A landlord who lets his property deteriorate imposes external costs on his neighbours. Cars create congestion and environmental costs. Much industrial activity pollutes and despoils the natural environment.

As far as *monopoly* is concerned, we have seen that monopolistic elements exist in the supply of schools, oil and in most labour markets. Whether such monopolies are an inevitable part of market allocation, or whether they are an aberration, is debatable. There are some circumstances in which the forces that drive a competitive market – the pursuit of self-interest – are likely to encourage the development of a monopoly. These include situations where economies of scale exist (enabling large firms to drive their smaller competitors out of business) and where imperfect information concerning product quality enables monopolies to develop (such as in health care). If such factors are important for any particular commodity, then it may prove impossible for a competitive market to avoid degenerating into a monopolistic one.

So, at least in the areas reviewed in this book, conditions (a) to (d) are unlikely to be met. Consequently, market allocation is unlikely to be efficient. Will it also fail to achieve other objectives, such as equity?

The Market and Equity

In the absence of any universally accepted conception of equity it is not easy to determine whether a particular method of resource allocation, such as the market system, achieves it. The best we can do is concentrate on the interpretations of the term that have emerged in our previous discussions. Most of these reflect either of two basic philosophies. The first emphasises the desirability of *equality* in the areas considered; it motivates, for example, the equal treatment for equal need objective of the National Health Service, educational policies designed to promote equality of opportunity, and policies aimed at reducing inequality in the distribution of income. The second philosophy concentrates only upon the attainment of *minimum standards* in each area. It is the philosophy underlying the concern that everyone should live in a 'decent home', and the perception of the poverty problem as one of simply bringing incomes of the poor above an arbitrarily defined line.

Whichever of those interpretations is preferred, it is unlikely that market allocation will achieve them. As we saw in Chapter 10, in a market system people's incomes – and hence their ability to purchase commodities – are determined by the resources they own and the prices they can obtain from selling those resources. Since the initial distribution of the ownership of resources is quite unequal, and since there are substantial barriers to competition in many resource markets (particularly that for labour), it would be remarkable if market processes produced an equal (or close to equal) distribution of income. Nor is there any reason to expect that minimum standards will necessarily be achieved; there will always be those with few resources and hence with levels of consumption below any reasonable minimum.

The Market and Other Objectives

Although we have concentrated on efficiency and equity as the principal objectives that a society will wish to pursue, we have seen that other objectives may also be important. The preservation of individual liberties and the promotion of altruism or co-operative behaviour are two that have emerged in some of our discussions. How does the market system perform in relation to these aims?

As with equity, the liberty objective has appeared in a variety of different forms. In the discussions of education vouchers and road pricing, for example, the desirability of *freedom of choice* was emphasised; for crime control, the preservation of *civil liberty* seemed important. Now it is often argued that competitive markets promote liberty, at least in the sense of freedom of choice. The existence of large numbers of small producers, each vying for the consumer's business, ensures that even the most idiosyncratic of consumers will be satisfied. Freedom of choice could also be enhanced by injecting market-type elements into existing areas of government policy. Under the education voucher scheme, for instance, parents would be free to choose whatever education they wished for their children, and not be compelled to accept the particular version provided by the government.

But, as we have seen, many markets contain considerable elements of monopoly. These, as well as impeding efficiency in the manner already described, also operate to limit freedom of choice. The freedom to enter the medical profession, and the freedom to choose from a wide range of different energy sources, are two examples in which the relevant monopolies act to restrict freedom of choice. Overall, therefore, while there is a strong presumption that markets encourage freedom of choice, we cannot state unequivocally that this will automatically occur in every situation.

We can be more definite concerning the other objective mentioned, the promotion of altruism. There can be little doubt that the market fosters personal attributes, such as greed and a lack of concern for one's neighbour, that are incompatible with altruistic behaviour. If this were the only consideration (which of course it is not) any reduction of the areas over which the market holds sway would be judged desirable.

In summary, therefore, we can say that market allocation without government intervention is unlikely completely to achieve either efficiency or equity, and may fail to meet certain other objectives as well. However, this does *not* necessarily imply that the government must therefore intervene. For it could be that such intervention may make things worse: it may create *more* inefficiency or *more* inequity than the market operating on its own. We need therefore to examine possible forms of government intervention and explore their ability to meet society's aims.

The State

Many people feel that state intervention in the market creates more problems than it solves. One line of criticism is that the *form* of intervention (provision, regulation, tax/subsidy) is often inappropriate – regulation being used where taxation would be more suitable, for instance. A more fundamental objection is that government by its very nature is bound to fail; it contains internal dynamics that will cause it to grow 'too big' and that this will have – indeed, has had – disastrous effects on economic efficiency and on liberty. Let us look at the arguments in more detail.

The Form of Intervention

The forms of intervention that have occupied us in this book has been provision, regulation and tax/subsidy policies. Government intervention generally takes the form of *direct provision* where there are extreme cases of external benefits – such as police services – and where equity considerations are important – such as education and health. While equity may be improved by such provision, it is often argued that efficiency is harmed. Governments are less responsive to consumers' preferences than is the private market; moreover there is no competition to ensure that private costs are kept to a minimum. Hence it is possible that any gains (in terms of either efficiency or equity) from government provision may be outweighed by accompanying efficiency losses.

A wide variety of different types of *regulation* have appeared in this book. These include traffic management schemes, pollution emission controls, and various forms of price control, such as energy cost controls, rent controls, and minimum wages. Let us examine them in turn, beginning with price controls.

Price controls are generally instituted as an attempt to promote equity. For instance, the aim of minimum wage legislation is to reduce the inequities involved in wage determination, while that of rent control is to reduce the inequities in housing allocation. In practice, however, such controls may have unintended consequences that reduce (or even reverse) their impact on equity and also create losses in terms of efficiency. For instance, consider those forms of price control that reduce the price *below* that which would be obtained in the market. Examples are rent control and energy price restrictions. These have the effect of increasing demand for the commodity and reducing its supply. Hence, while some consumers will still be able to buy the commodity and will benefit from the lower price, others will be deprived of it altogether. As a result the market will operate inefficiently, and there may be no positive gain in terms of equity. Similar problems arise if the price is fixed *above* the market level, such as the minimum wage. Then demand falls and supply increases, resulting in a surplus (unemployment, in the case of the minimum wage). Again efficiency has been reduced without any guarantee of an improvement in equity.

Other forms of market regulation are generally undertaken to promote efficiency. For example, traffic management schemes and pollution emission controls are all attempts to reduce the inefficiencies arising from the presence of external costs. However, they have been subject to the criticism that they do not eliminate such inefficiency. In Chapter 5, for example, we saw that direct regulation was not, in general, the least-cost method of reducing pollution, and similar objections can be raised about the use of restrictions to control urban congestion.

Given these problems with direct provision and with market regulation, many economists have argued that if government intervention is deemed essential it should take the form of *taxes* or *subsidies*. Thus, for example, instead of the government providing state schools, it should subsidise school students by giving them vouchers that they can spend on any private school they wish to attend. This could meet the equity objective and at the same time encourage competition, hence reducing costs and increasing efficiency. Instead of rent control, housing vouchers could be provided that would operate in a similar manner to the education ones. Income support should take the form of a negative income tax rather than a minimum wage. Traffic and pollution controls should be eliminated and a system of road pricing and pollution charges introduced.

However the case for such schemes is not open and shut. As we have seen, taxes and subsidy schemes often have their own inefficiencies associated with them. Moreover they may not be as equitable as other forms of intervention. For example, road pricing favours the better-off in a way that traffic management controls do not. And, of course, they may create more inefficiency or more inequities than the alternative of no intervention at all. What is needed is a careful empirical examination of the likely outcomes of different forms of intervention; the issues cannot be resolved by theory alone.

Is Government too Big?

It is often claimed that government intervention at its present level damages society and the economy. In Britain public expenditure is 44 per cent of the Gross National Product. This, it is argued, has a number of damaging effects. First it means that resources that could be used for 'productive' purposes, such as manufacturing goods for exports, are being diverted into essentially unproductive activities such as health care and education. Second, in so far as it is financed out of taxation, it creates an excessive tax burden that discourages work effort and encourages trade unions to make inflationary wage claims. Third, in so far as it is financed by increased government borrowing, it expands the government's deficit which also contributes to inflation.

Now these arguments have to be treated with some care. First the actual *resources used* by the public sector constitute only 25 per cent rather than 44 per cent of GNP, for the latter figure includes transfer payments that do not directly use up resources (such as unemployment pay or old age pensions). Moreover much of that 25 per cent goes into investment in 'human' capital (good health, educational skills) that does indeed have 'productive' potential; a skilled, healthy labour force can be as important a contributor to national production as any investment in capital machinery. Second, tax as a proportion of GNP in the United Kingdom is not high by international standards; it is lower than in Sweden, France or Germany for instance, countries not noted for their inefficiency. Third, the existence of links between either trade union wage claims or the government deficit and inflation is still a matter of considerable controversy.

A second criticism of government activity is that governments will inevitably grow too large. This derives from some of the work of a fairly recent development in economic analysis – that of 'public choice'. The public choice school interprets the actions of all the agents involved in government decisions, including voters, politicians and bureaucrats, as being motivated purely by self-interest. That is, instead of viewing politicians or civil servants as being selfless guardians of the public interest, adherents of this school view them as concerned only with their own welfare. Thus voters will vote solely on the benefits to themselves of particular parties; politicians will cater to voter preferences to the extent necessary to get themselves re-elected; bureaucrats will try to increase their salaries and power.

If this is correct then, it is argued, an inevitable result will be ever-increasing government activity. Groups of voters will vote for increasing public expenditure on particular services that benefit them, knowing they will not have to pay the cost since the extra taxation will be spread across the population. Politicians will support those policies because the voters do. And bureaucrats will favour any increases in government activity, for this permits them to create or expand their bureaucratic empire, increasing their power, status and income.

Although in some ways this is as simple a caricature of the motivations behind government actions as the opposing view that all the people involved are selfless agents dedicated to the public weal, it none the less contains much that is highly plausible. However, the theories involved have not as yet generated much by way of specific predictions that can be tested, so their usefulness as a means of analysing political behaviour – including the expansion of government activity – is still untested.

Both market and non-market systems of resource allocation thus have their advantages and disadvantages. Which system one ultimately finds superior will depend upon two factors: one's values concerning the relative weights that should be put upon society's various objectives, such as efficiency, equity, or liberty; and the extent to which the final allocation under each system departs from each objective. The first is a matter of value judgements about which economists – in their role as economists – have little to say. The second, however, is an empirical question to which economists have a great deal to contribute. What is needed is more empirical investigation to substantiate the competing claims of the different systems. If this book has succeeded in inducing any of its readers to pursue such investigations, one of its main objectives will have been achieved.

Summary

There are four conditions necessary for the market allocation of a commodity to be *efficient*: (a) there is *perfect information* and that individuals are the best judge of their own wants; (b) that the commodity does not generate *external benefits*; (c) that it does not generate *external costs*; and (d) that there are no *monopolistic* elements or barriers to competition in the relevant markets. For each of the problem areas investigated in this book, most of these conditions are violated. Moreover, market allocation will generally not be *equitable* and, while it may promote *liberty* in the sense of freedom of choice, it will also encourage self-interested behaviour and hence discourage *altruism*.

However, the fact that market allocation may fail in a number of areas does not imply that *government intervention* will do better – although it may. Direct government *provision* and market *regulation* can create inefficiency and do not necessarily promote equity. *Taxes* or *subsidies* seem to be more efficient in some contexts than are other forms of intervention, but again they are not necessarily more equitable. All forms of government intervention are likely to involve some restrictions on individual liberty, but by reducing the areas where the market predominates they may increase the possibilities for the exercise of altruistic behaviour. It can be argued that government will inevitable grow *too big,* but the theories this is based on have yet to be properly tested. Indeed, more empirical testing is required all round, for the relative merits of different systems cannot be assessed on theory alone.

Further Reading

An analysis of the reasons for market failure on broadly the same lines as this chapter can be found in Gordon (1982),

Chapter 11. For those with more economics, Culyer (1980), Chapters 2, 3 and 7 provide a more comprehensive treatment of market failure and include some discussion of the difficulties associated with non-market systems. Some of the issues are also discussed in Wilson and Wilson (1982), especially Chapter 2.

A vigorous assault upon the market system can be found in Titmuss (1970); and a yet more vigorous defence of it in Friedman and Friedman (1980). The major proponents of the argument that government is too big in the British context are Bacon and Eltis (1978). Public choice theories are discussed in Mueller (1979), but at a high technical level. A simpler version of some of the ideas can be found in Judge's contribution to the book on public expenditure edited by Walker (1982); this collection of readings also contains much other material relevant to the current debate on the role of the public sector.

Questions for Discussion

1. 'It is a happy coincidence that the form of economic organisation most likely to promote efficiency – perfect competition – is also that which involves the greatest decentralisation of power. The market is thus the cornerstone of liberty.' Do you agree?
2. Discuss the problems that imperfect information creates for market allocations.
3. Is the appropriate government response to externalities *always* to tax or subsidise the activity concerned?
4. What are the similarities between rent control and minimum wages as instruments of social policy?
5. 'There are shortages of doctors, nurses, policemen, etc., but none of food, shirts, cars, etc., because the market is used in the second case but not in the first.' Discuss.
6. Is government too big?
7. Discuss the view that the high tax rates necessary to finance public spending on social programmes encourages inflation.
8. Is all spending on the welfare state unproductive?
9. Some argue that, while the pursuit of self-interest in the

market generally promotes social welfare, its pursuit in government is invariably disastrous. Do you agree?
10. 'In all cases the comparison should be between an imperfect market and an imperfect [government], not some ideal abstraction' (Charles Schultze). Discuss.

Bibliography

Abel-Smith, B. (1976) *Value For Money in Health Services* (London: Heinemann).

Anderson, F. R., Kneese, A. V., Reed, P D., Stevenson, R. B. and Taylor, S. (1977) *Environmental Improvement Through Economic Incentives* (Baltimore: Johns Hopkins Press).

Anderson, R. (1976) *The Economics of Crime* (London: Macmillan).

Atkinson, A. B. (1969) *Poverty in Britain and the Reform of Social Security* (Cambridge: Cambridge University Press).

Atkinson, A. B. (1972) *Unequal Shares* (Harmondsworth: Penguin).

Atkinson, A. B. (1975) *The Economics of Inequality* (Oxford: Oxford University Press).

Atkinson, A. B. (ed.) (1980) *Wealth, Income and Inequality* (Oxford: Oxford University Press).

Atkinson, A. B. and Stiglitz, J. E. (1980) *Lectures in Public Economics* (New York: McGraw-Hill).

Bacon, R. and Eltis, W. (1978) *Britain's Economic Problem: Too Few Producers* (London: Macmillan).

Baumol, W. J. and Oates, W. (1979) *Economics, Environmental Policy and the Quality of Life* (Englewood Cliffs: Prentice-Hall).

Baumol, W. J. and Blinder, A. S. (1982) *Economics: Principles and Policy* (New York: Harcourt Brace Jovanovich).

Baxter, C., O'Leary, P. J. and Westoby, A. (1977) *Economics and Education Policy: A Reader* (London: Longman).

Becker, G. (1968) 'Crime and Punishment: An Economic Approach', *Journal of Political Economy*, 76, 169–217.

Beckerman, W. and Clark, S. (1982) *Poverty and Social Security in Britain Since 1961* (Oxford: Oxford University Press).

Bettman, O. (1974) *The Good Old Days – They Were Terrible!* (New York: Random House).

Blaug, M. (1972) *An Introduction to the Economics of Education* (Harmondsworth: Penguin).

Brown, A. J. (1972) *The Framework of Regional Economics in the United Kingdom* (Cambridge: Cambridge University Press).

Brown, A. J. and Burrows, E. M. (1977) *Regional Economic Problems* (London: George Allen & Unwin).

Burrows, P. (1979) *The Economic Theory of Pollution Control* (Oxford: Martin Robertson).

Butlin, J. A. (1981) *Economics and Resources Policy* (London: Longman).

Button, K. J. (1982) *Transport Economics* (London: Heinemann).

Carr-Hill, R. and Stern, N. (1973) 'An Econometric Model of the Supply and Control of Recorded Offences in England and Wales', *Journal of Public Economics*, 2, 169–217.

Central Statistical Office (1982) 'The Effects of Taxes and Benefits on Household Income, 1980', *Economic Trends*, 339, 97–126.

Central Statistical Office (1982) *Regional Trends* (London: HMSO).

Central Statistical Office (1981) *Social Trends* (London: HMSO).

Christopher, A., Polanyi, G., Selden, A. and Shenfield, B. (1970) *Policy for Poverty*, Research Monograph No. 20 (London: Institute of Economic Affairs).

Collard, D. (1980) 'Social Dividend and Negative Income Tax', in C. Sandford, C. Pond and R. Walker (eds) *Taxation and Social Policy* (London: Heinemann),

Cowell, F. (1977) *Measuring Inequality* (Oxford: Philip Allan).

Crew, M. A. and Young, A. (1977) *Paying By Degrees,* Hobart Paper 75 (London: Institute of Economic Affairs).

Cullingworth, J. B. (1979) *Essays on Housing Policy: The British Scene* (London: George Allen & Unwin).

Cullis, J. G. and West, P. A. (1979) *The Economics of Health* (Oxford: Martin Robertson).

Culyer, A. J. (1976) *Need and the National Health Service* (Oxford: Martin Robertson).

Culyer, A. J. (1980) *The Political Economy of Social Policy* (Oxford: Martin Robertson).

Dales, J. H. D. (1968) *Pollution, Property and Prices* (Toronto: University of Toronto Press).

Dasgupta, P. (1982) *The Control of Resources* (Oxford: Basil Blackwell).

Department of Employment and Productivity (1969) *A National Minimum Wage: An Inquiry* (London: HMSO).

Department of the Environment (1978) *English House Condition Survey,* 1976 (London: HMSO).

Department of the Environment (1981) 'Pollution Control Costs', unpublished.

Dorfman, R. and Dorfman, N. (1977) (eds) *Economics of the Environment: Selected Readings,* 2nd edn (London: W. W. Norton).

Ehrlich, I. (1973) 'Participation in Illegal Activities: A Theoretical and Empirical Investigation', *Journal of Political Economy*, 81, 521–65.

Freeman, C. and Jahoda, M. (1978) *World Futures: the Great Debate* (Oxford: Martin Robertson).

Friedman, D. (1978) *The Machinery of Freedom: A Guide to Radical Capitalism* (New York: Arlington House).

Friedman, L. (1976) *The Economics of Crime and Justice,* University

Programs Modular Series (Morristown, New Jersey: General Learning Press).

Friedman, M. (1962) *Capitalism and Freedom* (Chicago: University of Chicago Press).

Friedman, M. and Friedman, R. (1980) *Free to Choose* (Harmondsworth: Penguin).

Gordon, A. (1982) *Economics and Social Policy* (Oxford: Martin Robertson).

Gwilliam, K. M. and Mackie, P. J. (1975) *Economics and Transport Policy* (London: George Allen & Unwin).

Harbury, C. D. and McMahon, P. C. (1973) 'Inheritance and the Characteristics of Top Wealth Leavers in Britain', *Economic Journal*, 83, 810–33.

Heal, G. M. (1981) 'Economics and Resources' in Butlin, J. .A. (ed.) *Economics and Resources Policy* (London: Longman).

Holland, S. (1977) *Capital Versus the Regions* (London: Macmillan).

Holland, S. (1976) *The Regional Problem* (London: Macmillan).

Hunt, E. K. and Sherman, H. J. (1981) *Economics: An Introduction to Traditional and Radical Views,* 4th edn (New York: Harper & Row).

Judge, K. (1980) 'Beveridge: Past, Present and Future', in C. Sandford, C. Pond and R. Walker (eds) *Taxation and Social Policy* (London: Heinemann).

Kay, J. and King, M. (1980) *The British Tax System,* 2nd edn (Oxford: Oxford University Press).

Kent County Council Education Department (1978) *Education Vouchers in Kent.*

Kneese, A. (1977) *Economics and the Environment* (Harmondsworth: Penguin).

Lansley, S. (1979) *Housing and Public Policy* (London: Croom Helm).

Lansley, S. (1980) 'Housing' in Blake, D. and Ormerod, P. (eds) *The Economics of Prosperity* (London: Grant McIntyre).

Lecomber, R. (1979) *The Economics of Natural Resources* (London: Macmillan).

Lees, D. S. (1961) *Health Through Choice,* Hobart Paper No. 14 .(London: Institute of Economic Affairs).

Lees, D. S. (1967) 'Poor Families and Fiscal Reform', *Lloyds Bank Review,* 86, 1–15.

Le Grand, J. (1982) *The Strategy of Equality* (London: George Allen & Unwin).

Lipsey, R. (1979) *Introduction to Positive Economics,* 5th edn (London: Weidenfeld & Nicolson).

Loewy, E. H. (1980) 'Cost Should Not be a Factor in Medical Care', *New England Journal of Medicine,* 302, 697.

Maclennan, D. and Parr, J. B. (1979) *Regional Policy* (Oxford: Martin Robertson).

Maclennan, D. (1982) *Housing Economics* (London: Longman).

Manners, G., Keeble, D., Rogers, B. and Warren, K. (1980) *Regional Development in Britian* (Chichester: John Wiley).

Marin, A. (1979) 'Pollution Control: Economists' Views', *Three Banks Review,* 121, 21–41.

Marshall, A. (1980) *Principles of Economics* (8th edn London: Macmillan, 1961).

McInerney, J. P. (1981) 'Natural Resource Economics: The Basic Analytical Principles', in Butlin, J. A. (ed) *Economics and Resources Policy* (London: Longman).

McKenzie, R. and Tullock, G. (1978) *The New World of Economics,* rev. edn (Homewood, Illinois: Richard D. Irwin).

Meade, J. (1964) *Efficiency, Equality and the Ownership of Property* (London: George Allen & Unwin).

Meadows, D. H. *et al.* (1972) *The Limits to Growth* (London: Earth Island).

Mishan, E. J. (1969) *The Costs of Economic Growth* (Harmondsworth: Penguin).

Mueller, D. (1979) *Public Choice* (Cambridge: Cambridge University Press).

Myrdal, G. (1957) *Economic Theory and Underdeveloped Regions* (London: Duckworth).

Nash, C. A. (1982) *Economics of Public Transport* (London: Longman).

Packer, H. (1968) *The Limits of the Criminal Sanction* (Stanford: Stanford University Press).

Pearce, D. (1976) *Environment Economics* (London: Longman).

Phelps, E. (1973) (ed.) *Economic Justice* (Harmondsworth: Penguin).

Pond, C. (1980) 'Tax Expenditures and Fiscal Welfare', in C. Sandford, C. Pond and R. Walker (eds) *Taxation and Social Policy* (London: Heinemann).

President's Commission on Law Enforcement and Administration of Justice (1967) *Crime and Its Impact – An Assessment,* Task Force Report (Washington, D.C.: U.S. Government Printing Office).

Pyle, D. (1979) 'Crime Rates and Police Expenditure: An Introduction to the Economics of Crime', in S. Charles, D. Greenway and D. Pyle, *Case Studies in the Economics of Social Issues* (London: Heinemann).

Robbins, L. (1963) *Higher Education. Report of the Committee under the Chairmanship of Lord Robbins,* Cmnd 2154 (London: HMSO).

Robinson, C. (1982) 'Oil Depletion Policy in the United Kingdom', *Three Banks Review,* No. 135 September.

Robinson, R. (1979) *Housing Economics and Public Policy* (London: Macmillan).

Robinson, R. (1982) 'Housing Investment and Tenure Choice', in Cohen, C. D. (ed.) *Agenda for Britain. Vol 1* (Oxford: Philip Allan).

Routh, G. (1980) *Occupation and Pay in Great Britain* (London: Macmillan).

Royal Commission on Environmental Pollution (1972) *Third Report,* Cmnd 5054 (London: HMSO).

Royal Commission on the Distribution of Income and Wealth (1979) *Report No. 7,* Cmnd 6999 (London: HMSO).

Royal Commission on the National Health Service (1979) *Report,* Cmnd 7615 (London: HMSO).

Sandford, C. (1977) *Social Economics* (London: Heinemann).

Seldon, A. (1981) *Whither the Welfare State,* Occasional Paper No. 60 (London: Institute of Economic Affairs).

Smeed, R. J. *et al.* (1964) *Road Pricing: The Economic and Technical Possibilities* (London: HMSO).

Stafford, D. C. (1978) *The Economics of Housing Policy* (London: Croom Helm).

Thomson, J. M. (1974) *Modern Transport Economics* (Harmondsworth: Penguin).

Thomson, J. M. (1978) *Great Cities and Their Traffic* (Harmondsworth: Penguin).

Titmuss, R. (1970) *The Gift Relationship* (London: George Allen & Unwin).

Townsend, P. (1979) *Poverty in the United Kingdom* (Harmondsworth: Penguin).

Verry, D. (1977) 'Some Distributional and Equity Aspects of the Student Loans Debate', in *Education, Equity and Income Distribution* (Milton Keynes: Open University Press).

Walker, A. (ed.) (1982) *Public Expenditure and Social Policy* (London: Heinemann).

Walters, A. A. (1968) *The Economics of Road User Charges,* Occasional Paper No. 5 (Washington: International Bank for Reconstruction and Development).

Weale, A. (1978) *Equality and Social Policy* (London: Routledge & Kegan Paul).

Webb, M. G. and Ricketts, M. J. (1980) *The Economics of Energy* (London: Macmillan).

Weiller, D. *et al.* (1974) 'A Public School Voucher Demonstration: The First Year at Alum Rock (Santa Monica, California: Rand Corporation). Also reprinted in Baxter, C., O'Leary, P. T. and Westoby, A. (1977) *Economics and Education Policy: A Reader* (London: Longman).

Williams, A. and Anderson, R. (1975) *Efficiency in the Social Services* (Oxford: Basil Blackwell).

Wilson, T. and Wilson, D. T. (1982) *The Political Economy of the Welfare State* (London: George Allen & Unwin).

Ziderman, A. (1973) 'Does it Pay to Take a Degree? The Profitability of Private Investment in Education in Britain', *Oxford Economic Papers,* July. Also reprinted in Baxter, C., O'Leary, P. J. and Westoby, A. (1977) *Economics and Education Policy: A Reader* (London: Longman).

Index